# Conversations with Sherman Alexie

Literary Conversations Series
*Peggy Whitman Prenshaw*
*General Editor*

D0732332

# Conversations with Sherman Alexie

*Edited by*
*Nancy J. Peterson*

University Press of Mississippi
Jackson

www.upress.state.ms.us

The University Press of Mississippi is a member of the Association of American University Presses.

First printing 2009

∞

Library of Congress Cataloging-in-Publication Data

Alexie, Sherman, 1966–
    Conversations with Sherman Alexie / edited by Nancy J. Peterson.
        p.    cm. — (Literary conversations series)
    Includes index.
    ISBN 978-1-60473-279-5 (cloth : alk. paper) — ISBN 978-1-60473-280-1 (pbk. : alk. paper) 1. Alexie, Sherman, 1966—Interviews. 2. Authors, American—20th century—Interviews. I. Peterson, Nancy J. II. Title.
    PS3551.L35774Z46 2009
    818'.5409—dc22

                                                                2009015995

British Library Cataloging-in-Publication Data available

## Books by Sherman Alexie

*The Business of Fancydancing: Stories and Poems.* New York: Hanging Loose Press, 1992.
*I Would Steal Horses.* Niagara Falls: Slipstream Publications, 1992.
*Old Shirts and New Skins.* Los Angeles: American Indian Studies Center-UCLA, 1993.
*The Lone Ranger and Tonto Fistfight in Heaven.* New York: Atlantic Monthly Press, 1993; expanded edition: Grove Press, 2005.
*First Indian on the Moon.* New York: Hanging Loose Press, 1993.
*Seven Mourning Songs for the Cedar Flute I Have Yet to Learn to Play.* Walla Walla: Whitman College Book Arts Lab, 1994.
*Reservation Blues.* New York: Atlantic Monthly Press, 1995.
*Water Flowing Home.* Boise: Limberlost Press, 1996.
*Indian Killer.* New York: Atlantic Monthly Press, 1996.
*The Summer of Black Widows.* New York: Hanging Loose Press, 1996.
*The Man Who Loves Salmon.* Boise: Limberlost Press, 1998.
*Smoke Signals: A Screenplay.* New York: Hyperion, 1998.
*The Toughest Indian in the World.* New York: Grove Press, 2000.
*One Stick Song.* New York: Hanging Loose Press, 2000.
*The Business of Fancydancing: The Screenplay.* New York: Hanging Loose Press, 2003.
*Ten Little Indians.* New York: Grove Press, 2003.
*Dangerous Astronomy.* Boise: Limberlost Press, 2005.
*Flight.* New York: Black Cat-Grove, 2007.
*The Absolutely True Diary of a Part-Time Indian.* New York: Little, Brown, 2007.
*Face.* New York: Hanging Loose Press, 2009.

### Films by Sherman Alexie
*Smoke Signals.* ShadowCatcher-Miramax, 1998.
*The Business of Fancydancing.* 2002. Released on DVD: Wellspring Media, 2003.

# Contents

# Introduction

In his November 14, 2007, acceptance speech for winning the National Book Award for *The Absolutely True Diary of a Part-Time Indian*, Sherman Alexie acknowledged some of the influences that have shaped his career and love of books over the years. Among them, he paid tribute to his creative writing professor at Washington State University, Alex Kuo, who gave him a copy of a groundbreaking 1983 anthology edited by Joseph Bruchac, *Songs from This Earth on Turtle's Back*. In that book, Alexie read for the first time literary works written by Indian authors, and that encounter changed his life. Along with a poem about frying bologna, a poem by the Paiute writer Adrian C. Louis spoke to Alexie's experience as an Indian, growing up on a reservation. In his speech, Alexie quoted from one of Louis's poems—"Oh Uncle Adrian! I'm in the reservation of my mind"—and explained, "That line for me had all the cultural, historic, and artistic power of 'Because I could not stop for Death / He kindly stopped for me—.' It had all the power of 'Whose woods these are I think I know.' I knew right then, at that moment, when I read that line, that I wanted to be a writer" (Acceptance Speech).

Encapsulated in this moment from Alexie's acceptance speech are several prominent elements of his work: a strong commitment to communicating Native realities, often bleak ones, to a wide audience; an embracing of multiple and multifarious lines of influence (Emily Dickinson, Robert Frost, as well as Adrian Louis); a desire to spread encouragement and hope to young people of all backgrounds; as well as an insistence that books and literature are not mere entertainment or luxuries, but essential to survival and understanding.

Alexie has always had a finely tuned ear for poetic, comic, and sometimes radical truthtelling. He is a brilliant storyteller, whether the stories take the form of poems, short stories, novels, songs, or films. Born on October 7, 1966, in Spokane, Washington, Alexie grew up in the town of Wellpinit on the Spokane Indian Reservation. He is Spokane through his mother and Coeur d'Alene through his father. Today, he lives in the city of Seattle with his wife, Diane, and their two sons, Joseph and David. Alexie is a prolific author; as this volume goes to press, he has already published three volumes of short stories, five full-length volumes of poetry, five poetry chapbooks, four novels, two film scripts, and a new collection of poems, titled *Face*, has recently appeared.

The breakthrough year for Alexie was 1992: he was awarded a National Endowment for the Arts Poetry Fellowship; Hanging Loose Press published his first volume of poems, a collection titled *The Business of Fancydancing*; and Alexie was fortunate enough to have this collection discussed in a review essay of recent Native American writing in the *New York Times Book Review*. Better yet, reviewer James Kincaid singled out Alexie's poems and described him as "one of the major lyric voices of our time" (28). Soon afterwards, Alexie signed with an agent and found himself in a bidding war among publishers who wanted to bring out his first collection of stories. In recent years, Alexie's career has followed a trajectory he has described, in a tongue-in-cheek nod to Horatio Alger, as being "from rez to riches" (Hoback).

The interviews collected in this volume move from the earliest years of Alexie's career up to right before he won the National Book Award. They provide insights into Alexie's views on his life and writing, as well as his often controversial views on political issues and concerns confronting Native Americans today. They reflect a range of tones and attitudes: Alexie is oftentimes laughing or cracking jokes during these interviews, but sometimes he is offended, angry, bored, compassionate, and/or thoughtful. Occasionally he struggles toward the right words to describe something deeply felt or difficult to reckon with.

The diversity of interviewers and publication venues is also noteworthy. While most of the interviews were originally published in the United States, three interviews—from Canada, from the United Kingdom, and from Australia—reflect increasing international attention to Alexie's work. Alexie's interviewers also come from a variety of backgrounds and perspectives, which gives an indication of his immense following among different constituencies and audiences. Several of the interviewers included in this volume are Native or indigenous (Charlene Teters, Spokane; Tomson Highway, Cree; Lorena Allam, from the Gamilaroi and Yawalaraay peoples of northwest New South Wales in Australia). Several are academics (John Purdy, Åse Nygren, James Mellis), several are fellow writers (Tomson Highway, Joelle Fraser, Diane Thiel), some are bloggers (Tanita Davis and Sarah Stevenson), while many are full-time journalists and/or reviewers.

Alexie's early poems and stories, and the earliest interviews collected in this volume, offer insights into the depiction of reservation life that readers and reviewers have found so compelling and innovative in his work. "Reservation realism" is the phrase Alexie coins in the introduction to the 2005 expanded edition of his short story collection, *The Lone Ranger and Tonto Fistfight in Heaven* (xxi), and he acknowledges the double-edged quality of his success in depicting rez life by noting, "I was the first Alexie to ever become middle-class and all because I wrote stories and poems about being a poor Indian growing up in an alcoholic family on an alcoholic reservation" (xviii). The reservation life we glimpse in his early poems and stories is often painful, marked by poverty, alcoholism, despair, un- or underemployment. One of Alexie's most memorable characters, Victor Joseph, reflects on this aspect of reservation life, "It's hard to be optimistic on the reservation. When a glass sits on a table here, people don't wonder if it's half filled or half empty. They just hope it's good beer. Still, Indians have a way of surviving. But it's almost like Indians can easily survive the big stuff. Mass murder, loss of language and land rights. It's the small things that hurt the most. The white waitress who wouldn't take an order, Tonto, the Washington Redskins" (*Lone Ranger* 49).

Alexie also writes about how to survive the pain of the "small things" that Victor mentions. *The Lone Ranger and Tonto Fistfight in Heaven* in fact offers readers a poetic-mathematical formula for survival on the reservation: "Survival = Anger x Imagination" (150). These qualities resonate throughout Alexie's early stories and poems. And along with his depiction of stark reservation realities, Alexie tells of strong and beautiful aspects as well: we find passion and love, dancing, Indi'n humor, storytelling, powwows, basketball, and above all, fry bread.

But some reviewers of Alexie's early work were not always even-handed in their assessment of his reservation realism, and many times the negative aspects of reservation life are emphasized without much understanding of the context for his depictions or without acknowledging the love and hope that can be found in the stories and poems as well. In several of the interviews collected in this volume, Alexie responds to criticisms concerning the depiction of alcoholism, despair, and stereotypes in his early work. In his 2006 radio interview with Lorena Allam, for instance, Alexie insists, "The idea of the drunken Indian is not a stereotype— it's a damp reality." In his 1997 interview with Charlene Teters, Alexie talks about being "accused of exaggerating the despair on the reservation" in his written work, which he goes on to refute by pointing to "the alcohol and drug problems" he sees there and the level of denial that makes it difficult to address these concerns effectively. He positions himself as a writer who is trying to protest the situation ("Hey, that's not right!"), while also admitting that he's a "mouthy kind of guy" who sometimes rubs people the wrong way. To understand the complexity of Alexie's positions, it is also important to note that, along with pointing to problems in his conversation with Teters, Alexie evokes a wonderful image of the reservation—"The Spokane Rez, in my experience, is one of the most beautiful in the country. . . . [I]t's the most beautiful place in the world"—and he mentions several specific details that make it so. The Alexie who emerges in these interviews is sometimes a vehement critic, calling attention to social and political problems on reservations. At the same time, he remains a strong advocate for Indian peoples.

As these interviews make clear, Alexie resists pandering to those readers and publishers who prefer nostalgic depictions of traditional Indian life. He continually reminds interviewers that he does not write the "corn pollen, eagle feathers, Mother Earth, Father Sky" kind of Indian literature that is easy to market. He also reveals a strong ethical dimension in what he chooses to include in his own novels, stories, and poems. His interview with John Purdy, for instance, reveals an Alexie who wants to avoid promoting "a traveling road show of Indian spirituality" in his work, while also paying homage to drums, powwows, and the stick game through his eloquent descriptions of them. Similarly, in his interview with Joelle Fraser, Alexie underscores the point that sacred practices and beliefs should not be rendered on the page: "I don't write about anything sacred. I don't write about any ceremonies; I don't use any Indian songs." He tells Fraser that, instead, "I write about a drunk in a bar, or a guy who plays basketball." Interview comments such as these suggest that readers of Alexie's work have to be careful not to read the spiritual themes and conflicts of his poems and stories as necessarily being signs of a failure of belief or a loss of tradition, for they could also be linked to the deliberate decisions of an author unwilling, for ethical reasons, to reveal sacred matters to a reading public.

Like the author himself, the settings of Alexie's stories have migrated from the reservation to the city. He is careful to point out this shift in his work and perspective to interviewers, telling Jessica Chapel in 2000 that the stories in *The Toughest Indian in the World* (2000) reflect his concern with urban perspectives and urban Indians: "I was very much thinking about urban Indians as I worked on this collection. Sixty percent of all Indians live in urban areas, but nobody's writing about them." The stories in his subsequent collection of short stories, *Ten Little Indians* (2003), are set mostly in Seattle, and many of Alexie's Indian protagonists are upwardly mobile or middle class—college students, entrepreneurs, lawyers. As he tells interviewer Williams Cole in 2002, "I live in a white collar Indian world now. And you don't see any representation of white collar Indians in any kind of media." He explains to Cole that he wants to advance "the idea of twenty-first-century Indians as lawyers and doctors and engineers and architects" and to talk about "the ordinary ways in which we live our lives." But Alexie has not left behind his long-standing interest in depicting Indian people struggling to survive: the most acclaimed story of the collection, "What You Pawn I Will Redeem," features a homeless Spokane Indian named Jackson Jackson, who roams the city in search of enough money to buy back his grandmother's powwow regalia from a pawn shop. Seattle as a setting for the stories of *Ten Little Indians* offers an urban, multiethnic space inflected with post-NAFTA, post 9/11 tensions. In other words, Alexie has chosen to situate his contemporary Indians in a time and place where they can attempt to carve out their own twenty-first-century ways of living indigenously.

The geographical shift from Spokane to Seattle, from the rez to the city, both personal and fictional, may help to explain Alexie's evolving views on tribalism. Talking with Doug Marx in 1996, Alexie directly says, "I have a very specific commitment to Indian people, and I'm very tribal in that sense. I want *us* to survive as Indians." To Kelley Blewster in 1999, Alexie insists, "Good art is not universal. Good art is tribal." But more recently, Alexie has mentioned to interviewers that the events of September 11, 2001, changed his outlook on tribalism. In his 2003 interview with Matt Dellinger, Alexie comments that "the worst part about tribalism is its tendency to fundamentalize, and if I can fight fundamentalism in any of its forms I'm happy." In his conversation with Timothy Harris of *Real Change* that same year, Alexie describes his work as becoming "less and less Indian-centric." And yet, he emphatically tells Diane Thiel in 2004, "I am never, not even in my most intimate moments, completely free from my tribe." While Alexie occasionally indicates that being free from tribal identity and affiliation is something to be desired, in his 2004 conversation with Åse Nygren, he reiterates how important his own sense of tribal identity is to him, saying, "I'm very aware of my Spokaneness. I grew up on the Spokane Indian reservation, and my tribe heavily influences my personality and the ways in which I see the world." What Alexie seems to be calling for in his current comments on this issue is a recognition that one can be a member of many different tribes, not all of them racially or ethnically based. He explains to Tanita Davis and Sarah Stevenson in the most recent interview included here, "Ever since 9/11, I have worked hard to be very public about my multi-tribal identity. I think fundamentalism is the mistaken belief that one belongs to only one tribe; I am the opposite of that." Alexie's self-positioning in this comment has much to say about the depictions of Zits and Junior, and their search for new forms of identity and multiple lines of affiliation in his most recent novels, *Flight* and *The Absolutely True Diary of a Part-Time Indian*, both published in 2007.

These interviews offer valuable insights into Alexie's own description and evaluation of his written work and his writing process. Early in his career, Alexie felt a sense of urgency about writing, and indeed in the first few years of publication, he wrote quickly and furiously. In a 1994 autobiographical essay, "One Little Indian Boy," Alexie writes about his drive: "I know this. I know this. I have so much left to say and I don't know how much time I have left to say it all" (62). Or, as he explained to reporter Wishelle Banks in 1995, when he was just twenty-eight years old: "The average life expectancy of Indian men is like forty-nine, so I'm already middle-aged. How much time do I have left?" Some readers have commented that Alexie's early works can feel rushed at times. *Indian Killer*, in particular, was written in an intense burst, and it is the book that most often makes reviewers and interviewers uncomfortable. The reviewer for *Time* magazine, for example, wrote that "Alexie's tale is septic with what clearly seems to be his own unappeasable fury" (Skow), a line that Alexie occasionally quotes and mocks in some of these interviews. He defends the novel in his conversation with Kelley Blewster by explaining that he wrote *Indian Killer* intending to make white people uncomfortable, so that the novel could portray how "Indians are culturally, psychologically, physically, and emotionally killed. Still." Alexie's protest against the colonizing forces that devastate Native peoples across the Americas is a recurring theme in these interviews. At times, he speaks with intensity about the violence of American history, and he is especially effective in the interview conducted by Åse Nygren in pointing to genocide and Holocaust as a part of Native history that has never been fully recognized and appropriately addressed in the United States. "I want our dead to be honored," he adamantly tells Nygren.

Another aspect of colonialism that Alexie speaks out about in his interviews concerns literary appropriations: he frequently critiques nonnative writers such as Tony Hillerman, Barbara Kingsolver, Larry McMurtry, and others, who portray Indian culture and Indian characters in their novels. As he explains in his interview with Tomson Highway, Alexie is appalled that their fiction sells so well across America while the work of Native writers remains less visible and less marketable, especially when Native writers do not dwell on the kinds of romanticized scenes and characters that unfortunately appeal most to American audiences. The interviews also show Alexie's outrage at nonnatives who pass themselves off as Indian writers; in his interview with Lorena Allam, for example, Alexie talks about the writer known as "Nasdijj," who turned out to be a fraud. Alexie has called for "non-Indians" to "quit writing about us until we've established our voice—a completely voluntary moratorium," as he terms it in his conversation with Jessica Chapel. "If non-Indians stop writing about us," he adds, "they'll have to publish us instead."

At this point in his career, Alexie has become emblematic of an Indian writer who is not only published, but who is also widely popular and critically acclaimed. Winning the National Book Award for *The Absolutely True Diary of a Part-Time Indian* is the most recent recognition of Alexie's immense talent, which also includes his being named one of "Twenty Best American Novelists Under the Age of 40" by *Granta* magazine in 1996 and being included on *New Yorker* magazine's June 1999 list of the top twenty writers to watch in the twenty-first century. (See the Chronology in this volume for further information about Alexie's major awards.) As he has become one of the most prominent voices in contemporary American Indian literature, Alexie has also used his stature to mentor and encourage younger Indian writers. "The responsibilities of being an Indian writer are enormous," Alexie admits to John Purdy in 1997, and he has addressed this responsibility in various ways through the years, as these interviews demonstrate.

The interviews in this collection also reveal Alexie to be a self-aware, self-critical writer. Speaking with John Purdy, for instance, Alexie assesses his 1996 collection of poetry, *The Summer of Black Widows*, as being "technically good," "probably my best book," but he also expresses concerns that the poems are not the kind that "Indian people" can "relate to." Kelley Blewster reports in her profile of Alexie that he was "shocked" at the critical success of his 1995 novel, *Reservation Blues*, and that if he were grading it, he would give it a mere "C-minus." In his interview with Jessica Chapel, Alexie describes his short story "The Sin Eaters" (from *The Toughest Indian in the World*) as a "failed novel." In his 2007 conversation with Dave Weich, Alexie surprises the interviewer by suggesting that "*Flight* has been so extensively rewritten in my mind that we think I'm going to rewrite it extensively and republish it in a year and a half." Alexie is sometimes a tough critic of his own work.

Although Alexie defends *Indian Killer* in many of the interviews included here, he reveals in a 2002 conversation with Duncan Campbell that the novel "still, to this day, troubles me the most because I can't even get a grasp on it. It's the only one I re-read." More recently, in a keynote address to the Native American Literature Symposium in 2007, Alexie expressed his ongoing dissatisfactions with *Indian Killer*, going so far as to call it "racist" and suggesting that he wrote *Flight* as an "answer" to that novel. Indeed, both novels depict a boy who grows up cut off from his Indian heritage and who suffers immensely because of those circumstances, and both novels depict stark moments of violence. But *Flight*, in notable contrast to *Indian Killer*, ends with hope that the main character, Zits, who renounces violence in the end, will be able to create a meaningful, hybrid identity for himself.

Throughout these interviews, Alexie offers insights into all the major literary works he has published. He has also had an active involvement in filmmaking, especially with the success of *Smoke Signals* (1998), which not only won major awards at the 1998 Sundance Film Festival, but also was the first feature-length film written, directed, and produced by Native Americans to be nationally distributed in the United States, a fact that Alexie is quite proud of. His second full-length film, *The Business of Fancydancing* (2002), was not commercially successful but earned critical acclaim. This collection includes two interviews that focus primarily on Alexie as a filmmaker: Dennis West and Joan M. West's interview with Alexie about *Smoke Signals* for *Cineaste*, and Aileo Weinmann's interview with Alexie about *The Business of Fancydancing* for Filmcritic.com. In other interviews, readers gain insight into lesser-known aspects of Alexie's filmmaking involvement: he discusses his role of being a "script doctor" for Hollywood projects, and he talks about film projects he hoped to be able to make but could not for various reasons (such as a film version of *Indian Killer*).

Along with films that were not made (or have not yet been made), Alexie occasionally describes book projects that have not (yet) been published. His idea for a novel tentatively titled *Al Capone's Bones*, about the Mafia and Indians, comes up in a couple of the interviews. He talks with Williams Cole about an abandoned novel that would have told a story about what the United States would be like now if the British had won the Revolutionary War. Elsewhere he mentions working on a biography of Jimi Hendrix, a family memoir, and plans for some other narrative projects.

What also becomes clear in this collection of interviews is that poetry is the genre Alexie takes most seriously. He acknowledges that writing fiction, especially novels, earns him a comfortable living, but it is poetry "that's the constant," as he states to Joelle Fraser, and it's poetry that he makes sure to write every day, he tells Lorena Allam. Throughout these interviews Alexie claims the influence of a diverse group of poets on his own writing—Native poets such as Joy Harjo, Luci Tapahonso, Simon Ortiz, Leslie Silko, Adrian Louis, Louise Erdrich, as well as nonnative poets, including Emily Dickinson, Walt Whitman, Gerard Manley Hopkins, Shakespeare, Theodore Roethke, Allen Ginsberg, Langston Hughes, Lucille Clifton, and many others. He is perhaps most forthcoming about his work as a poet in the interview with Diane Thiel, revealing the ways in which form, rhyme, rhythm, repetition, and image can work together to create emotionally intense poems about Indian life. "I can sometimes make English sound like Salish," Alexie remarks. He also expresses an interest in finding surprising ways to lighten the gravitas of poetry with infusions of humor.

Indian humor is one of the most enduring qualities that readers have come to expect and admire in Alexie. For Alexie himself, as these interviews demonstrate, humor is one of the essential elements of his work. In several of the interviews, he displays great pleasure in being the World Heavyweight Poetry Champion, and he discusses his penchant for performing stand-up comedy rather than offering typical literary readings on his book tours. He tells Åse Nygren that "being funny breaks down barriers between people. I can get up in front of any crowd, and if I make them laugh first I can say almost anything to them." His humor in fact often has a serious edge. A good example of this complexity comes up in Alexie's interview with Lorena Allam, when he connects humor to trauma and survival: "the two funniest groups of people I've ever been around are Native Americans and Jewish folks," Alexie says and then pointedly adds, "so I guess there's something inherently funny about genocide." It is perhaps in his most recent and widely acclaimed novel, *The Absolutely True Diary of a Part-Time Indian*, that Alexie strikes a masterful balance between great pain and humor.

As is the custom with this series, the interviews are reprinted in their full versions, with minimal editing. All book and film titles have been regularized and italicized. Misspellings and small inaccuracies in the originals have been corrected silently; clarifications or substantial corrections have been noted using brackets. The interviews appear in chronological order, and readers of this volume in its entirety will note some repetition among the interviews, understandably so given the standard questions Alexie is often asked. Most interesting, however, are the moments when Alexie looks back at his previous work (such as *Indian Killer*) or positions (on tribalism, for example) and critiques or qualifies them. By reading the volume as a whole, scholars, students, and general readers will be able to locate themes and issues that have remained at the forefront of Alexie's work, while also noting the ways in which his thinking on other topics has changed over the years. Intriguing narrative arcs emerge in this collection of interviews, as do many complicated moments that defy any easy translation into potential "soundbites."

I wish to acknowledge the assistance of many people who helped out with this project at crucial moments. Thanks go to Jeff Berglund, Stephanie Fitzgerald, and Richard Pearce for encouraging my work on Alexie. I appreciate the support of my colleagues and friends at Purdue University; in particular, Dorsey Armstrong, Kristina Bross, John Duvall, Wendy Flory, Christian Knoeller, Bill Mullen, Bich Minh Nguyen, Aparajita Sagar, Marcia Stephenson, and Irwin Weiser have generously shared their time and interest in this project. The Interlibrary Loan staff of the Purdue Libraries helpfully provided copies of interviews from many difficult to locate publications. The College of Liberal Arts Dean's Office at Purdue deserves special recognition for funding my travel to libraries and other sites to work on this volume.

I am especially grateful to all of the interviewers and publishers who agreed to allow their work to be reprinted in this volume. Seetha Srinivasan and Walter Biggins, my editors at the University Press of Mississippi, offered advice and encouragement at the right moments. Samuel Drews capably assisted me with proofreading and fact checking. Putting together an accurate and helpful Chronology for this volume proved to be a daunting task, but I thank both Bob Hershon of Hanging Loose Press and Christy Cox of FallsApart Productions, who provided key pieces of information. Most important, I offer heartfelt appreciation to Sherman Alexie for the strength of his writing and his vision, which bring together honesty, anguish, humor, and hope, ever so powerfully, and for so many readers.

NJP

## *Works Cited*

Alexie, Sherman. Acceptance Speech. National Book Awards. New York City. 14 Nov. 2007. Available online at http://www.nationalbook.org/audio_video.html#sherman. Accessed 9 June 2008.

———. Introduction. *The Lone Ranger and Tonto Fistfight in Heaven*. Expanded ed. New York: Grove, 2005. xi–xxii.

———. Keynote Address. Native American Literature Symposium. Mount Pleasant, MI. 9 March 2007.

———. *The Lone Ranger and Tonto Fistfight in Heaven*. Expanded ed. New York: Grove, 2005.

———. "One Little Indian Boy." *Edge Walking on the Western Rim: New Works by 12 Northwest Writers*. Ed. Mayumi Tsutakawa. Seattle: Sasquatch Books/One Reel, 1994. 53–63.

Banks, Wishelle. "Alexie Finds Inspiration in His Home, Humor in His Family and Their Life." *Native Voice* [a student publication of the Native American Journalists Association] 1995. http://www.fallsapart.com/art-nv.html. Accessed 10 May 2008.

Bruchac, Joseph, ed. *Songs from This Earth on Turtle's Back*. Greenfield Center, NY: Greenfield Review Press, 1983.

Hoback, Jane. "Native Tongue." *Rocky Mountain News* 25 July 2003. http://www.rockymountainnews.com/news/2003/Jul/25/native-tongue/. Accessed 10 May 2008.

Kincaid, James. "Who Gets to Tell Their Stories?" *New York Times Book Review* 3 May 1992: 1, 24–29.

Skow, John. "Lost Heritage." Rev. of *Indian Killer*, by Sherman Alexie. *Time* 21 Oct.1996: 90.

# Chronology

1966      Sherman Joseph Alexie Jr. is born on October 7 in Sacred Heart Hospital in Spokane, Washington, to Lillian Agnes Cox Alexie (Spokane, Flathead, Colville) and Sherman Joseph Alexie (Coeur d'Alene). He is diagnosed with hydrocephalus, undergoes surgery at six months, and suffers from seizures until he is seven years old. Grows up on the Spokane Indian Reservation in the town of Wellpinit (located about fifty miles northwest of the city of Spokane). Learns to read by the age of three.

1972–80    Attends school in Wellpinit on the reservation.

1981–85    Transfers to Reardan High School (located approximately twenty miles south of Wellpinit). Plays basketball for the "Reardan Indians" and becomes team captain; joins the debate team, Future Farmers of America, and many other clubs. Experiences athletic and academic success. Graduates in 1985.

1985–87    Attends Gonzaga University in Spokane, Washington. Shortly after his arrival on campus, Alexie begins drinking to excess.

1987      Moves to Seattle briefly, with the intention of enrolling in the University of Washington, but is robbed at knife-point one night and returns home.

1988–91    Transfers to Washington State University in Pullman. Originally intends to study pre-medicine, but begins to study creative writing under Alex Kuo. Eventually graduates (in 1994) with a B.A. in American Studies.

1988      The *Journal of Ethnic Studies* publishes eighteen of Alexie's poems in the summer issue (vol. 16, no. 2).

1990      Alexie's poem "Distances" appears in issue number 56 of *Hanging Loose* magazine, beginning his long and successful relationship with the press.

1991      Alexie works as an assistant for People to People, a student ambassador program based in Spokane, for nine months until his career as a writer develops. Receives a Washington State Arts Commission Fellowship for poetry ($5,000). Stops drinking as he begins to receive attention as a writer.

1992    *The Business of Fancydancing* (poems and stories) is published by Hanging Loose Press. Alexie is awarded a National Endowment for the Arts Fellowship for poetry ($20,000). Alexie's manuscript for *I Would Steal Horses* wins the Fifth Annual Chapbook Contest sponsored by Slipstream Press and is published in March. In May, reviewer James Kincaid describes Alexie as "one of the major lyric voices of our time" in an omnibus review of recently published Native American literature in the *New York Times Book Review*.

1993    *Old Shirts and New Skins* (poetry) is published in March by the American Indian Studies Center at UCLA. *The Lone Ranger and Tonto Fistfight in Heaven* (short stories) is published in September by Atlantic Monthly Press. *First Indian on the Moon* (poetry) is published in December by Hanging Loose Press.

1994    Alexie marries Diane (Hidatsa, Ho-Chunk, Potawatomi) and moves to Seattle permanently. *Seven Mourning Songs for the Cedar Flute I Have Yet to Learn to Play*, a long-poem by Alexie with prints by James Lavadour (Walla Walla), is published by the Whitman College Book Arts Lab. Alexie's story "This is What It Means to Say Phoenix, Arizona" is selected for *The Best American Short Stories 1994* (ed. Tobias Wolff). In December, Alexie wins a Lila Wallace–*Reader's Digest* Writers' Award ($105,000); for his outreach project, he works with the United Indians of All Tribes Foundation to organize a series of writing workshops for Native peoples in Seattle.

1995    *Reservation Blues* (novel) published in June by Atlantic Monthly Press. *Reservation Blues: The Soundtrack*, a musical collaboration between Alexie and Jim Boyd (Colville), is released by Thunderwolf Productions. "That Place Where Ghosts of Salmon Jump," a piece of public art based on Alexie's poem, is installed adjacent to the downtown Spokane Public Library overlooking the falls.

1996    *Water Flowing Home* (poetry chapbook) published in January by Limberlost Press. *Reservation Blues* wins the Before Columbus Foundation American Book Award. *Granta* magazine selects Alexie as one of the twenty "Best Young American Novelists" for issue 54. *Indian Killer* (novel) is published in September by Atlantic Monthly Press. *The Sum-*

*mer of Black Widows* (poetry) is published in October by Hanging Loose Press. "Capital Punishment" from *The Summer of Black Widows* is included in *The Best American Poetry 1996* (ed. Adrienne Rich).

1997    Son Joseph is born.

1998    *Smoke Signals* (dir. Chris Eyre, Cheyenne/Arapaho) debuts at Sundance and wins the Sundance film Festival Audience Award and the Filmmakers Trophy in January. *The Man Who Loves Salmon* (poetry chapbook) is published by Limberlost Press. Alexie enters the World Poetry Bout Association competition in Taos, NM, and wins his first (of four consecutive) World Heavyweight Poetry championship. Alexie is one of eight panelists invited to participate in "A Dialogue on Race with President Bill Clinton," which airs on PBS's *Lehrer News Hour* on July 9. *Smoke Signals: A Screenplay* is published in July 1998 by Hyperion, an imprint of Miramax Books, just as Miramax Films puts *Smoke Signals* into nationwide release.

1999    Alexie debuts as a stand-up comic at the Foolproof: Northwest Comedy Festival in Seattle in April. In June, Alexie is included in the *New Yorker*'s "Future of American Fiction" issue and is named one of the "twenty best young fiction writers in America."

2000    *The Toughest Indian in the World* (short stories) published in May by Grove/Atlantic. *One Stick Song* (poetry) published in September by Hanging Loose Press.

2001    Alexie's *Toughest Indian* shares the 2001 PEN/Malamud Award for Short Fiction with Richard Ford. Son David born.

2002    *The Business of Fancydancing,* Alexie's second feature-length film, premieres at the Sundance Film Festival in January and goes into limited release at independent film festivals.

2003    On January 30, Alexie is a guest on the *Oprah Winfrey Show* and is presented reissued medals of honor his grandfather earned while fighting in World War II. In March, Alexie's father dies. *The Business of Fancydancing: The Screenplay* is published by Hanging Loose Press, and the film is released on DVD in July. *Ten Little Indians* (short stories) is published in June by Grove/Atlantic. In October, Alexie receives the Regents' Distinguished Alumnus Award from Washington State University.

2004    "What You Pawn I Will Redeem," a story from *Ten Little Indians* is selected for inclusion in *The Best American Short Stories 2004* (ed. Lorrie Moore). Alexie becomes an Artist in Residence at the University of

Washington, teaching courses in American Ethnic Studies, an appoint-
ment he also accepts in 2006 and 2008.

2005 "What You Pawn I Will Redeem" is selected for the *O. Henry Prize
Stories 2005*. An expanded edition of *The Lone Ranger and Tonto Fistfight in Heaven* (short stories) published in February by Grove/Atlantic.
*Dangerous Astronomy* (poetry chapbook) is published in July 2005
by Limberlost Press. The poem "Avian Nights" (from *Dangerous Astronomy*) wins a Pushcart Prize and is included in *The Pushcart Prize
XXIX (2005)*.

2007 *Flight* (novel) is published in April by Black Cat books, an imprint
of Grove/Atlantic. *The Absolutely True Diary of a Part-Time Indian*
(young adult literature) is published in September by Little Brown. In
October, Alexie receives the Western Literature Association's Distinguished Achievement Award for 2007. In November, *Absolutely True
Diary* wins the 2007 National Book Award for young people's literature.

2008 *Absolutely True Diary* wins the 2008 American Indian Youth Literature
Award from the American Indian Library Association and is chosen for
the seventh annual "Spokane Is Reading" event.

2009 *Face* (poetry) is published by Hanging Loose Press.

Conversations with Sherman Alexie

# Sherman Alexie, Literary Rebel

John and Carl Bellante/1993

From the *Bloomsbury Review* May–June 1994: 14–15, 26. Reprinted by permission of the interviewers.

Sherman Alexie is a robust and powerful writer in his mid-twenties who has taken the literary world by storm. The *New York Times Book Review* has described his work as "so wide ranging, dexterous, and consistently capable of raising your neck hair that it enters at once into our ideas of who we are and how we might be, makes us speak and hear his words over and over, call others into the room or over the phone to repeat them." Distinctly unfaint praise for a personable, well-spoken, scholarly-looking fellow who spends the vast majority of his time in Spokane, Washington, and whose sense of self-deprecating humor disguises the fierce fealty he feels towards his people, the Spokane/Coeur d'Alene.

By his own admission, Alexie is still learning his craft as a writer. He started off as a poet (*The Business of Fancydancing*, Hanging Loose Press, 1992) whose verses possess a strong narrative proclivity, and moved on to short fiction as manifested by *The Lone Ranger and Tonto Fistfight in Heaven* (Grove Atlantic, 1993), whose compelling stories concerning growing up Indian in America contain a powerful poetic undercurrent. His first crack at a novel, currently titled "Coyote Springs," is due for publication by Grove Atlantic in 1995, and is the source of much speculation about what literary legerdemain this burgeoning artist is capable of producing next. This fall two limited editions of his poetry will be released: *Water Flowing Home* (Limberlost Press, Boise, ID) and *Seven Mourning Songs for the Cedar Flute I Have Yet to Learn to Play* (Whitman College Press, Walla Walla, WA).

Throughout his books the reader encounters a complex sensibility simultaneously embracing the Indian way of life but which nevertheless has been profoundly influenced by white American culture, books and movies in particular. As such, Alexie finds himself irrevocably torn between two loyalties, which lends a dynamic tension to his evocative and deceptively straightforward writing. Speaking with the inside knowledge of a person who has grown up in and around the reservation—or "the rez" as he tends to refer to it—Alexie manages to chronicle indelibly what he perceives as the severe plight of Native Americans.

Getting together with Sherman Alexie, as we did over lunch last fall, is to discover an engaging personality whose quick wit and finely developed sense of irony permeate his conversation with equal regularity as each turns up in his prose and poetry. Neither is he hesitant to talk quite bluntly about his life.

**The Bloomsbury Review:** One's immediate impression of you as a writer is that, in your role as storyteller, you have an unmistakable poetic streak. Was the transition from poet to writer of fiction at all tricky for you?

**Sherman Alexie:** The evolution came pretty naturally because, as you say, my poems are stories. There's a very strong narrative drive in all my poetry. It felt natural for me to evolve into a larger form. Not to say it wasn't difficult for me at first, though. Definitely. I had this thing about going beyond one page, typewritten. I'd get to the bottom of a page and freak out, because I wouldn't know what to do next. But the stories kept getting bigger and bigger, as did the lives of all my fictional characters. They began to demand more space than a poem could provide. So it was natural to move on to short stories and now to a novel.

**TBR:** Your prose appears to be pared down quite scrupulously. Very focused, even stark.

**SA:** I don't like the term "minimalism" because it implies you're not telling the whole story. But minimalism is sometimes what I do. I'm interested in the details that *matter*. You'll notice there's not much landscape in my stories, not much physical description of anybody or anything. I suppose I'm more interested in interior landscapes, which is where poetry comes in.

**TBR:** Would it be going too far to speculate that Victor, the protagonist in many of your stories, is your fictional alter ego?

**SA:** My editor and I were talking about my characters, and I told him I think I'm going to kill some of them off in my novel. And he said, "Yeah, when it's all over we'll know which ones are you." But then he added, "Victor will be alive." So I suppose that means something.

**TBR:** What about Thomas Builds-the-Fire? Is he based on somebody you know, or is he an aspect of your personality?

**SA:** An aspect of me. The three major male characters in the book are Victor, Junior, and Thomas Builds-the-Fire. I call them the holy trinity of me.

**TBR:** Sometimes Victor's stories are told in the first person, sometimes in the third person. How do you decide when it's appropriate for the narrative to be subjective or objective?

**SA:** Whether or not Victor is going to tell the truth. When I'm writing in the third person, I'm looking at *everybody* with a larger eye than what just Victor could provide. Victor's a storyteller himself, so he has a tendency to exaggerate.

**TBR:** Would you explain the nature of what storytelling means to Native American culture?

**SA:** People keep asking me how my work is influenced by the oral tradition. I always say, "Well, my writing has nothing to do with the oral tradition, because I typed it." [Laughter.] On the most basic level I'm telling stories on the page, certainly, but it's really a far evolution from storytelling of the past, which was done in a very extemporaneous fashion.

**TBR:** But your stories do have a spontaneous flow. And many of your characters engage themselves in the art of storytelling, implying it continues to be a compelling force. Is one of the grievances you hold against television, another recurring image in your fiction, that it helps destroy the oral tradition?

**SA:** I don't really have much against television as long as I can get cable TV. [Laughter.] Indians tell a lot of stories. At powwows, in houses, at gatherings. It ties people together.

All of the stories aren't necessarily hundreds of years old either. My family tells stories from twenty years ago over and over again. But then again, in my family we're heavily influenced by TV and movies too. Just like the larger white culture. That's all in my stories too.

**TBR:** One of your poems would appear to be directed at Jack Crabbe, the hero of *Little Big Man*, the book by Thomas Berger and the movie directed by Arthur Penn. We gather you don't exactly approve of the way Native Americans are characterized in cinema and books.

**SA:** To be honest, I've never read the novel. But the movie is the best portrayal of Indian life I can think of. Far superior to *Thunderheart* or *Dances With Wolves*. Certainly the best Indian movie ever made by Hollywood.

**TBR:** With all the fuss being made about what a groundbreaking movie *Dances With Wolves* was, *Little Big Man* covered much of the same territory first. Seeing white actors play Native American parts really bothers you, doesn't it?

**SA:** Val Kilmer can play Jim Morrison, but he can't play an Indian [in

*Thunderheart*]. Of course that bothers me. One of the poems in the new book
I'm working on has a section where it says the Motion Picture Academy of Arts
and Sciences has announced a new category for this year's Academy Awards—best
performance by a non-native in a Native American role. [Laughter.] I keep waiting for the day when an Indian gets to play a white guy.

**TBR:** How do you feel about Tony Hillerman's novels?
**SA:** I know some Navajos have given him their seal of approval or whatever. But
it's colonial writing. No matter what his political leanings are, it's still colonial
writing. They're fine detective novels, and he does his research for the Navajo culture part. It's basic Navajo Culture 101 stuff. But he's in the way. As long as people
like Tony Hillerman continue to write about Indians, publishers are going to pick
up white writers, because what they have to say is sanitized and simple.

All that appropriation, not just writing, but New Age culture, the men's movement and stuff, take all the good of native culture or native images or native spirituality without accepting any of the bad. The good has to be earned. Tony Hillerman is taking shortcuts, as are any dozens of others you could name, like Barbara
Kingsolver.

**TBR:** Time is a recurring image in your stories. You'll describe a woman who
hasn't smiled for two hundred years. Or a character who's stood in line for five
hundred years. Are you suggesting that an Indian's experience of time is different
from what a white's might be?
**SA:** Yes. The past is still here for us. We carry all of that with us. Otherwise they
wouldn't keep repeating the same mistakes.

**TBR:** So your perception is that there are certain elements of Native American
culture that are immutable, which won't or shouldn't change.
**SA:** We carry good and bad with us. The whole romantic myth of the Indian warrior and Indians of the past damages Indians just as much as it damages New
Agers. In some ways, it's bad we carry that past with us because it's not here and now.

You try to live up to some ideal that's impossible. You can't be that *Dances
With Wolves* kind of Indian. In my novel there's a moment where characters are
talking about religion, and one guy says, "Well, I'm not going to be a Christian.
I believe in my Native spirituality." To which another character responds, "Yeah,
but all *you* know about Native spirituality is what you learned from *Dances With
Wolves.*"

**TBR:** Is the concept of time a topic that arises in your conversations with other
Native Americans?

**SA:** I worry about such things, but that's how I am. There's not a conscious effort by Indians to think about time, but it's my observation that's how a lot of people in my tribe live their lives.

One point I want to make clear is that I don't claim to be a spokesperson for all natives. I know of my family, my tribe. And I've known Indians from other tribes with similar stories. As a writer I look at people and how they communicate and talk.

**TBR:** One of the risks you artfully skirt in your fiction is confirming certain Indian stereotypes—such as the idea Indians can't hold their liquor, or that they have difficulty assimilating into American society.

**SA:** I'm busting those stereotypes too. If you pay close attention to characters in *The Lone Ranger and Tonto*, most of them *don't* drink. Only one of the women characters in the book drinks. She's in "Crazy Horse Dreams." Thomas Builds-the-Fire has never drunk. There are certainly drinkers in my book, just as there are drinkers on my rez, in my tribe. But there are non-drinkers too. The time frame is all skewered, but the three main characters, Thomas, Victor, and Junior, are all not drinking in the present.

**TBR:** You just mentioned Crazy Horse, who's referred to frequently in your stories. What makes him such a focal figure for you?

**SA:** He's an Oglala Sioux, which makes him from a different tribe and culture entirely. But I use him as a spiritual figure, a savior whose example we need to aspire to.

**TBR:** Yet, as a writer your attitude towards Jesus is ambivalent, to say the least.

**SA:** Not towards Jesus himself. I'd say I'm ambivalent towards Christians. [Laughter.] Mostly I'm ambivalent toward churches, who haven't been very good to Native Americans and reservations in this country. They've participated fully in the genocide of Native Americans culturally. The priest and nuns at boarding school beat kids for speaking their native language. There *have* been public apologies made in the Pacific Northwest, and different areas, for the Church's actions. But that doesn't make me any less suspicious of churches. Or most institutions, for that matter.

**TBR:** You apparently distrust tribal councils who preside over reservations.

**SA:** [Laughing.] If there's one thing we've assimilated fully as Native Americans, it's political corruption. For the most part, the tribal council people I've known have been self-serving, manipulative capitalists. And certainly tribal councils themselves are no different. After being powerless all their lives, they acquire a little power on the rez, and it corrupts them, makes them do horrible things to their people. That's the worst kind of assimilation, when you're hurting members of your own tribe.

**TBR:** A powerful image in your writing is dancing, which serves as a symbolic link between Native American and white culture.
**SA:** For almost every culture, with the possible exception of America, dancing was a very important part of religion, of social life. In Native American culture, especially, there are so many different kinds of dancing, a dance for everything. I still think that's the case, or at least I want it to be. One of my characters says, "I'm not interested in how things are, I'm interested in how things *should* be." And you know, a dance is not just your feet moving.

**TBR:** It's an attitude. Just as your characters' visions and storytelling are a form of attitude.
**SA:** Dancing and believing in or listening to your dreams.

**TBR:** How much genuine communication takes place, in your experience, between tribes?
**SA:** There are hundreds of tribes in this country, some of whom still hold strong animosities towards one another. I don't think *anybody* likes the Pawnee yet. [Laughter.] Certain tribes are friendly because they've been friendly a long time. Like any other communities, how they relate to each other depends on their histories together. The Spokane and Coeur d'Alenes, the two tribes I belong to, get along, because they've always been so close together. There was never an issue of any wars going on between them. But some Plains tribes are bitter enemies. They've been fighting forever. And on a certain level those feelings are as strong as ever. It doesn't mean when you see someone from that tribe at a powwow, you run up and hit him over the head. Some of it's just joking stuff. Playful.

**TBR:** Basketball is another subject that pops up frequently in your writing. Do Indians like to take credit for inventing it, much as the Russians once claimed to have originally created baseball?
**SA:** Just me fooling around. But in fact the Incas probably invented it, or a form of basketball. They had these huge sunken pits they played it in, and this rock they had to throw through a hole dug in the wall. The team that lost got killed. Now *that's* basketball. We may not have invented it, but it's been in the air for a long time.

**TBR:** Why haven't Native Americans made their way into the NBA, given the legendary talents they display at an early age in your stories?
**SA:** College.

**TBR:** The fact that not enough attend?
**SA:** For the ones who do, the culture shock is too great. Being so far away from home, the sense of isolation affects you. Being on a reservation, or even in an urban area, you have the closeness of your family and other Indians around. Things run differently in college. You feel very alone.

**TBR:** How do the friends you grew up with respond to your having become a writer who's made an impression on white culture? For that matter, has your writing had much impact among your own people?
**SA:** I sold almost two hundred copies of *Fancydancing* on my rez. Not as many of the other books.

**TBR:** Do they respond to your work differently than non-native readers?
**SA:** I talk to a lot of Indians who come to my readings. They like the stuff. After all, I'm talking to them. I'm telling stories they know, or know about, telling shared jokes, puns, the shared inside information. Indians appreciate that. Of course, the irony is on my own rez, I was an outsider mostly when I was growing up.

**TBR:** Due to literary inclinations on your part?
**SA:** Most writers are alienated little kids. The joke I always tell is when we played cowboys and Indians on the rez, they always made *me* be the cowboy. [Laughter.]

**TBR:** A fascinating ingredient of the humor in *The Lone Ranger and Tonto* is how distinct and different it is from white humor. There seem to be many varieties of inside jokes where people laugh at observations funny to them, but probably not to anyone else who's not tuned into their wavelength. Are you suggesting people starved for positive elements in their lives will laugh at anything, or does Indian humor run deeper than that?
**SA:** What makes it so different is gallows humor. If you weren't laughing, you'd be crying. It's good in many ways, telling stories and laughing, having a good time together. But in some ways, humor is also used by people to hide. They can't be serious. Like James Many Horses when he gets cancer.

**TBR:** He wears people out with his jokes.
**SA:** That's a large part of Indian humor.

**TBR:** Maybe it all comes down to an equation you propose in the book. That survival equals anger times imagination.
**SA:** Exactly what my attitude towards life is.

**TBR:** Precisely what about white culture makes you so angry?
**SA:** Pretty much anything patriarchal.

**TBR:** Then you don't perceive Indian societies as being patriarchal?
**SA:** Now they are. [Laughter.] There used to be a sense of matriarchal power. That's not the case anymore. Not in my tribe anyway. We've resisted assimilation in many ways, but I know we've assimilated into sexism and misogyny.

**TBR:** That's surprising, considering how women are generally portrayed—totally subservient to their husbands and other men of the tribe. Certainly that's true of the women in *Little Big Man.*
**SA:** That's just those Lakotas. [Laughter.] Traditions differ from tribe to tribe. But think of a tribe like the Iroquois. The U.S. system of government is directly lifted from the Iroquois nations. Men served as government officials, but the *women* picked them all. As with anything else, women always have power. Women are the creators. We get into trouble when we try to deny that. So I'm angry toward this patriarchal country that creates an environment totally hostile toward women. If we can't love our own mothers and sisters, how can we start loving?

**TBR:** Do you imagine anger will always be a source for your fiction, your reason to create?
**SA:** Or as one person put it, "Now that you've got a six figure contract, can you still be angry?" [Laughter.] The answer is, "Yeah," because of family members, friends, whole tribes, the whole country of Indian people, let alone all the other disadvantaged groups who *don't* have six figure contracts. I'm thinking about them.

**TBR:** One problem with using anger for inspiration is the way it wears you down. Do you ever worry about anger becoming a negative force?
**SA:** Anger in itself can be positive or destructive. That's why you need to use imagination to make it positive. A quote by Gandhi pretty much sums it up: "Anger as a positive force can change lives." The phrase "angry young man" suggests senseless anger. That's not the case with me. Anger without hope, anger without love, or anger without compassion are all-consuming. That's not my kind of anger. Mine is very specific and directed.

**TBR:** In the first story of your collection, "Every Little Hurricane," you draw a direct correlation between the weather and people's emotional lives, as if they're inextricably linked.

**SA:** Just because we're on top of the food chain doesn't mean we're not affected by weather. It's extremely arrogant of us. Recent floods in the Midwest demonstrated how powerful nature is and how strongly it influences us. The reason we're sitting inside right now is because it gets hot sometimes. Or windy. We forget we're *part* of nature, as subject to its whims and purposes as any other animal.

**TBR:** You take that image a step further, though. When people fight, the storm isn't just metaphorical, it's the genuine article.

**SA:** That's right. Humans fighting with one another is a pretty common, natural occurrence.

**TBR:** You're implying it's especially prevalent among Native Americans, however?

**SA:** When one Indian kills another, nobody notices because that's natural selection. There is a lot of infighting, Indian against Indian. If you can't fight the bigger power, which seems so invincible, you're going to fight each other. Even among writers, there's a lot of that. I'm catching a lot of crap because of the success I'm having. About whether I'm really Indian or not. How traditional I am. I was at an Indian school the other day, and one of the students wanted to know, "Do you speak your language? What's your band?" Narrowing me, as if my not knowing those things made him a better Indian than I am. That kind of thing happens all the time, not just in the writing world. For example, if you're a rez Indian, you're superior to an urban Indian. If you speak your language, you're superior to people who don't. If you dance, you're superior to people who don't.

**TBR:** A similar form of stereotyping exists in your stories, as far as white characters are concerned. In the first place there are very few whites of major importance. Secondly, those depicted remain sketchy at best in their fictional development. Do you feel uncomfortable getting under the skin of white characters?

**SA:** No, I have fun making them sketchy. Because Indians have been sketchy for a long time. I enjoy playing with them as one-dimensional characters. That's on purpose. They're flat cardboard cut-outs, the kind you get your photograph taken with at Disneyland. [Laughter.] The whole idea gets my mind working. It'll probably even end up in a story now. White people cut-outs at the trading post: "Come get your photo taken with a white person. Only a dollar fifty!"

**TBR:** Let's talk about who your literary influences were.

**SA:** I had no idea there was any such thing as contemporary Native American literature when I started my writing career. Alex Kuo, my writing teacher at Washington State, who was friends with a number of these people, introduced me to all this contemporary native writing. Adrian C. Louis, Linda Hogan, Simon Ortiz, Scott Momaday, people who have careers now. He gave me this anthology with seventy-two native writers in it. I went home that night and pored through it. Bam-bam-bam-bam! I was amazed and stunned that these people were writing poems and stories *about* me.

**TBR:** Was it similar to what you were writing yourself?

**SA:** It went across the board. Some of it I liked then, because I was seeing it for the first time, although I don't necessarily care for that style now. To paraphrase Adrian C. Louis, he calls it "the corn pollen and eagle feather school of poetry." It's that traditional poetry anybody can write. If you had a nine-year-old white kid from Brooklyn, say, write an Indian poem, he'd turn out Mother Earth-Great Spirit stuff. I don't care for that kind of native writing. It's poetry white writers try to copy.

**TBR:** To some extent *The Lone Ranger and Tonto* resembles Sherwood Anderson's *Winesburg, Ohio*: the stories feature certain central figures and all take place within the same locale. Which is to say that even when Victor's not in the story per se, you can still feel his presence, his consciousness, if you prefer.

**SA:** People find themselves wondering whether it's a novel or a book of short stories. I tell them, it's like a big house with twenty-two rooms, and they're all happening at the same time.

**TBR:** Were you also a storyteller at an early age?

**SA:** My whole family is good at that. The funny thing is they're better at it than I am. And I'm the one getting published. [Laughter.]

**TBR:** Perhaps because you're the only one who wrote it down.

**SA:** I was always like that. Always read voraciously. I'd read the whole reservation library by the time I was in fifth grade. I taught myself to read. I remember, before I could actually read, seeing a sentence and a paragraph and *understanding* them. Not knowing the words, but understanding the form.

**TBR:** Which writers particularly impressed you?

**SA:** I liked John Steinbeck a lot. When I was in third grade, I read *Cannery Row* and thought, "Wow! That's a great book." The third grade year is when I really got

"Steinbecked." We had seven or eight different books by him in the rez library. *Of Mice and Men, The Pearl, The Red Pony.*

**TBR:** There's a particular allegorical aspect to those books that is reflected in your work.
**SA:** It's amazing. I haven't thought about John Steinbeck in I don't know *how* long. Your asking me that question brought it all out. And yeah, when you think about it, there's a really serious parallel to what I'm doing and what Steinbeck did. Oh, no! A white guy influenced me! [Laughter.]

**TBR:** Without question there are certain books one reads growing up that subtly alter our perception of the world, in that we begin to comprehend what it is to view life through adult eyes. Harper Lee's *To Kill a Mockingbird* was such a book for us. Were there any other books which were formative in your development?
**SA:** Scary books. I liked Stephen King. I still do.

**TBR:** In a seminar we did with Clarissa Pinkola Estés and Paolo Coelho, called "The Dark Side of Children's Literature," we discussed how the gorier aspects of the Grimm fairy tales, or Mother Goose nursery rhymes, offer children their first glance at death, providing an initial contemplation about mortality. No doubt Stephen King served a similar purpose for you.
**SA:** I didn't need to learn more about people dying.

**TBR:** You're working on a novel now. How's it coming and what's it about?
**SA:** A reservation Catholic rock 'n' roll band. It's pretty much done, but I can't find the ending.

**TBR:** Have you ever had a difficult time finding an ending before?
**SA:** No, never.

**TBR:** Could part of the problem be that the novel is a longer, more complex form than you're used to?
**SA:** Yes. I had a couple endings that were very *cute*, which didn't feel right. I'm *trying* to write a positive novel, because I've noticed in Native American literature—almost all literature, for that matter—there are no healthy male/female relationships. Although there's a lot of horrible stuff going on around it, at the core of this novel I wanted a strong relationship between a male and female. I also wanted to have very strong women, as I do in the short stories, but to have their roles be more active. I've focused on father/son, brother/brother relationships in my work so far, and I want to change that. I'm really dealing with Indian women

a lot now. The book deals with a romantic relationship, but it's also about the way Indian men treat Indian women.

**TBR:** Does your struggle have to do with filling out your canvas, being more descriptive?
**SA:** That's the whole point. I still haven't done that. The hardest part about a novel for me is you're doing all these pages, pages, and pages examining people, and they're still mostly undescribed. A big description for me is saying somebody had blue jeans on.

**TBR:** How long have you been working on the book?
**SA:** About a year. It'll be done about the first of next year. I just want to get the next one going. It's already jumping around in my head. A murder mystery.

**TBR:** Will your approach be, as Ross MacDonald recommended, to come up with the ending first, then work the plot back to the beginning?
**SA:** Maybe. I'm going to bust the genre apart. The novel will speak in the plural, and you won't know if the narrator is a man, a woman, or a lot of people. So that there's a tribal sense. That's one difference. I've only written the first page. It works on the first page, but I'm not sure I can carry it off for two hundred more. We'll see.

**TBR:** In your work so far, you don't appear to worry much about genres. So this ought to be a real challenge.
**SA:** I plan to blow the formula apart. One writer I really like who does that is Walter Mosley with the Easy Rawlins mysteries. His hero is a black detective in Los Angeles during the 1940s. While it's still formula writing, there's some sly social commentary, real insidious stuff. Not that I want to be sly or insidious. [Laughter.]

**TBR:** Does that mean you've surrendered to the necessity of having to sell books to make a living as a writer? Or don't you worry about that?
**SA:** Now I do. Especially with this present book. There's so much gossip, so many rumors about it. People are talking about me at New York cocktail parties. Jay McInerney mentioned my name on the Charlie Rose show! One night I couldn't sleep, so I turned on the TV, PBS. And a second after I turned it on, Charlie Rose asks, "So, Jay, who have you been reading? Who do you recommend?" And Jay goes, "Well, there are a lot great books coming out by multi-ethnic writers. One in particular I really like, a *great* book, is Sherman Alexie's *The Lone Ranger and*

*Tonto Fistfight in Heaven."* [Laughter.] Here's this cultural icon mentioning my name on national television. I thought I was dreaming. I have a hard enough time telling the difference between my dreams and reality. This was too much.

**TBR:** Did you pinch yourself?
**SA:** I did more than that. I banged my head against the wall. [Laughter.]

# Sherman Alexie:
# A Reservation of the Mind

Doug Marx/1996

From *Publishers Weekly* 16 September 1996: 39–40. Reprinted by permission.

Six years ago, as a twenty-four-year-old student at Washington State University, Sherman Alexie, a Spokane/Coeur d'Alene Indian, set down his career goals at the insistence of a friend: 1) to publish ten books by age thirty; 2) to see a book on the silver screen by thirty-five; and 3) to receive a major literary prize by forty.

With *Indian Killer*, his third prose work, a tragic thriller about the ravages of cultural dilution and dissolution, out this month from Grove/Atlantic, and *The Summer of Black Widows*, his seventh collection of poetry, out in October from Hanging Loose Press, the first goal will be achieved. Three of Alexie's books— his first short-story collection, *The Lone Ranger and Tonto Fistfight in Heaven* (Atlantic Monthly, 1993); his novel *Reservation Blues* (Atlantic Monthly, 1995); and *Indian Killer*—are the subject of ongoing film negotiations. As for a major literary award, if review acclaim from such established masters as Reynolds Price, Leslie Marmon Silko, and Frederick Bausch, not to mention inclusion in the recent "Best of Young American Novelists" issue of *Granta*, means anything, Alexie could well win his prize.

When asked how sudden success has affected him, Alexie flashes a quick smile and quips: "I like room service." The remark—even coming from a sometime stand-up comic—is revealing. Self-described as "mouthy, opinionated, and arrogant," Alexie betrays no squeamishness about the mix of art and commerce. He loves the limelight, and his readings are known for their improvisational energy, costume changes, and singing. Six years sober after a six-year binge that began the day he entered college, he explains: "Today, I get high, I get drunk off of public readings. I'm good at it. It comes from being a debater in high school, but also, crucially, it comes from the oral tradition of my own culture. It's in performance that the two cultures become one." Then he laughs, adding: "The most terrifying phrase in the world is when an Indian man grabs a microphone and says, 'I have a few words to say.'"

Alexie has more than a few words to say. His memory runs deep. Whether cast in poetry or prose, his work offers a devastating and deeply human portrait of contemporary Indian life. Greeting *PW* in the modest Seattle apartment where he lives with his wife of two years, Diane, a beautiful, private woman of Hidatsa/Ho Chunk/Pottawatomi descent, Alexie proves to be affable and generous, ready to sit down around the kitchen table and talk about his life and art.

Tall, handsome, his long black hair tied in a ponytail, dressed casually in a beige knit shirt and khakis, Alexie, who played basketball in high school, has a shooting guard's easy movements and soft touch. One would never suspect that he was born hydrocephalic, endured a brain operation at six months that should have left him mentally retarded—if not dead—and for his first seven years was beset with seizures and medicated with regular doses of lithium, phenobarbital, and other sedatives.

The son of Sherman Sr. and Lillian Alexie (his father is Coeur d'Alene, his mother Spokane), Alexie was born and reared in Wellpinit, the only town on the Spokane Indian Reservation—a place he describes as a landscape of "HUD shacks and abandoned cars"—which lies some fifty miles northwest of Spokane, Washington. Alcoholism, a central concern of Alexie's work, afflicted his family, but there was love in the house, along with a mix of traditional and contemporary culture. "I've come to realize my parents did a damn good job, considering the cards they were dealt," he says.

Then there was his maternal grandmother, Etta Adams, who died when Alexie was eight, and who appears as the eternal, wise, and practical "Big Mom" in *Reservation Blues*. "She was one of the great spiritual leaders of the Spokane tribe," Alexie says, "one of the most powerful figures to visit the Northwest, and in her last days thousands came to pay their respects." The need for female strength and wisdom is a primary theme of Alexie's, sounded early on in "Indian Boy Love Songs," four poems collected in *The Business of Fancydancing* (Hanging Loose, 1992).

Alexie began reading in earnest at an early age. Because he was unable to participate in the wild athleticism of a young male Indian's rites of passage, books became his world. "I knew what a paragraph was before I could read the words," he says, claiming that at age six, he began working his way through *The Grapes of Wrath*. Steinbeck's final image of a starving man being breast-fed is fixed in his mind: "Ah, so *that's* the way a story's supposed to end," he recalls telling himself. "With that kind of huge moment, which is the way the stories we tell ourselves end." Through grade and high school, he devoured every book in the school libraries, reading and re-reading Steinbeck until the copies fell apart in his hands. "I was a total geek," Alexie recalls, "which automatically made me an outcast, so

in order to succeed I had to be smarter than everybody else. My sense of compet-
itiveness came out that way. I was fierce in the classroom, I humiliated everybody
and had my nose broken five times after school for being the smart kid."

## Playing the Good White Indian

Alexie's view of Indian life acquired more complexity when, in 1981, he enrolled
at an all-white high school in Reardan, a reservation border town unfriendly to
Indians. With his world turned upside-down, he became the "perfect Reardan
kid": an honor student and class president and the only ponytail on the crew-
cut Reardan Indians basketball team. "I kept my mouth shut and became a good
white Indian," he acknowledges. "All those qualities that made me unpopular on
the reservation made me popular at Reardan. It got to the point where I don't
think they saw me as Indian."

The hard work and conformity earned Alexie a scholarship to Gonzaga University in Spokane, where he enrolled with vague intentions of becoming a doctor
or lawyer—"the usual options for a bright, brown kid"—and promptly fell apart.
Feeling lost, lacking a life plan, he began drinking heavily. His misery found con-
solation in poetry, which he began to read avidly—Keats, Yeats, Dickinson, Whitman. "I didn't see myself in them," he says, "so I felt like I was doing anthropology,
like I was studying white people. Obviously, something was drawing me in that
I couldn't intellectualize or verbalize, and then I realized that the poems *weren't*
just about white people. They were about everybody. I also realized that the poets
were outcasts, too," he chuckles.

After two years, Alexie packed his bags and left Gonzaga for the University
of Washington. Newly arrived in Seattle, he was robbed and soon found himself
back in Wellpinit, on the verge of joining the long history of young Indians who
come home to a slow death by alcohol. Waking one morning on the steps of the
Assembly of God Church, hungover, his pants wet, he staggered home to mail off
an application to WSU [Washington State University] in Pullman. It was a poetry
class at WSU taught by Alex Kuo that finally helped him to get his bearings as a
writer, he recalls.

The boozing didn't stop, but the words poured out. Kuo, who became a father figure to Alexie, gave him a copy of the anthology *Songs from This Earth on
Turtle's Back*. "In an instant I saw myself in literature," Alexie recalls. A line from
an Adrian C. Louis poem called "Elegy for the Forgotten Oldsmobile" changed
his life forever: "O Uncle Adrian! I'm in the reservation of my own mind." "I
started crying. That was my whole life. Forget Steinbeck, forget Keats. I just kept

saying that line over and over again. I sat down and started writing poems. And they came. It was scary."

Under Kuo's guidance, his first semester manuscript became his first book, *I Would Steal Horses*, which was published by Slipstream in 1992. With Native poets such as Adrian Louis and Simon Ortiz, Joy Harjo and Linda Hogan as models, he began to write his own story in his own voice. Lyrical, angry, poignant, socially engaged, the poems found their way into small literary magazines such as Brooklyn's *Hanging Loose*. Eventually, Hanging Loose Press brought out *The Business of Fancydancing*, which received a strong critical reception and has sold 11,000 copies, an astounding number for a book of poems from a small press. Serendipitously, the letter accepting the manuscript for publication arrived the day Alexie decided to quit drinking.

During his student days, and at Kuo's urging, Alexie began to experiment with prose—some of which appeared in *Fancydancing*. Other fictions were later collected in *The Lone Ranger and Tonto Fistfight in Heaven*, half of which was written in a four-month burst when agents, alert to his poetry, began calling with requests for fiction.

A friend introduced Alexie to Nancy Stauffer, who remains his agent to this day. "Nancy's really been good at helping me develop a career," he says. "We really have a plan. We're not just going book to book. First and foremost, I want to be a better writer, and I want a larger audience." In short order, Alexie found himself with a two-book, six-figure contract with Morgan Entrekin at the Atlantic Monthly Press at a time when, he says, he "didn't even have an idea for a novel."

The idea did come, in the guise of *Reservation Blues*, a novel that imagines legendary bluesman Robert Johnson arriving on a reservation seeking redemption from "a woman," in this case Big Mom. Johnson's magic guitar carries four young Indians off the reservation and into the world of rock and roll. The book explores differences between reservation and urban Indians and the effects of the church on traditional people, among other themes. It's also a bleak novel that's leavened by Alexie's signature black humor. "I'm not trying to be funny," he explains. "I don't sit down to write something funny. In my everyday life I'm funny, and when I write it comes out. Laughter is a ceremony, it's the way people cope."

There isn't much laughter in *Indian Killer*, which depicts John Smith, an Indian without a tribal affiliation. Adopted off the reservation and reared by a white couple, he becomes a suspect in a string of brutal scalpings that terrify Seattle. Tangent to Smith are a host of characters, including a racist talk-show host, a white professor of Native American studies, and a defiant female Indian activist, all of whom are struggling with their senses of identity. The picture is of a man divided by culture, a culture divided by its tragic history, a city divided by race, and a nation at war with itself. And it is a vision Alexie paints with excruciating clarity.

The perception of being an outcast among outcasts contributes to Alexie's complex portrait of reservation life, a view rife with ironies and a sense of complicity that has come under fire from Indian writers for its apparent emphasis on hopelessness, alcoholism, and suicide. "I write what I know," he says, "and I don't try to mythologize myself, which is what some seem to want, and which some Indian women and men writers are doing, this Earth Mother and Shaman Man thing, trying to create these 'authentic, traditional' Indians. We don't live our lives that way."

Well aware that his poems and novels have angered Indians and whites alike, Alexie enjoys walking a kind of cultural highwire. "I use a racial criterion in my literary critiques," he says. "I have a very specific commitment to Indian people, and I'm very tribal in that sense. I want us to survive *as* Indians."

That said, Alexie's Indian characters are never guileless victims. Echoing Big Mom, who continually reminds her neighbors in *Reservation Blues* that their fate is in their own hands, he explains: "It's a two-way street. The system sets you up to fail, and then, somehow, you choose it."

# Spokane Words: Tomson Highway
# Raps with Sherman Alexie

Tomson Highway/1996

From *Aboriginal Voices* January–March 1997: 36–41. Reprinted by permission.

This interview between Sherman Alexie and Tomson Highway, a Cree playwright and novelist, took place at the Seventeenth Annual International Festival of Authors in Toronto on October 28, 1996.

**Tomson Highway:** Good afternoon, ladies and gentlemen. My name is Tomson Highway, and I am both your host and interviewer for today's interview. I am a writer here in this fabulous city of Toronto! Please welcome, from the United States of America, Mr. Sherman Alexie.
**Sherman Alexie:** Thank you.

**TH:** I'm curious—your name, where does it come from?
**SA:** Sherman? I'm a junior. I'm Sherman Joseph Alexie, Jr. Junior's a very common name on reservations. Go onto any reservation and say, "Hey Junior!" and seventeen men and three women turn around.

My dad was Sherman, my grandfather was Alphonse, my great-grandfather was Adolph; had another great-great-grandfather who was Aristotle. . . .

**TH:** Really?
**SA:** Not *those* ones—different ones!

**TH:** Well, thank the living Lord Jesus you ain't called "Jim." Now, your tribal affiliation . . .
**SA:** I'm enrolled Spokane from my mother's side. My father's Coeur d'Alene. The name means "heart of—"

**TH:** Alene. Who, in this country, is the Prime Minister's wife!
**SA:** Oh, we predicted her arrival, then.

My other tribe is the Spokane, where I grew up, on the Spokane reservation. It's Spo-kan-ee, actually, and it means "children of the sun."

**TH:** Why do you say "my other tribe"? Are you half and half?

**SA:** My mother's side is Spokane, Salish, Kootenay, and Colville Indian, which are all Salish; they are all related—speak the same language.

**TH:** How many people live on the Spokane Indian Reservation?

**SA:** About a thousand. There's about 2,500 Spokanes altogether. Most of the others live in the city of Spokane, which is just off our reservation.

**TH:** Tell us a little about the Spokane Indian Reservation.

**SA:** We're a Salmon people. Our religion, our culture, our dancing, our singing—had everything to do with the salmon. We were devastated by the Grand Coulee Dam. It took away seven thousand miles of salmon spawning beds from the interior Indians in Washington, Idaho, and Montana. We've had to create a religion for many years.

We have fish hatcheries so now our salmon are homegrown. People often ask me, "Why didn't they build a fish ladder?" I say, "You haven't seen the Grand Coulee Dam, have you?"

**TH:** The principal source of economic survival today on the Spokane Indian Reservation is . . . ?

**SA:** Forestry. And now casinos and bingo halls. Yes, we are casino-owning Americans.

**TH:** Really? How's it doing?

**SA:** Very well, thank you. On my reservation unemployment was about 90 percent before the bingo hall and casino; now it's about 10 percent. They worry about the Mafia coming in and taking over the casinos. I say, Indians couldn't tell the difference between the Mafia and the United States government. Even if the Mafia did come in and take over, we'd welcome them, because we'd be better organized and the government wouldn't mess with us. And we'd have much better pasta! No more Kraft macaroni and cheese.

**TH:** The Spokane language, do you speak it?

**SA:** No, I understand it. My parents are both fluent in Salish but they didn't teach us.

**TH:** Why not?

**SA:** When I was very young, my mom told us, "English will be your best weapon." My own language wasn't going to save me. English would. And it has. I'm a writer, making my living off writing in English. I do use Spokane language in my work where I would use it myself like in phrases or dirty words. I can tell people what I think of them in two languages.

**TH:** Fantastic! Tell us about your education. There was an elementary school on your rez . . .
**SA:** I went to the tribal school until eighth grade, and then I transferred off the reservation to a border town high school, which was an all-white high school and very German. It was a German immigrant community.

**TH:** What do you mean by border town?
**SA:** A town; a not-Indian town on the border of the reservation.

**TH:** So there was half-white, half-Indian?
**SA:** No, it was me and all the rest of the—

**TH:** You and the Germans!
**SA:** Me and the Germans.

**TH:** Oh my God!
**SA:** I started worrying, you know. I started thinking, "They're not going to start *those* things here, are they?" I thought the whole world had turned blonde overnight!

**TH:** That was a very traumatic time in your life?
**SA:** Terrifying. There's a rez accent. I don't know if all these people here have heard it—it sounds vaguely Canadian, actually.

**TH:** Can you just give us a taste?
**SA:** Okay. Idt's sorda like dis—sordof a liddle sing-song qual-*I*-ty to it. And dere's a lot of "enit," which means "ain't it." "Eh" is a word we use a lot, too. I hear people here saying it. I heard this camera guy say, "eh," and I thought, "Is he Indian?"

So I walk off the reservation into this small German immigrant high school and start talking like this. This very pretty blonde woman looks at me and says, "You talk really funny." I didn't speak again for a month and a half.

**TH:** How long were you in this linguistic cultural hell—to paraphrase Adrienne Clarkson?
**SA:** Exactly what I was thinking. I was thirteen years old and I was thinking, "Ya know, I am in a linguistic hell."

It ended up being fine. All those qualities about me that made me an ugly duckling on the reservation—ambitious, competitive, and individualistic—these are not necessarily good things to be when you're part of a tribe. I was into books. I've always loved reading. I planned on becoming a doctor, a pediatrician.

**TH:** You weren't sporty?

**SA:** I played basketball, but I was more interested in books. I wasn't a guy who did dangerous things. I remember once we set up this wooden ramp. We'd go down this sand hill and jump over the ramp on our bicycles. The jump took us over an open sewer pit. If you didn't do this, you weren't a man. So, we're these nine-year-old Indian kids jumping over open sewer pits, and we didn't always make it.

**TH:** This is when you became . . . intellectual.

**SA:** It was either in the sewer or intellectual. It was either smell like this or smell like that.

**TH:** Well thank the living Lord Jesus for that sewer, otherwise we wouldn't have your books. Then you went to high school in Spokane, I take it?

**SA:** No, I went to high school at Reardan; I went to college in Spokane at a Jesuit university. I am Catholic. I'm not sure exactly why I went for more punishment.

**TH:** Hang on. You were raised Roman Catholic?

**SA:** Not Roman.

**TH:** What kind of Catholic?

**SA:** Spokane Indian Catholic.

**TH:** You were raised a Catholic, and then you went to a Jesuit Catholic school, which is a Roman Catholic School. What happened when you first walked in that door?

**SA:** The Jesuits were trying to hold on to their original mission to educate the Indians, and I was the only Indian there, so they really tried to educate me. I'd skip class, they'd call me up, "Hey Sherman, why'd you skip class?" "Well, because I was tired." "Why were you tired?" "Well, because I was sleepy." They didn't understand the simplest things.

**TH:** These Jesuits were the people who first missionized that area, right?

**SA:** One of my great-great-great-great grandmothers (Christine Polotkin) first saw the coming of the black crows. She had a dream about European contact. She dreamed about three ravens with white stars at their necks showing up and coming to the people, and the ravens saying, "If you don't listen to us and do what we say, you're all going to die."

A week later, three Jesuits showed up, in black, with white stars at their necks. And everybody said, "All right. . . ."

**TH:** So you got a degree at this university?

**SA:** No, I transferred—well, I ran. I fled. They're chasing me still. They were running after me—the Jesuits—trying to save me; they lifted up their cassocks and they were wearing Nikes. I didn't realize God had a shoe deal.

  I went to Washington State University where I got a Bachelor's in American Studies. That is a real degree. People sometimes think, "What is American Studies?"

**TH:** What is American Studies?

**SA:** It's where you study the United States.

**TH:** History, literature, sociology, anthropology, all that stuff.

**SA:** I was majoring in most everything. I couldn't figure out what I wanted to be. I was going to be a doctor, a lawyer, an accountant, an English major. One day I sat down, added up all my credits and looked at the American Studies degree. I realized, "I've got most of those credits." American Studies is for those people who are . . . eclectic.

**TH:** Congratulations! You're a success! When did you start writing?

**SA:** I started writing because I kept fainting in human anatomy class and needed a career change. The only class that fit where the human anatomy class had been was a poetry writing workshop. I always liked poetry. I'd never heard of, or nobody'd ever showed me, a book written by a First Nations person, ever. I got into the class, and my professor, Alex Kuo, gave me an anthology of contemporary Native American poetry called *Songs from This Earth on Turtle's Back.* I opened it up and—oh my gosh—I saw my life in poems and stories for the very first time.

**TH:** Who were some of the writers in the book?

**SA:** Linda Hogan, Simon Ortiz, Joy Harjo, James Welch, Adrian Louis. There were poems about reservation life: fry bread, bannock, 49s, fried baloney, government food, and terrible housing. But there was also joy and happiness.

  There's a line by a Paiute poet named Adrian Louis that says, "Oh, Uncle Adrian, I'm in the reservation of my mind." I thought, "Oh my God, somebody understands me!" At that moment I realized, "I can do this!" That's when I started writing—in 1989.

**TH:** The poetry that you would have studied in American Studies, for instance, the poetry of Wallace Stevens or e. e. cummings or Emily Dickinson, never influenced you at all?

**SA:** Of course it did. I loved that stuff. I still love it. Walt Whitman and Emily Dickinson are two of my favorites. Wallace Stevens leaves me kind of dry, but the other poets, they're still a primary influence. I always tell people my literary influences are Stephen King, John Steinbeck, my mother, my grandfather and the Brady Bunch.

**TH:** Then you moved on to short stories.

**SA:** I'd written a couple of them in college. After my first book of poems, *The Business of Fancydancing,* was published by Hanging Loose Press in Brooklyn, New York, I got a great *New York Times* book review. The review called me "one of the major lyric voices of our time." I was a twenty-five-year-old Spokane Indian guy working as a secretary at a high school exchange program in Spokane, Washington, when my poetry editor faxed that review to me. I pulled it out of the fax machine beside my desk and read, ". . . one of the major lyric voices of our time." I thought, "Great! Where do I go from here!?" After that, the agents started calling *me.*

**TH:** Where did that book of poetry come from?

**SA:** It was my first semester poetry manuscript. Part of the assignment was to submit to literary magazines. The one I liked in the Washington State library was *Hanging Loose* magazine. I liked that it started the same year I was born. The magazine, the press, and I are the same age. Over the next year and a half they kept taking poems of mine to publish. Then they asked if I had a manuscript. I said, "Yes!" and sent it in.

It was a *thousand* copies. I figured I'd sell a hundred and fifty to my family. My mom would buy a hundred herself and that would be about it. But it took off. I never expected it. Sometimes I think it would have been nicer if it had not been as big, because my career has been a rocket ride. There's a lot of pressure.

**TH:** That would have been about six years ago?

**SA:** The book came out in 1992. It was accepted in late 1990.

**TH:** Then you moved on to short stories—how did that transfer?

**SA:** The agents started calling me after the book of poems was published. They asked me if I had a fiction manuscript because that's what they could sell. I said, "Yes," and then went and wrote short stories. I had some from college, but I wrote about half of my first book of short stories, *The Lone Ranger and Tonto Fistfight in Heaven,* in three months—in between the review and when I submitted the book to agents.

It was an economic move, I'm not ashamed to say. In fact, you can tell which stories were pre-*Fancydancing* and post-*Fancydancing*. The ones pre- are much more like poems. The ones post- are much more straight narrative stories.

**TH:** Fantastic! Tell us a little bit more about the *Lone Ranger and Tonto*.
**SA:** The title, *The Lone Ranger and Tonto Fistfight in Heaven*, came to me in a dream. In this dream, I was sitting in a huge arena. I could see people boxing, miles away it seemed. This gentleman with a hawk face, dressed completely in red, everything was red—boots, shoes, cap, top hat—sat down beside me. I said, "What's going on down there?"

He said, "Oh, that's the Lone Ranger and Tonto. They're boxing. The winner gets to go to heaven and the loser has to go to hell."

I said, "Oh, my gosh." Then I realized this was the devil. (Some people have therapists, I have audiences.) I really started getting into it, "Go, Tonto, hit him, hit him!"

I woke up before the fight was over, saying, "Wow, that's a great dream." I thought, "That's a title for a story, or it is a story." I wrote the story as the dream was but it seemed too much a parable. I thought the title would work better as a contemporary story, so I wrote about an interracial romance between an Indian man and a white woman. The theme of the story is the Lone Ranger and Tonto fistfight in heaven. I think this is the theme between all Indian-White relationships, not only as individuals, but as races, as colonials to colonized.

**TH:** Not a relationship of equals, a relationship of subservience.
**SA:** Subservience and antagonistic.

Kemosabe in Apache means "idiot," as Tonto in Spanish means "idiot." They were calling each other "idiot" all those years; and they both were, so it worked out. It's always going to be an antagonistic relationship between indigenous peoples and the colonial people. I think the theme of *The Lone Ranger and Tonto Fistfight in Heaven* is universal.

**TH:** How did your first novel come about?
**SA:** I had a two-book deal with Atlantic Monthly Press. I had a one-sentence description of a novel; it was an all-Indian Catholic rock-and-roll band. That's what the novel ended up being about—an all-Indian Catholic rock-and-roll band called Coyote Springs. The novel was called *Reservation Blues*.

It is a sequel because many of the same characters and situations that existed in *The Lone Ranger and Tonto Fistfight in Heaven* are in it. It's set on my reservation with three main characters: Thomas Builds-the-Fire, a misfit storyteller of the Spokane tribe; Victor Joseph, an alcoholic angry Indian guy; and Junior Polotkin, the happy-go-lucky failure. I called them "the unholy trinity of me."

*Reservation Blues* is also about a deal with the Devil. Robert Johnson, the blues guitarist, plays a prominent role in the book. His guitar bewitches Thomas, Victor, and Junior into becoming a blues band that ends up auditioning for Cavalry Records in Manhattan.

**TH:** What about *Indian Killer*?
**SA:** *Indian Killer.* I wrote this first and foremost because people—critics and audiences—kept talking about *The Lone Ranger and Tonto Fistfight in Heaven* and *Reservation Blues* as if they were dark, depressing, Kafka-ish, cockroach-nightmare-crawling-across-the-floor kind of books. Actually they're very funny. I think they have happy endings. I thought, "Okay, you want dark and depressing? Here you go. Here's *Indian Killer.* You're going to look back with fondness at the whimsical *Reservation Blues*, the lighthearted *The Lone Ranger and Tonto Fistfight in Heaven*." I abandoned my trademark humor and went for the full thriller, murder mystery.

The plot-line is a series of murders of White men in Seattle that look as though an Indian is doing them. The bodies are ritually mutilated, scalped, and certain objects are left at the scene. John Smith, the main character, as a newborn was adopted by an upper middle-class White family, and in his adulthood is struggling to find a connection to Indian people, any sense of connection to anybody. He gently goes mad during the course of the book.

I've met a lot of people like him—"lost birds"—Indians adopted out by non-Indian families—we call them lost birds. One of my cousins was adopted out. I wanted to write a book about a character like that to get this out into the public.

The Indian Child Welfare Act in the States in 1974 prevented such adoptions. The social problems and dysfunctions of these Indians adopted out are tremendous. Their suicide rates are off the chart, their drug and alcohol abuse rates are off the chart. There's a book here, called *Inside Out*, a national bestseller.

**TH:** James Tyman, from Saskatchewan.
**SA:** James Tyman. Someone handed it to me last week and I just read it. His story is very typical, and is not as bad as many of the stories I've heard.

**TH:** This concept, this identity crisis, misplaced birth, was the germ for the book, the Indian germ?
**SA:** It was the germ of the novel. I was going to write a novel about just a lost

bird. I didn't realize it was going to be a murder mystery. I had an idea about a suspected Indian serial killer for a long time.

It's also a novel about, not just physical murder, but the spiritual, cultural, and physical murder of Indians. The title, *Indian Killer*, is a palindrome [double-entendre], really. It's "Indians who kill" and it's also "people who kill Indians." It's about how the dominant culture is killing the First Nations people of this country to this day, still.

**TH:** Well, congratulations on the publication of *Indian Killer*.
**SA:** Thank you.

**TH:** With the little bit of time we have left, let's open the discussion to the floor. If there's anybody who has questions, please ask now.

**Question:** The Colville tribe is made up of twelve tribes. Do you have any blood related to any of the tribes? Were you influenced by the Lakes Colville Indian writer Mourning Dove, who wrote a book called *Cogewea*?
**SA:** No, and no. Mourning Dove, the *Cogewea* book, is an example of a book written by a White person which is disguised as an autobiography of an Indian person. Other examples are *Black Elk Speaks*, written by Black Elk, supposedly, and John Neihardt—an autobiography that Black Elk himself disavowed before he died, a fact which is conveniently omitted in any discussion of the book.

There's *Lame Deer, Seeker of Visions* and *Lakota Woman*, two other supposed autobiographies, really written by White men. *Lakota Woman* has gone on to be a movie and an international bestseller. As far as I know, Mary has not received any sort of royalties. The same man who wrote that book also wrote *Lame Deer, Seeker of Visions*. Once again, these autobiographies are not really autobiographies, they're translations. Both writers of those books have freely admitted to poetic license. Poetic license and manifest destiny are often the same thing.

**Question:** Why are many Indian writers not getting national attention?
**SA:** We're not the appropriate kind of stories. If you write about Lakota Indians or horse cultures, you have a better chance of a bestseller. If you write about pre-twentieth-century Indians; if you use a "corn pollen, four directions, Mother Earth, Father Sky" sort of language; or if you write about the wonderful relationship between an Indian and a White person: love affair, friendship, mentoring relationship, you have a better chance of selling a lot of books.

If you are of—now I'm not saying these people aren't Indian—if you are of a very mixed-blood, you have a better chance of selling a lot of books. It's a particular kind of Indian experience. They have more access to the educational and publishing channels. If you write the appropriate kind of material, you have a better chance. The second you don't, your chances decrease.

I'm very fortunate. I'm writing these highly political books about reservation Indians. I'm telling rez jokes in my books. I think most non-Indians don't have a clue about half the jokes in there. I'm selling a lot of copies and doing well. I'm an anomaly.

Other writers are writing stories that aren't getting told and not because of their writing ability. Ninety percent of the books in any bookstore are not written very well. It's the approach. Any non-Indian writer writing about Indians is going to automatically get a better critical and commercial reception than any Indian. Tony Hillerman, for instance, any one of his novels, has sold more copies than all the books written by Indians, ever.

**Question:** Do you resent the fact that he writes about Indians?

**SA:** Yes. I resent that he's made a career off Indians, and as far as I know, has not given much back. I'm on the Board of Trustees of the American Indian College Fund—I haven't heard his name mentioned. I'm resentful that there are many writers out there making careers off Indians and doing absolutely nothing in return. There's a guy I'm reading with tomorrow evening—Mr. Kinsella—who's making a career writing books about Indians, and as far as I know, he's doing nothing for Indians. People ask me and I give hard-core answers. You're making money, give it back. Donate 10 percent of your royalties to the Native College Fund. How about giving 10 percent of your royalties to the tribe you're writing about?

**Question:** Do you feel bound to writing just about your Native self, as opposed to non-Native issues?

**SA:** I hate that question more than any other. It's an incredibly racist, colonial question. Nobody ever asked Raymond Carver if he was going to write about anything other than poor white people. Nobody ever asked Faulkner if he was going to write about anything more than poor, white Southern people. People don't ask those questions of non-Brown writers. I'm shocked *you* asked that. [The question was asked by a non-White person.] The author of *Remains of the Day* wrote that precisely because he was tired of the ghettoization of his work about British-Japanese people.

I'm not limited by writing about Spokane Indians. Every theme, every story, every tragedy that exists in literature takes place in my little community. *Hamlet* takes place on my reservation daily. *King Lear* takes place on my reservation daily.

"Because I could not stop for death, death kindly stopped for me." That is a total Indian couplet.

I feel challenged by trying to write about Spokane Indians. They're a powerful people, and it's a powerful place. I'm never going to run out of stories or themes. To suggest otherwise, or to suggest I should be interested in something else, is ridiculous.

# The Reluctant Spokesman

Erik Himmelsbach/1996

From the *Los Angeles Times* 17 December 1996: E1, E6. Reprinted by permission of the interviewer.

*With the success of his new book, Sherman Alexie finds himself cast as the poster boy for all things American Indian. Trouble is, he's not much liked by his own tribe.*

Sherman Alexie is ready to play cards with Satan.

The thirty-year-old author is hunkered down at the Beverly Prescott, in town to discuss the film rights to his latest novel, *Indian Killer* (Atlantic Monthly Press), a slyly subversive potboiler about a serial murderer whose actions spark a modern battle of cowboys and Indians in Seattle. It may seem like perfect big-screen fodder, but Alexie, a Spokane Coeur d'Alene, harbors no illusions and is prepared for the inevitable raw deal from Hollywood.

"The real problem is that there's no white hero in my book," he says. "They want loincloths. They want sweat lodges and vision quests. They want *Dances With Wolves*, and I don't write that."

If producers aren't sensitive to the particulars of the late twentieth-century American Indian, at least no one's mentioned Lou Diamond Phillips.

"I think he's done with the Indian thing," Alexie says with a grin. "He's done four or five of them, and they all flopped. Hopefully, he hasn't read the book and won't be interested."

While they're busy keeping Diamond Phillips off casting lists, Hollywood types also would be wise to avoid calling Alexie a "Native American." The author dismisses the term as meaningless, a product of liberal white guilt.

"I'm an Indian," he says. "I'll only use 'Native American' in mixed company."

*Indian Killer* is Alexie's second novel; the first was *Reservation Blues*. (He's also written an acclaimed book of short stories, *The Lone Ranger and Tonto Fistfight in Heaven*, and several volumes of poetry.)

It's a multilayered work. While it satisfied Alexie's desire to explore the mystery genre, it also highlights the tenuous thread of civility that exists between white and American Indian cultures, how we are only a flash point away from igniting a racial powder keg—even in progressive Seattle, where Alexie lives with his wife, Diane.

"If you look at the history of the U.S. and chart what's happening, we are brewing a revolutionary stew," he says, comparing the present disparity among classes and races to France just before the French Revolution. "There's a tremendous level of anger out there, and the anger in the Indian community has not really been talked about. There's a huge open wound."

Healing would require apologies and reparations from the U.S. government, but Alexie isn't holding his breath. "It would change the whole myth of America, the rugged individual, the courageous pioneer, this whole American dream," he says. The government "would have to admit that there were terrible evils committed here, comparable to any evils ever."

Alexie has done his share of myth debunking. His earlier work, especially *Lone Ranger and Tonto*, is notable for its honest and humorous character studies of modern tribal life. His stories are candid snapshots of a culture that has long been ignored.

In *Indian Killer* he leaves the reservation to examine the plight of the urban Indian, like himself, displaced from the tribe. He notes that 60 percent of the Indians in this country live in urban areas. But that presented new challenges, as Alexie struggled to develop some of the characters, especially white characters, whose life experiences are foreign to him.

"I grew up in a culture where you are taught that songs and stories have specific owners and you can't tell them without permission," he explains. "Growing up with those cultural constructs, the whole idea of the artist as the individual is totally outside my concept of who I am. I'm always operating with some sort of tribal responsibility, so here I am writing about people way outside my tribe, and it got uncomfortable."

While Alexie has enlightened the world at large about the contemporary American Indian experience, his tribe has essentially shunned him. Back at the Spokane Reservation in Wellpinit, Washington, people have strong, often unfavorable opinions about the author who, as a child, often whiled away his days alone in his room playing Dungeons & Dragons or Nerf basketball.

"I was a divisive presence on the reservation when I was seven," he recalls. "I was a weird, eccentric, very arrogant little boy. The writing doesn't change anybody's opinion of me. If anything, it's intensified it."

Alexie says one tribal elder resents him not for anything he's written, but because he was a "ball hog" on the tribe's basketball team.

Part of the animosity stems from Alexie's decision to leave his tribal school and transfer to Reardan High, a virtually all-white school twenty miles from his home.

Alexie was terrified when he arrived at Reardan—he was the school's first and only Indian until his twin sisters joined him after a year. To assimilate, he had to abandon certain characteristics, including his reservation accent and some of his hair, which fell far below his shoulders.

"People think it's a trivial thing, and it's not," he says. "The physical act of cutting parts of yourself off to fit in, that's what it is."

Ultimately, though, Alexie succeeded at Reardan for the same reasons he was outcast by his tribe—his "insane ambition."

He drew on his experiences at the school when developing John Smith, a central character in *Indian Killer*. Unlike Alexie, however, Smith was tormented by his lack of tribal identification: He was adopted by a white couple and never knew his heritage.

"Indian children adopted by non-Indian families have tremendous social problems," Alexie says.

Although ostracized by his tribe, Alexie has been embraced by many other American Indians, judging by the number of events and commencements he's asked to speak at.

He jokes that his "little books about one little reservation in Washington state" have come to represent all Indians everywhere. As such, he's not allowed to merely write books. He has had to become a poster boy.

"It's very interesting. Nobody ever asked Raymond Carver to speak for every white guy," Alexie says. "I end up having to be a spokesperson for Indian people. I've become a politician and a sociologist and psychologist and cultural critic, and all these jobs I have to fulfill simply based on the fact that I am an Indian writer getting a lot of attention."

Being selected as one of *Granta* magazine's "20 best American novelists under 40" has added to the author's laundry list of accolades, although he takes this sort of recognition with a grain of salt.

"There are hints I got on there because of some affirmative action policy," he says. "How many spots are reserved in the literary world for Indian people? None. If I was on there because of some newly invented Indian quota in the literary world, great. I hope we get lots more quotas."

While he doesn't shun his profile-building extracurricular responsibilities, Alexie prefers the solitude of his craft. "Writers and artists are by and large selfish bastards. It's isolated, individualistic. In that sense, it was a job I was perfectly suited for."

In this way, Alexie identifies with *Indian Killer*'s Marie Polatkin, an angry, righteous Indian who will grant no quarter to the white intellectuals who think they understand the Native American experience.

But sharing his writing with the world has had a profound effect on this self-proclaimed selfish bastard. "I had no idea about the very quiet ways in which art works," he says, explaining the letters of support he receives from all over the country.

"I was in the Seattle airport, and this ten-year-old Indian boy came up to me and he said, 'I like your poem,' and he told me which poem he liked," Alexie says. "And at that moment, all the wonder and magic of what art is supposed to be about is contained there. For just a few moments, you forget about slogging through airport after airport. It sounds clichéd and romantic and sentimental, and it is, but it's great. It's those little moments that save you."

As the day turns dark, and Hollywood's bright lights wink seductively at Alexie from his eleventh-floor view at the Beverly Prescott, his thoughts suddenly turn from idyllic to pragmatic. Nothing, it seems, can save him from the dread of the meetings with the movie people. He'll hear about how his writing can be sliced and diced and marketed and compromised in the name of mass-market entertainment.

It's times like these that he wraps himself in the security of what he considers his true calling: poetry. (His latest book of poems, *The Summer of Black Widows* [Hanging Loose Press], was published in September.)

"There is no possible way to sell your soul because nobody's offering," he says with a laugh. "The devil doesn't care about poetry. No one wants to make a movie out of a poem."

# Crossroads: A Conversation with Sherman Alexie

John Purdy/1997

From *Studies in American Indian Literatures* 9.4 (1997): 1–18. The interview originally appeared in a special issue focusing on Sherman Alexie. Reprinted by permission of the interviewer.

This conversation took place on 4 October 1997, a rainy, early autumn morning in an east Seattle café near Sherman Alexie's home. It is an interesting neighborhood, for it sits on a clearly demarcated boundary: on one side, the intercity struggle for survival—economic and otherwise—and on the other the affluent mansions lining Lake Washington. The café sits directly on the line.

My colleague and former student, Frederick Pope, went with me to talk with Alexie, who is in much demand; in fact, that evening he was scheduled to read at Left Bank Books, for a benefit to provide books for Native American inmates of this country's prisons. As always, it was an interesting and dynamic discussion and, on our trip home, Fred and I agreed; it was candid, wide ranging, profoundly playful.

We began with a discussion of his recently completed movie. As with his writing career, his film involvement seems to be progressing rapidly. Two weeks after our meeting, the film was screened at Sundance for the annual film competition, and later for the major film distributors of the country. There can be no doubt that Sherman Alexie is wonderfully full of ideas, and that those ideas will work their way into art that will be both imaginative and engaging.[1]

**John Purdy:** I understand the filming of the movie went well?
**Sherman Alexie:** We're premiering, screening at Sundance October 15. We'll know shortly after that if we're in [the final competition] or not.

**JP:** Fantastic. . . .
**SA:** We developed it there, so . . . we're in, but we need to get in the competition, and that's only sixteen films. We need to be up for the awards. [The film made the final sixteen.]

**JP:** Lots of good films have come out of Sundance.
**SA:** Yeah, but ours is better.

**JP:** Tells us a bit about the movie.
**SA:** It's a story; it's from *The Lone Ranger and Tonto*, "This is What It Means to Say Phoenix, Arizona," that story. Victor and Thomas go to Phoenix to pick up Victor's dad's remains, so it's a buddy movie. It's pretty funny. Thomas is Thomas. The actor who plays him is amazing. Evan Adams. He's had small roles in Canadian productions; he's a First Nations guy from up there. He's just amazing. He's sort of taken Thomas. I can't write about . . . I tried to write a short story with Thomas in it but I couldn't. I kept seeing him. . . .

**JP:** Seeing Adams?
**SA:** He's taken him away from me. He's so convincing, so real, so Thomasy. He's an adjective now.

**JP:** So he's type-cast . . . as Thomas?
**SA:** He's so right for the role it's scary to think that he's always going to be playing some weird Indian.

**JP:** I don't recognize the name.
**SA:** No. The movie has Gary Farmer in it, from *Pow Wow Highway*, Tantoo Cardinal. . . .

**JP:** *North of Sixty.* . . .
**SA:** Yeah. Adam Beach who was Squanto. Irene Bedard. Michelle St. John, Elaine Miles, from *Northern Exposure* . . . am I missing anybody? Cody Lightning, who was in *Grand Avenue* on HBO. Baker, who's on *North of Sixty*. Tom Skerritt has a role, Cynthia Geary, who was on *Northern Exposure*. . . .

**JP:** That's a good cast. And what kind of role did you have in it? Did you have much control over it?
**SA:** Oh yeah. I wrote the screenplay; I was the co-producer. Five songs of Jim Boyd's and mine are in there. Two '49s in there I wrote. So. . . .

**JP:** You can do it all. . . . You're doing '49s now?
**SA:** For good or bad, whatever, is in there.

[Interruption]

**JP:** So, did you have fun making the movie?
**SA:** No (laughs). Yeah, yeah I did. The scary thing is that it was so fun, and so

intense, so immediate, that if I start doing really well at this, I might wind up being a good screenwriter. I'm going to direct *Indian Killer*. I'm scared that if I make
it I'll give up writing books.

**JP:** Whoa. And move to Hollywood. . . .
**SA:** No (emphatically). The thing I think about is that probably 5 percent of
Indians in this country have read my books. *Maybe* that much. Probably more
like 2 percent, or 1. You take a thing like *Pow Wow Highway* and 99 percent of
Indians have seen it.

**JP:** Well. It's a powerful medium. So you didn't make Gary Farmer wear a wig did
you?
**SA:** For the first scene. Then he doesn't have it. Then we let him be Gary. But, he
gets to be young in the movie. Twenty years difference.

**JP:** It's just that the one he wore in *Highway* was so much a wig. So you're directing *Indian Killer*? Are you dealing with the same [film] people? I hadn't heard
about that.
**SA:** It's not official yet, we haven't signed the contracts, but it's happening.

**JP:** Where will you shoot it?
**SA:** Seattle. Right here.

**JP:** This all sounds time consuming. Do you get to write, other than what you're
working on [for the movies], or is the schedule so intense that it takes you away
from writing?
**SA:** I'm working on a new novel.

**JP:** Want to talk about it?
**SA:** Yeah, but I don't know if it's going to be the next one published. I've sold it,
but I don't know if it's going to be the next one. Essentially what it's about is . . .
it's set in the future, although it's set in the 1950s, an alternate 1950s, and I don't
want to give too much of it away, basically scientists have discovered the cure for
cancer involves the bone marrow of Indians.

**JP:** Carrying the cure for the world, huh?
**SA:** Yeah, essentially we start getting harvested.

**JP:** You and the yew tree.
**SA:** It's called *The Sin Eaters*. Pretty intense. And I'm working on one about the
Mafia in the '20s and '30s and Indians, but I don't want to give away more than
that, though.

**JP:** I think that's what they call the tease. . . .
**SA:** And it's based on a true story about the Mafia and the Spokane Indians in the 1920s.

**JP:** Oh no. Well, we have our research cut out for us now. Interesting.
**SA:** Well, actually, it's based on a true *sentence*. There's only one sentence that mentions this Mafia connection in one book. I came across it and I can't find anything else about it. I'm taking that one sentence to create a whole story.

**JP:** So it's the greatest cover-up in the world. One sentence and all the other information's yours.
**SA:** Exactly.

**JP:** I love the life of a novelist, right?
**SA:** I'm going to use that one sentence as the first sentence in the book.

**JP:** The one set in the alternate '50s, you say you've already contracted that. When do you think that will come out?
**SA:** Next year. Same press: Atlantic.

**JP:** And now into movies and writing '49 songs.
**SA:** I've been doing that forever, did that long before I ever wrote a book.

**JP:** Did you play around with songs, then, when you were young?
**SA:** Yeah. I quit for a long time, sort of getting back into it again, and realizing I forgot how to sing. Maybe it's a mental or emotional block.

**JP:** You were playing with the language, then? Is that attractive to you? My son and I do that all the time. We take a song and rewrite it, play with the language, it's fun.
**SA:** Exactly. '49s are just fun that way.

**JP:** Well, I didn't know you were doing a movie of *Indian Killer.* You did the script *and* you'll direct?
**SA:** I'm doing the screenplay right now. Just about done.

**JP:** One of the questions I wanted to ask you is what you have envisioned for your future. It sounds like you don't have time to envision a future.
**SA:** Yeah, well, movies, definitely. I mean, I feel the only concept for me is poetry. I kind of get bored with other things. Novels take so much energy; it's so *hard.* Hundreds and hundreds and hundreds of pages of writing. They're *hard.* I think I'm just a decent fiction writer. I tell good stories, but sentence to sentence, verb to

verb, noun to noun, I don't think I'm all that, you know. . . . Everybody else seems to think more highly of my work than I do. Suppose that's a good thing, eh? But I like the poetry; I think I'm good at that.

**JP:** So you still work at it?
**SA:** Oh yeah.

**JP:** What have you done with it?
**SA:** Publish it. I just had a new book out last year, which makes seven books of poems now.

**JP:** True. I remember when *Fancydancing* came out, I was on a flight, one of those small commuter flights, practically falling out of my chair. I had a colleague sitting in front of me who said "What are you laughing at?" and I said, "Here, read this." Spoonfeeding bits and pieces of the book to him, and not just the humorous ones. Comes pretty quickly though doesn't it? A lot's happened to you since then.
**SA:** That was published in January of '92. Yeah, I mean five and a half years later I'm an eight-hundred-pound gorilla. (Laughter, of course.)

**JP:** One of the things that came to mind as we e-mailed back and forth about this interview is the memory of hearing you read, at places like Village Books. It's fun. But when you read at Bellingham High a few years ago, with Dian Million, Tiffany Midge, Ed Edmo, it was a different thing. Do you see your audiences as different in some sense?
**SA:** Oh yeah. When you're inside a bookstore, it's much more static; there's many more expectations of what's going to happen. I like to play with them. I've come out and done my characters, or come out and been Angry Indian Guy, or Funny Indian Guy, took on a persona and messed with the crowd.

**JP:** And you do it well, by the way. I want you to know. When you read with Linda Hogan that one time, you could hear the hackles on the back of their necks going up. And you, just looking back at them, with a smile on your face.
**SA:** Oh yeah, I had a good time with that reading. Part of that was good time, part of it was just a *bad* mood. It depends on the environment. At Village Books, everybody's crowded into such a little space, you have so little room to work with up in front, it's really much more of a reading reading, but if I'm on a stage, I'll get nuts.

**JP:** It was fun that night at the high school. Jim Boyd was there, too. You were working on *Reservation Blues*, then. You were running some things by us, and there were a couple of times when you'd stop and say, "Yeah, that works. The audience bought that. Let's try something else over here."

**SA:** That's a way of doing it. I mean, you always get tired of the question, y'know, of "How does your work apply to the oral tradition?" It doesn't. I *type* it! (Laughter.) And I'm really, really quiet when I'm doing it. The only time when I'm essentially really a storyteller is when I'm up in front of a crowd. Growing up with traditional and nontraditional storytellers, and they're always riffin' and improvvin'. . . .

**JP:** That's the fun of it.

**SA:** Sure. You can just imagine! The reason, I tell people, that Indians . . . that whites beat Indians in wars was not because they were tougher; I mean, we'd beat them, on any one given day. But then the whites would want to fight the next day again, and we just didn't want to do that. We'd want to go talk about it. You can hear the stories, the next day the warriors going "Man, remember when you dodged that bullet?" and the day after that it was "Hey, remember when that guy shot you nine times and you survived?" After the next day "Remember when you jumped over that cactus, got shot nine times, grabbed that horse, crawled inside of it, hid for nine hours while they stampeded around you, jumped back out, grabbed the general by the throat, slapped him twice and ran away?" *Yeah*. . . .

**JP:** Yeah, tell it again.

**SA:** I come from a long line of exaggerators.

**JP:** One of the problems with editing a journal is we have people who get interested, get caught by those stories and then read a lot, but all of a sudden someone comes through with a new novel that does something else, something that comes around for the first time, and we're right back to where we were in the '60s and there's a raging debate about "Is this Indian?"

**SA:** Actually *SAIL* is just fine. I've been subscribing for the past four years. Some essays are great; I've never seen a wider difference between good or bad in any academic journal. The bad ones are even more interesting, because they embrace, hang on to old ideas. I mean they're not bad scholarship, they're not badly written. What I mean is that no one has figured out a new way to look at Indian literatures. Above all *Indians* aren't looking at Indian literature. There are very few Indian scholars, very few Indian literature critics examining it. Those who do, like Gloria Bird, or Robert Warrior, or Liz Cook-Lynn, are still using the same old lit-crit tools. I think we have been far too nice to each other for too long now. I think Indian writers have grown enough, that we're not going to get any better unless we really start hammering on each other.

**JP:** I think that's true in the scholarship, too. One of the things we try to do in the journal is that, rather than get everyone to follow in lock-step, to take articles with widely varying points of view so sometimes we have two essays in one issue that give opposing arguments. It is tough, too, not only for the people who submit but for the people who read the submissions, because those people cover the spectrum, too. We often have two readers, one who will say publish, this is great stuff, the other saying throw it out. O.K. What do you do now?
**SA:** The thing that gets me with that is the Vizenor thing. I mean he's the god of the Indian lit-crit people.

**JP:** Why do you think so?
**SA:** It's obtuse prose, a lot of word play and word masturbation, essentially, that results in, nothing.

**JP:** Did you ever read his *Narrative Chance?*
**SA:** Yeah. I mean, I can get into it, it's fine, but I've sort of been struggling with this idea, what does Indian literature mean? If Indian literature can't be read by the average twelve-year-old kid living on the reservation, what the hell good is it? You couldn't take any of his books and take them to a rez and teach them, without extreme protestation. What is an Indian kid going to do with the first paragraph of any of those books? You know, I've been struggling with this myself, with finding a way to be much more accessible to Indian people.

**JP:** I was at a workshop once in Santa Fe and Vizenor was there, Owens, Anna Lee Walters was there, and some other people from the Navajo reservation. Someone asked her, "So who are you writing for, Anna?" She said, "Young Indian kids on the rez."

One thing I like about my classes is that sooner or later students are going to be asking that same question: "What is this Indian literature?" And then they wrestle through all those questions of audience, and definitions, by biology or whatever, and just when they start to feel comfortable, then we complicate it. Take the book for the book.
**SA:** But see, that doesn't work.

**JP:** What?
**SA:** Taking the book for a book.

**JP:** In what way?
**SA:** In an Indian definition, you can't separate the message from the messenger.

**JP:** That's not the same. I think "the book" can carry that. Your work carries it.
**SA:** Yeah. But I think you're referring to identity questions and such.

**JP:** Oh. That's how the issue shakes out, because that's what the students are interested in, but the question is how to take them back to the book, to the story itself.
**SA:** Most of our Indian literature is written by people whose lives are nothing like the Indians they're writing about. There's a lot of people pretending to be "traditional," all these academic professors living in university towns, who rarely spend any time on a reservation, writing all these "traditional" books. Momaday—he's not a traditional man. And there's nothing wrong with that, I'm not either, but this adherence to the expected idea, the bear and all this imagery. I think it is dangerous, and detrimental.

**JP:** It's the nineties, and now it's time to move on. So, we get back to the discussion of what "it" is.
**SA:** Well, I want to take it away. I want to take Indian lit *away* from that, and away from the people who own it now.

**JP:** I think you do, in your writing.
**SA:** That's what I mean. I'm starting to see it. A lot of younger writers are starting to write like me—writing like I do, in a way, not copying me, but writing about what happens to them, not about what they wish was happening. They aren't writing wish fulfillment books, they're writing books about reality. How they live, and who they are, and what they think about. Not about who they wish they were. The kind of Indian they wish they were. They are writing about the kind of Indian they are.

**JP:** Sure, and it makes sense. Whenever you have any group of individuals in any literature who start to define the center, then everybody has to ask whether or not that's sufficient over time.
**SA:** We've been stuck in place since *House Made of Dawn*.

**JP:** But there's some interesting work coming out. Have you read Carr's *Eye Killers*?
**SA:** I hate it.

**JP:** You did? Well, that's right, it does have that traditional thing going on, but to move into the genre of the vampire novel I thought was interesting.

**SA:** That's fun, but I thought that book was blasphemous as hell to Navajo culture, the way he used ceremonies and such. I have a real problem with that. I don't use any at all. And a white woman saved everybody.

**JP:** But she *was* a teacher. (Laughter.)
**SA:** But it read like a movie turned into a novel. I was supposed to review it, and I didn't.

**JP:** Tell me this. What do you see coming out right now that is doing what needs to be done?
**SA:** Irvin Morris. I like his book [*From the Glittering World: A Navajo Story*]. I think Tiffany Midge has a good future, once she stops copying me.

**JP:** She did a great reading that night in Bellingham High.
**SA:** The thing is she was so into my work then, she's not so much now. That night, ask the people who saw me read before that night, she read exactly like me. So even that night I had to change the way I read. I'd never heard her read in public before, and she got up and read and I thought, "O my god, that's me, that's my shtick." So I, literally, had to figure out a different way to read.

**JP:** Do you see anybody coming up through Wordcraft Circle?
**SA:** I'm in Wordcraft Circle; I'm a board member and all that. But I get worried. I think it's focusing too much on the idea of publication. The idea of writing as a career. It's becoming very careerist.

**JP:** So you either make it . . . if you don't publish and not doing it for your whole life then you shouldn't be doing it? Is that the danger you see?
**SA:** Well, it's becoming less and less about art. The whole thing is full of publication opportunities, money to win, scholarships, news about Indian writers publishing. . . .

**JP:** "Done good."
**SA:** Done good, yeah. Which is all fine. We're having a meeting soon and I just want to share my concerns with them that I'm worried that the focus has gone wrong.

**JP:** That the joy of it is not there?
**SA:** Exactly. One percent of one percent of the people in Wordcraft are going to have a book published. I think it's setting up unrealistic expectations.

**JP:** There's a group that Liz Cook-Lynn is involved with, a storytellers' circle, and they publish what they come up with, themselves. The focus isn't on selling it, but on doing it.

**SA:** Yeah. The act is the thing. I know people who would rather be where I'm at now, but I'm jaded as hell. About publication, about the "art" of it. I sound like I'm complaining. I'm glad to be where I'm at; I worked hard to get where I am. But there's also a lot that's shady about it. Being a successful Indian writer, and being an Indian, a "good Indian" (in quotes) are often mutually exclusive things, and there's a lot of pressure. I spend a lot of time alone, working. Selfish. My friendships suffer, my relationships with my family suffer, my health suffers. To be where I'm at, to do what I do, you'd have to be an obsessive compulsive nut (much laughter) and I don't think we should be encouraging our children in that direction. (More laughter.) Or at least letting them know. I mean, Wordcraft should be talking about the ugliness, too. This is what happens. Hard truths about publishing.

**JP:** The reality rather than the ideal image of the author dashing about the world, vacationing on sunny beaches.
**SA:** Exactly.

**JP:** But there are other rewards, right? The joy?
**SA:** Money and attention.

**JP:** Besides that.
**SA:** Don't let any writer fool you.

**JP:** Now, a little bit ago you said the poetry was still there, that that's. . . .
**SA:** Yeah, but nobody buys that.

**JP:** Yeah, true. I almost said that. But they buy movies and they buy novels.
**SA:** First and foremost, writers like to get attention. Don't let any writer tell you different.

**JP:** Yeah, well, in my world it's tenure and promotion, so. . . .
**SA:** Which is attention. We want to be heard. We're standing on street corners shouting. If that's not a cry for attention, I don't know what is. And Indian writers, all writers in general, but Indian writers, too, were the weird kids, the bizarre kids. The ones who question institutions, the ones who were not all that popular. The ones who people looked at weird. There are big burdens involved in all of this, you know.

[Interruption]

**JP:** You were on the state governor's book award board, and one winner was Carolyn Kizer. She has a great poem, "Afternoon Happiness." It says the poet's job is to write about pain and suffering, all that is "grist for me," but all she wants to do is write a poem about being content, and this poem does it.

**SA:** Actually, I'm doing it, too. My next book is all happy rez poems.

**JP:** That ought to start a buzz.

**SA:** Yeah. All the joy I remember from growing up.

**JP:** Good. Think it will sell well in Europe?

**SA:** It's not corn pollen, eagle feathers, Mother Earth, Father Sky. It's everyday life. Remembering taking our bikes and setting up ramps to jump over the sewer pit. That kind of stuff.

**JP:** And making it!

**SA:** Yeah, yeah. Or *not*. (Laughter.) And some of it a little sad. I'm working on this poem; it's not very good right now, I just wrote it last night, but I remember, I remember, I dreamed it a couple of nights ago, but during the winter we would, in winter, we'd take our gloves and put them on the radiator in the old school whenever they'd get wet. But I remembered some kids didn't have gloves, because they couldn't afford it, they were too poor. And I didn't have gloves this one winter, and I remembered that. And so I had this dream where I was sitting in the classroom and there were twelve pair of gloves on the radiator and thirteen kids in the classroom, and so everybody's looking around trying to figure out who's the one who doesn't have gloves, so everybody's hiding their hands. So, I'm working on that poem, and that image of everyone hiding their hands so nobody will know who didn't have gloves. Kind of sad, kind of nostalgic. . . .

**JP:** But positive in ways. . . .

**SA:** And that is also funny, I mean. Another one's about . . . there's this series of lullaby poems, actually, that I've written, they're really rhymey lullaby poems. Pow-wow lullaby poems, I call 'em, 'cause where we live on the Spokane rez the pow-wow ground is a couple of miles away, and at night you can hear the drums and the stick game players playing all night long, and that would put me to sleep at night during pow-wows. I'm writing poems about that feeling, or walking in the dark back from the pow-wow grounds, hearing the drums or walking to the grounds at night, or falling asleep in teepees, or in Winnebagos, or when we were real little, at a pow-wow in Arlee or wherever, and you'd end up sleeping in cousins' teepees in just a big pile of Indian kids. Those are the kinds of poems I've been writing.

Like the last book, *The Summer of Black Widows*, I thought was technically good. My last book of poems, technically good. I thought it was probably my best book. But very few of the poems Indian people would relate to. Whereas a book like *Fancydancing* I think is incredibly Indian. I want to go back to writing the kind of poems I wrote in *Fancydancing*. I'm more happy now. I'm a happier person. When I wrote these books . . . I'm getting happier and getting healthier. Some people say I always write about drunks. Well, no I don't, but if you look at the books you can see a progression, actually. The alcohol is dropping out of the books, because the alcohol is dropping farther and farther out of my life, as I've been sober for more and more years.

**JP:** And I can see a bunch of kid poems coming out in the near future, then?
**SA:** No. No, I won't write about him, I mean I write about him but I won't publish them unless he's old enough to let me know it's O.K.

[Interruption]

**JP:** What's needed, then, is a new press.
**SA:** I'm going to do it. Actually, next year I'm going to start up a literary journal that's called *Skins: The Poetry Journal for Indians and People We Wish Were Indians*. I figure to start publishing books out of that.

**JP:** Fantastic. Great. It's been done. Lots of people have started presses that way.
**SA:** I've the money and the influence. I can print a thousand copies of a poetry book, I'll be able to do that kind of thing, and I can get distribution. Poetry books will still only sell three hundred copies, but I can get them out there.

**JP:** Well, even one, two or three.
**SA:** One a year, two a year maybe.

**JP**: How long have you been thinking about this?
**SA:** Since the beginning. I just had to get to a place where I had the finances to do it. I didn't want a little mimeograph, I wanted a very, very professional journal, ah, very beautiful. The very best paper and the very best design. I wanted to wait until I had the finances there to have the best looking journal possible. I just said *Skins* and I can see it. *The Poetry Journal for Indians and People We Wish Were Indians*.

**JP:** People have talked about it over the years and presses have come and gone, presses have had interest in it and other times none, and I bring that up because we get back to that model "if it's not like this . . ." we don't buy it. The reason some young writers get caught in trying to write like that, the convention, is that they might get published.
**SA:** That's all they know. That's all they've read or been shown. I don't know

about you, but growing up all I got exposed to was Mother Earth-Father Sky stuff, or direction stuff. That's how I thought Indians wrote. I didn't know I could write actually about my *life.* (Laughter.)

**JP:** The first revelation, right?
**SA:** Yeah, I could write about fry bread and fried bologna. And the great thing is I didn't know you could combine, the traditional imagery and fried bread and fried bologna. The way I lived my life, and the way inside me, and the way I thought, which is a mix of traditionalism and contemporary culture.

**JP:** Right, which is reality.
**SA:** Which is reality. I didn't realize I could do that, something you can. I can write about, you know, Raybans and pow-wows.

**JP:** How soon do you think you will do that, *Skins?*
**SA:** Next year some. We haven't figured out submission policies, yet. For a while I think we'll just recruit, get it established and then open it up to submissions. But with editorial guidelines—"no lyric poetry." (Laughter.) "We want narrative."

**JP:** No lines that end with the word "blue."
**SA:** Right.

**JP:** Well, the *Bellingham Review* has been around for seventeen years or so, started by a colleague of mine, who has retired.
**SA:** Yeah—a guy named Knute.

**JP:** Yeah Knute.
**SA:** He rejected me like ten times while I was in college. I bet eventually he probably rejected half the *Fancydancing* manuscript.

**JP:** Oh, wow. "Click!" That's interesting. He wasn't the colleague on the plane with me who I showed the book to, but he did, though, what you're talking about. He set up a press with just that idea, that out of the journal submissions he took some poets and made them books. And it worked.
**SA:** Do you know Jim Hepworth? Confluence Press? He rejected *Fancydancing,* the book.

**JP:** Good. I mean, oh, that's too bad.
**SA:** No. I harass him constantly. He goes, "Oh I didn't read it, I couldn't have read it, one of my readers must have. I would have remembered it." And I started laughing. I said, "Jim, you sent me the letter. I still have the letter. You said, 'This is encouraging, this shows lots of potential. But not ready for publication yet.'"

**JP:** Yeah. I know. So do you send him reviews of the book on the back of royalty reports?

**SA:** Well, he knows what happened.

**JP:** Wish you the best of luck on that project. It's good.

**SA:** It's going to . . . the reception we get at literary journals is terrible. The standard literary journal rarely publishes us. And when we do it's always part of a "special issue," or a special section. "The Literary Reservation." I'm looking for new young writers, the undiscovered voices, who are telling us things. I want to read poems where I recognize the characters, and I recognize the words. Where, ah, I'd also like to publish poems that people will not get, at all.

**JP:** Insider jokes.

**SA:** Yeah, I load my books with stuff, just load 'em up. I call them "Indian trap-doors." You know, Indians fall in, white people just walk right over them.

**JP:** I thought it was supposed to be the other way around. Hmm.

**SA:** Ah. So that's the kind of thing I'm imagining. Poems that work in all sorts of ways, but I really want the subtext for Indians.

**JP:** This is exactly how, as we were talking earlier, it will be done, how it will move on. Others have been at work doing it, like *Greenfield Review*. Now that things are established, it's time for the next phase. *Skins.*

**SA:** And just stay with poetry, because fiction costs too much.

**JP:** Yeah, yeah. Takes up a lot of space: more short stories, you have fewer poems.

**SA:** And I'm sorry, but I think generally speaking, Indians just don't write good fiction: it's not in us.

**JP:** I take it then, that you're not going to do a serial of *Almanac of the Dead?*

**SA:** No. I just don't think . . . it's just not natural for us. I think we're meant to write poems. All of our traditional communication, it's about poetry. So I think in some sense, genetically, we're poets. Culturally speaking, we can become fiction writers. We can sort of . . . but it's one of the problems with some of the criticism, some of the criticisms directed by Liz Cook-Lynn, and Gloria Bird, and Robert Warrior talking about how there needs to be more tradition in Indian writing. I thought. . . .

**JP:** What's "more tradition"?

**SA:** But also, I mean, we're writing in English, 99 percent of our audience is going to be non-Indian, so how the hell do we do that?

**JP:** And, if you take that a step further, then should you?

**SA:** Exactly. We shouldn't be writing about our traditions, we shouldn't be writing about our spiritual practices. Not in the ways in which some people are doing it. Certainly, if you're writing a poem or story about a spiritual experience you had, you can do it. But you also have to be aware that it's going to be taken and used in ways that you never intended for it to be. I think it's dangerous, and that's really why I write about day-to-day life.

The responsibilities of being an Indian writer are enormous. Even more so than any other group of people because we have so much more to protect.

**JP:** (An aside to Fred: "You ever heard this before?")

**SA:** I mean and it's so funny, people, like some of these writers, will think of me as being this very contemporary, very nontraditional guy, and I am, but I'm a lot more conservative in my take on Indian literature than any of those people are. I think . . . like some of the Navajo stuff and some of the traditional chants, or like some of Momaday's stuff, when rendered into English, means nothing. Means *nothing.* Our traditions are all about being, about taking place in a specific time and a specific geography. But when in a book that goes everywhere to anybody, it's like a traveling road show of Indian spirituality.

**JP:** Think of it this way, too, one of the elements behind that is the impetus for putting it in English and putting it in a book.

**SA:** To sell it. There's no Indian who would stand—well very few—on a roadside singing traditional songs to make money. Yet they will put it in a book and sell the book. To make money. I think the passage of money invalidates any sort of sacredness of any of the ceremonies that are placed within a book.

**JP:** Someone asked, I think it was Vine Deloria, Jr., how to tell a plastic shaman, and he said to just ask how much they charge. Pretty well says it.

Well, I'm glad you're going to do that; it's a really good idea, the journal and the press, and to put out the poets who come through who have promise. That's good.

**SA:** Yeah, I'd like to nurture careers. And to have a space for Indian writers to develop. I mean like this idea of featuring a poet per issue, a young, unknown person, featuring them, and also charting the growth of these young poets over a few years, and then into a book. I've seen a number of first books by Indian poets recently that really needed editing help.

**JP:** I've noticed that, too, lately. Even fairly well-established presses are putting out things maybe too quickly, not carefully enough.

**SA:** And then the books, because they're bought, disappear, and it does a disservice to the writers. That's one of my problems with Wordcraft, it's rushing people into print before they're ready. And when you get a bad poem published, or a flat poem published, you don't learn anything. They've published bad poems of mine, and I've suffered for it. There are bad poems of mine in books.

**JP:** It becomes embarrassing later as well. (Laughter.)
**SA:** "Oh my god, I wrote that? No, somebody slipped that in there when I wasn't looking."

**JP:** It's a strange business, isn't it? I'm glad that you're keeping at the poetry, some balance. So when's the movie coming out?
**SA:** We're doing distributor screenings over the next couple of weeks, for Miramax, Sony, and all of that. All the big ones. If there's been an independent movie over the last five years, whoever's released it, they're coming. It's a good movie, comparable in level and quality to *The Full Monty*, the performances are amazing. These actors finally got a chance to play human beings, rather than wind-o-bots. I think it's really going to go. I thing we'll get an awakening here, and we'll get about a three-year window to make Indian films.

**JP:** The doors will open quickly. . . .
**SA:** And close quickly. What's going to happen is there will be a flood of Indian movies, most of them will be bad, they won't make money, and then the door will close again. We'll have the chance for a couple years here I think.

**JP:** Just like we were talking about a while ago, things get rushed into production instead of. . . .
**SA:** What I'm hoping to get from this movie is so, . . . we told the story but at the same time it is also very subversive, to take on "Indian cinema" and the images in the movies: about the Warrior, about storytelling, there's all sorts of little jokes along the way about the ways Indians get viewed in the movies, and in culture, as we're telling the road movie stories. I'm hoping it will kill, make it impossible for anybody to make this type of movie again. Like the way *Blazing Saddles* killed the Western for twenty years.

**JP:** If it accomplishes just ten years, it'd be wonderful.
**SA:** Six months, three days, two hours. For dinner after they see the movie, if they can see Indians as nothing else but human beings, it'll be a success.

**JP:** We could boycott the whole thing, Hollywood. One day.
**SA:** One day. One day of no anti-Indian thoughts. Not going to happen. I can dream.

**JP:** So you have a something going on tonight?

**SA:** It's called for Books for Prisoners. It's affiliated with Left Bank Books.

**JP:** Well, I hope you have fun.

## Note

1. Aaron Gorseth did the initial transcription of the audio tape of this conversation. It has been edited slightly from the audio, mostly to remove slight repetition and the usual, inconsequential utterances, like "oh" and "ah," which unfortunately includes most of the laughter. Even more sadly, there is no way to convey the inflections, grins, and body language that animated most of the conversation with a playful edge.

# Sherman Alexie:
# Poet, Novelist, Filmmaker

Charlene Teters/1997

From *Indian Artist* Spring 1998: 30–35. Reprinted by permission of the interviewer. Charlene Teters, a member of the Spokane Nation, is an artist, teacher, writer, and activist.

Thirty-one-year-old writer Sherman Alexie is sitting in Seattle's Occidental Park, across from the Elliott Bay Book Company. At the moment, he is seated among some of Seattle's homeless, many of whom are Native people and some of whom are inspirations for the characters in his bestselling novel, *Indian Killer*.

"Remember Marie and her sandwich van?" he asks, referring to a character in his book. "This is the park."

Alexie writes about personal experience and real places. His main characters in *Indian Killer* all suffer from such afflictions as alcoholism, anger, self-loathing, and other symptoms of internalized racism. Alexie knows of these things firsthand. He has lived with his characters and shared their pain.

Alexie is one of the current generation of "new storytellers." His stories are about memories, about survival, about what life on the rez was like during a time of great change. He says he is not traditional, but Indian and non-Indian readers alike respond to the genuine Indian voice in his work. Far from romanticized, his writings are brooding and ironic, with a sharp edge. And sometimes this edge causes his readers to confuse the writer with the work.

Besides *Indian Killer*, Alexie has authored the novel *Reservation Blues*, four books of poetry, and a collection of short stories. The latter, titled *The Lone Ranger and Tonto Fistfight in Heaven*, has just been made into a movie titled *This Is What It Means to Say Phoenix, Arizona*. Coproduced by Alexie and Cheyenne-Arapaho filmmaker Chris Eyre, the movie premiered at the Sundance Film Festival in January and will be distributed by Miramax. Says actor Michael Horse, "It's not just one of the best Indian films, but one of the best films I've seen." Extremely prolific, Alexie is currently working on another book of poetry, *The Man Who Loves Salmon*, and the screenplay for *Indian Killer*, which he will also direct.

Alexie writes constantly. Whether at home or on the road, he's always tapping his latest memories and experiences into his laptop computer. He also thinks in pictures, he says, which facilitates his screenwriting and producing roles. In the past, his speaking engagements have taken him from San Francisco to New York and Paris. But now that he and his Hidatsa wife, Diane, have become parents of a baby boy, he stays much closer to home.

**Charlene Teters:** Tell me about your home and early life.
**Sherman Alexie:** The Spokane Rez, in my experience, is one of the most beautiful in the country: pine trees, streams, lakes, the Columbia and Spokane Rivers, Tshimakin Creek, deer walking through the middle of town, bear falling asleep on the church roof. Physically, it's the most beautiful place in the world. And then it has all the social problems that a reservation has: the alcohol and drug problems, family dysfunction, domestic violence. And so I grew up in that. It's isolated, and unlike a lot of reservations, it's mostly Indian, and most everybody is Spokane Indian. It's really more of a mono-culture. So that's who I dealt with for the first eighteen years of my life, and that was good. It was like a little island.

Myself, growing up, I was weird. I was smart. From the earliest time that I can remember, I had this need to be better than everyone else. I don't know where that comes from, but that's not a good thing when you're an Indian—to assert yourself as an individual, to rise out in the crowd, to not fall into peer pressures to behave in a certain manner. Our tribe is very reserved, very conservative. I was not reserved. From the very beginning, I was this socialist-communist-artist guy.

In my books, which are based on personal experiences and history, I get accused of exaggerating the despair on the reservation. But in the face of tremendous social problems, there is a great deal of denial there. That conservatism is like blinders. And when someone like me says something, they get into trouble. I've been getting into trouble since I was very little, because I'd be standing up and saying, "Hey, that's not right!"

**CT:** You have a reputation for being arrogant. Are you aware of that?
**SA:** [Laughing.] Oh, yes. Because I am. Well, because I am to some degree. What I am is really, really confident. Of course I've got my insecurities—I've built this shell of defenses around myself to survive growing up—but I'm very confident. People think of me as being this extroverted, funny, arrogant, mouthy kind of guy. I'm actually afraid of things, even scared of meeting new people. But people have said these things about me before they even met me.

**CT:** Do you think people develop a perception of you based on stories they've read or heard?

**SA:** Yes, I'm sure people are afraid to meet me. They think I'm this big scary Indian, this big mean guy, but I'm not. It goes back to when I was a kid on the rez. I wanted to leave, and everyone knew that. I was very verbal about it. I knew that if I stayed there, I'd die. A lot of my friends on the rez have died—from car wrecks, cirrhosis, suicide, murders. So in a sense I never fit in, and I was always individualizing myself.

A lot of it has to do with the rumor mill, too. A friend of mine was at this writer's conference in Florida where there were no Indians at all. They were talking about my book, and this white scholar stood up and said that I had no authority to speak about the reservation because I grew up with white people. The rumor was that my folks had adopted me out to white people.

Also, not many Indian writers have achieved the level of success I have in such a short time. But I haven't met an Indian writer out there who isn't arrogant—or a writer in general who isn't arrogant. It's part of what we do. The very act of creating art is arrogant. To think that what we think is important enough that everyone should see it, or that everyone should buy it and read it, that's an arrogant act in itself. So a succinct answer as to why people think I'm arrogant: because I don't pretend I'm not.

**CT:** Tell me about your Grandma Etta.

**SA:** Ah, Big Mom loved me, my grandma loved me. All my other grandparents were dead before I was born. She was my only link to the past. I'd go and visit her. She'd tell me these stories. Not traditional stories in the sense of coyote, eagle feathers, or talking birds; she would give me the history of my family. She'd tease, she would lie and flirt, talking about how so and so was so handsome. And she would talk about when she was a little girl, the salmon in the Spokane River swam so thick that you could walk across the river from shore to shore on their backs.

She knew I was weird. She was always teasing me. She would call me up on the phone and say, "Come down here, I need to make you Indian!" She was really supportive of who I was. Big Mom would go Goodwill shopping or garage-sale shopping, and she would always bring back books for "Junior." She wouldn't even look at what kind of books they were; she would just see a book and bring it home. So I'd end up with these Harlequin romances, or auto-repair manuals—it didn't matter.

Big Mom's other grandkids were dancers or singers—more traditional.

Everybody was into powwows except me, but she didn't care. That's what I miss, that kind of support from an elder. She was my strongest link to tradition, and I lost her when I was thirteen. I miss her every day.

**CT:** Who are your favorite authors?

**SA:** In terms of novels and fiction writing, James Welch is who I looked towards: works like *The Death of Jim Loney*, which is a great book, and *Winter in the Blood*. That was the first Indian novel I read where I recognized the characters.

Adrian C. Louis is another one. He's really got this angry-reservation-Indian-guy writing going on. He's another writer whose characters I recognize. Simon Ortiz I like. Luci Tapahonso writes some really beautiful poetry—and some really funny ones, too, like "Raisin Eyes." In her new book, she has a poem about being in the airport in Texas trying to look good because George Strait might show up.

Joy Harjo is a great poet. She's moved into music. I love her music, but I think she's neglecting her poetry. Her poems "Woman Hanging from the Thirteenth Floor Window" and "She Had Some Horses" are two of the great poems of the twentieth century. I wish she wrote more.

**CT:** How do you go about getting a book made into a screenplay and a film?

**SA:** My books have done well in non-Indian terms, so people have been calling me from the very beginning, interested in my works and in me as a possible film writer. But they were also interested in changing the stories to fit the idea of commercial Indianness. They wanted more loincloths, more visions. They wanted *Thunderheart* or *Dances With Wolves*, so I kept my rights, because I wasn't interested in those kinds of changes.

Chris Eyre, a Cheyenne/Arapaho filmmaker, first became interested in my work as a graduate student at New York University. And that's what I'd been waiting for: Indian filmmakers and directors coming to me. When Eyre and I started working together, we became twice as effective. We went through many potential producers, then took the project to ShadowCatcher, a Seattle film-production company founded by veterans of Hollywood. They were interested in Northwest writers and interested in me, so we decided to go with them.

*This Is What It Means to Say Phoenix, Arizona* is based on my book *The Lone Ranger and Tonto Fistfight in Heaven*. It's about two young Coeur d'Alene Indians, Victor Joseph and Thomas Builds-the-Fire, who travel to Arizona to retrieve the remains of Victor's estranged father. In going from book to screenplay, I found that to be an easy process because it's more like poetry, about images. The production company almost went overboard in allowing Chris and me to tell this story. They deferred to our judgments in the material. The producers did a great job making sure we told the story right, but what is on screen, for better or worse, belongs to Chris and me.

**CT:** There seems to be a lot of excitement about the release of the film.
**SA:** Yes, I sense excitement and also some grumbling. [Laughing.] You know how Indians are. But once again, it's the fact that all these filmmakers have been struggling for years to get a film done, and here is Chris who's twenty-seven and me being thirty-one, we get it done. It's great, I love it.

*Indian Killer* is up next. I'm going to direct that project. We're developing it now. Chris is moving on to other projects, but I'll be writing, directing, and co-producing it along with ShadowCatcher, filming in Seattle. I still have a lot to learn, but I realized that I want to direct, and I want to protect what I write.

**CT:** It seems that Indians, for the most part, continue to be just the subjects of films rather than the creators of films.
**SA:** This is a first. Chris and I coproduced it, so this is the first feature film written, directed, and coproduced by Indians that's also based on a book written by an Indian. This is it, the first! Everybody wanted to be in it. Gary Farmer, Tantoo Cardinal, Adam Beach, Evan Adams, Irene Bedard, Michael Greyeyes, Michelle St. John, Elaine Miles, John Trudell, Leonard George, Darwin Haine, Cody Lightning, Simon Baker. Michael Greyeyes, who is this incredibly talented, successful actor, took a part with only three lines. I was really honored. Actors came in to do small parts because they wanted to be associated with it—and more important, to support it. I'm proud and honored that they would do that.

**CT:** Will *Indian Killer* have an all-star cast like this one?
**SA:** Oh, yes, 99 percent of the cast in *This Is What It Means to Say Phoenix, Arizona* is Indian. We also got stars to do the white roles—like Tom Skerritt of *Alien* and *A River Runs Through It*. Also Cynthia Geary of *Northern Exposure*. Because of the casting process for *Phoenix*, we sort of know who we want for roles in *Indian Killer*. We're not saying now, but we have good ideas about who we want.

**CT:** Even with new films done today by Indian directors, there are new stereotypes developing. Films start with flute music, pan to a campfire, maybe go to the drum.
**SA:** Yes, it's pan-Indianism, generic Indianism that Indians have adopted and somehow think is traditional or real. Like the vision quest in the third act. Whether it's made by an Indian or not, there is always the vision quest, where some Indian is standing on a mountain like this. [Alexie raises his hands.] I'm sorry, but I've met thousands of Indians, and I have yet to know of anyone who

has stood on a mountain waiting for a sign. I don't know anyone who's done it. If you told someone on the reservation, "I want you to go out on Lookout Mountain and wait for a sign," they'd say, "You want me to do what? Hell, no! It's cold! I want to watch football." It's almost the twenty-first century. The way of being Indian now is vastly different than it was a hundred years ago.

CT: Your work has a distinctively Indian voice—not someone talking "for my people," but a genuine Native voice.

SA: Let me just say that there is a great deal of posing out there. I think a lot of Native writers are pretending, writing about the kind of Indians they wish they were, not the kind of Indians they are. They're posing as something they're not. And then they have to construct a personal history that coincides with that. I write about the kind of Indian I am: kind of mixed up, kind of odd, not traditional. I'm a rez kid who's gone urban, and that's what I write about. I've never pretended to be otherwise.

# Sending Cinematic Smoke Signals:
# An Interview with Sherman Alexie

Dennis West and Joan M. West/1998

From *Cineaste* 23.4 (1998): 28–31, 37. Reprinted by permission.

Every few years or so, press kits arrive at the offices of film magazines announcing that a forthcoming film about Native Americans decisively breaks with the stereotypes of the past. *Smoke Signals* is the latest film to advertise itself so, but, unlike most of its predecessors, *Smoke Signals* delivers on its promises. A prime component of its success is that it is the first feature to have been written, directed, and coproduced by Native Americans, and also features Native Americans in all the lead roles.

The storyline is a variation of the odyssey theme. In this instance, rather than focusing on a warrior/father struggling to return to his home, the plot turns on a warrior/son struggling to physically and emotionally find an alcoholic father who fled his home and died in self-exile. Victor Joseph (Adam Beach), an abandoned son who has grown up on the Coeur d'Alene reservation in Idaho, must undertake a journey to collect the ashes of his father, Arnold Joseph (Gary Farmer), who has died in Phoenix, Arizona. Thomas Builds-the-Fire (Evan Adams) provides Victor the money he needs for the trip on condition that he is allowed to go along. Unlike Victor, Thomas has numerous positive memories of Arnold Joseph, ultimately derived from the circumstance that, when he was only an infant, Arnold had saved him from a burning building.

Their road together turns out to have a number of detours and moments of truth, all of which are interesting in and of themselves. More important than the incidents and challenges per se, however, are the effects they have on the emotional development of the two sojourners. Sherman Alexie, who wrote the script based on sections of his best-selling *The Lone Ranger and Tonto Fistfight in Heaven*, has noted that American popular culture recognizes only two major Native American profiles: the warrior and the shaman. He goes about subverting these stereotypes with various images, stories, and songs. Although some aspects of the odyssey are somber, humor often finds its way into the darkest moments. Victor and Thomas constantly jibe with one another and outsiders about what it means to be a contemporary Native American. Thomas proves to be a genuine storyteller, but his tales never dissolve into the usual hocus pocus surrounding shamans; and Victor is indeed a warrior, but he is neither stoic nor silent. Both characters are decidedly Native American, but Native Americans rooted in this time and place and not a fictionalized past.

The literary talent of Sherman Alexie, who is coproducer as well as the scriptwriter of *Smoke Signals*, is very much in evidence throughout the film. Words count for him, whether for the sheer joy of wordplay, or as a means of revealing a character. But the film is never talky in the sense of a stage play. Rather, it has the kind of intelligent and clever dialog characteristic of the best studio films of yore. In this sense, Alexie has been extremely successful in moving from writing for the printed page to writing for the screen. And his considerable success in the former bodes well for his future as a writer for the cinema. Throughout the 1990s, Alexie has garnered numerous writing awards, steadily gaining recognition as one of America's leading fiction writers. His second novel, *Indian Killer*, a current best seller, is being developed as a feature film by ShadowCatcher Entertainment, the producer of *Smoke Signals*.

In addition to his prose, Alexie is a well-known poet. His first book of poetry, *The Business of Fancydancing*, was chosen in 1992 by the *New York Times Book Review* as its Notable Book of the Year. He has since won a poetry fellowship from the National Endowment for the Arts and a Lila Wallace/*Readers' Digest* Writer's Award. Not coincidentally *Smoke Signals* features an original contemporary poem as its coda. The first line sounds one of the film's major themes: "How do we forgive our fathers?" The film concludes with a voice-over recitation of the poem that is a refreshing break from the dumbing-down and action-oriented approach of so many contemporary films. That the poem's author, Dick Lourie, is not a Native American also fits into the film's pattern of breaking with the expected ethnic response. Using a Native American poem for this purpose would have been far more predictable and problematic.

*Smoke Signals* is all the more impressive for being the debut feature of director Chris Eyre, a twenty-eight-year-old Cheyenne/Arapaho filmmaker from Oregon who has previously written and directed seven short films. He keeps the film moving at a brisk but not a hurried pace, taking time to get the most out of a scene involving frying bread, while allowing spectacular outdoor vistas to speak for themselves rather than being framed as picture postcards. Eyre gets a particularly strong performance from Evan Adams, who credibly renders Thomas as an engaging cross between a mama's boy and a traditional seer, a sometimes nerd in funny glasses who is no one's sidekick. Eyre also makes effective use of Irene

Bedard, as Suzy Song, who has an understanding and affection for the deceased Arnold Joseph that his son must deal with.

No single film can be expected to undo the misinformation about Native Americans that has accumulated over many generations. Since the politically turbulent Sixties, there has been an ongoing movement by Native American film actors to combat ethnic stereotyping. In their wake have come Native American producers, directors, actors, and scriptwriters. *Smoke Signals* belongs to and advances this continuum. Hopefully, it will prove to be the first of a new wave of diverse Native American films. The ethnic group that has been featured more than any other in the history of American films is finally beginning to speak in its own voice. During the 1998 Seattle Film Festival, *Cineaste* was able to speak with Alexie about the many cultural issues embodied by and explored in his debut feature film effort, *Smoke Signals*.

—Dan Georgakas

**Cineaste:** You have called your screenplay "groundbreaking" because of its portrayal of Indians. Why?

**Sherman Alexie:** Well, it's a very basic story, a road trip/buddy movie about a lost father, so I'm working with two very classical, mythic structures. You can find them in everything from the Bible to *The Iliad* and *The Odyssey*. What is revolutionary or groundbreaking about the film is that the characters in it are Indians, and they're fully realized human beings. They're not just the sidekick, or the buddy, they're the protagonists. Simply having Indians as the protagonists in a contemporary film, and placing them within this familiar literary, and cinematic structure, is groundbreaking.

**Cineaste:** Do you think *Pow Wow Highway* (1989) was one of the more worthy previous efforts?

**Alexie:** When it came out, I loved it, and I saw it three times at the Micro Movie House in Moscow, Idaho. But I saw it again on Bravo recently and, after working on this film, and seeing what we could do, *Pow Wow Highway* now seems *so* stereotypical. The performances are fine, but it trades in so many stereotypes, from standing in a river singing, to going up on a mountaintop to get a vision, and the generic AIM political activism. Every stereotypical touchstone of a contemporary Indian art film is there. Two scenes especially really made me cringe. When Philbert goes up on a mountain, he's supposed to leave something that means so much to him, and he leaves a Hershey bar! Then there's the scene with A Martinez, as Buddy Red Bow, where the police car's coming, and Buddy has a piece of metal or something in his hand. He jumps in the air, and there's this brief flash shot of him dressed in the full costume of an Indian warrior, throwing a tomahawk, and I just thought, "Oh God!"

Our expectations of movies about Indians were so low then that we embraced a movie like *Pow Wow Highway* simply because there was no other option. Looking back, *Thunderheart* is a far superior movie, just in terms of its representation. I mean, it's a generic white guy saves the day movie, but I think it's better in terms of its representation of contemporary Indians. Except for John Trudell changing into a deer [laughs]. I've never seen an Indian turn into a deer. I mean, I know thousands of Indians, I've been an Indian my whole life, and I've yet to see an Indian turn into an animal! And I know some very traditional Indian folks.

**Cineaste:** Would you comment on your fundamental approach in adapting your collection of short stories, *The Lone Ranger and Tonto Fistfight in Heaven*, for the screen?
**Alexie:** I've never been one of those people who compared the book and the movie of the book. That's never interested me because I've always separated them as two very distinct art forms, so I never got mad if the movie wasn't the book, or vice versa. I knew from a very young age that it was impossible to do that. I mean, you're talking about a three-hundred-page novel versus an hour-and-a-half or two-hour movie. It's impossible to convey in a movie the entire experience of a novel, and I always knew that.

Knowing that going in, I didn't have any problems with mutating my own book. I treated my book of short stories in adapting the screenplay as though I didn't write it. Right from the get-go, I said, "OK, Sherman, you're going to do composite characters, compress time, take bits and pieces from stories you need for this screenplay, and you're not going to care." The narrative integrity of any one story was never the point, it was all about taking situations from the twenty-two short stories—it actually ended up being adapted from four short stories—taking the best you can find in this book to make the screenplay.

**Cineaste:** How did you think about structure?
**Alexie:** The cheapest kind of independent film to make is either people in a room talking . . .

**Cineaste:** *My Dinner with Andre*?
**Alexie:** Yeah, or *Clerks*. It's either that or a road movie, and I didn't want to make a talking-heads movie, because that's a tough sell to begin with. It's hard to reach a large audience with a talking-heads movie and, if you put Indians in the talking heads, only four people are going to want to see it. But I knew the road movie was

a very time-honored structure, and also very cheap to do. Put two guys in a car or a bus, get a camera rig, and you're fine, it's easy to film.

**Cineaste:** And it can be visually interesting.

**Alexie:** Exactly. You can let the landscape tell a lot of story. And if it's a road/buddy movie, you're going to have a lot of music, and I always knew music was going to be a part of this. There are specific music cues in the screenplay about traditional music or rock and roll music, or a combination of the two. "John Wayne's Teeth," for example, is a combination of English lyrics and Western musical rhythms along with Indian vocables and Indian traditional drums. I also wanted to use Indian artists, so as not only to make a revolutionary movie for Indians, but also to use Indian artists on the soundtrack, which fits well with the road/buddy movie structure.

There was always a template in my head for this, which was these two odd buddies, sort of Mutt and Jeff on a road trip, *Midnight Cowboy* on a bus ride. One of the original drafts of the screenplay, in fact, contained many more overt references to *Midnight Cowboy*. Joe Buck and Victor—beautiful, stoic, clueless guys—are very much alike. At the Sundance Institute, I saw a documentary about Waldo Salt, the screenwriter of *Midnight Cowboy*, that really affected me in the way I wanted to make the movie. In an interview in the documentary, Salt talked about his use of flashforwards in *Midnight Cowboy*, so that while the story is going, you learn more and more about Joe Buck and his experiences back home. It was always flashforwards, that's what he called them, that continued the story and gave you more information. Rather than stopping the movie to be expository, they kept the drama going. So in writing the screenplay, I always knew there were going to be flashforwards. *Midnight Cowboy* was really a template for me in a lot of ways, not only in its structure, but also in the screenwriting philosophies of Waldo Salt.

**Cineaste:** Would you comment on the screenplay's semiautobiographical elements?

**Alexie:** My friend and I took a trip to Phoenix, Arizona, to pick up his father's remains. At the Sundance Festival, quite a few people asked, "Were you influenced by *Pow Wow Highway*?" because that film's also about a trip by two Indian guys to the Southwest. "It wasn't really an influence," I said, "unless you can say that my friend's father died because of *Pow Wow Highway*." The basic creative spark for *Smoke Signals* came from the trip I took with my friend. It's not my friend's story, but I placed my characters within that framework of going to pick up a father's remains. That's how the short story came about. It's more about my relationship with my father than about my friend's relationship with his father. My father is still alive, but he's had to struggle with alcoholism, as I have. It's also about the struggle within myself of being this storytelling geek like Thomas, as well as this big jock masculine guy like Victor, so it's a sort of schizophrenic multiple personality of myself that I develop within the movie.

**Cineaste:** Storytelling, dreams, and visions are key motifs in your book, *The Lone Ranger and Tonto*, and in *Smoke Signals*. Would you comment on their cultural and artistic significance for you?

**Alexie:** In the book itself, I'm rarely interested in traditional narrative. My beginnings are as a poet. My first form of writing was poetry. While there's certainly a strong narrative drive in my poetry, it was always about the image, and about the connection, often, of very disparate, contradictory images. When I began working on the screenplay, and not knowing anything about screenplays, I started reading all the typical books—you know, Syd Field and all those people—but I was not interested in their formulas for successful screenplays. In fact, after reading them and all the screenplays they admired so much, I realized that the qualities they were talking about were not what made those movies or screenplays great. It was always something that exploded outside the narrative or the structure that made the movie great, so I was always interested in going outside the narrative and traditional formats.

In my books, I've always been fascinated with dreams and stories and flashing forward and flashing back and playing with conventions of time, so in adapting the screenplay, I always knew I would use those elements. I knew there would be moments when the camera would sit still and somebody was going to talk, but I didn't want just talking heads, as I mentioned earlier. I always knew that while the person was talking, we were going to see images from the story he or she was telling. I even develop that motif, and the fact that the story of the movie is told by Thomas, so at certain points he's telling the story about himself telling the story about somebody else telling a story. So I wanted to keep those complicated layers going.

It's all based on the basic theme, for me, that storytellers are essentially liars. At one point in the movie, Suzy asks Thomas, "Do you want lies or do you want the truth?," and he says, "I want both." I think that line is what reveals most about Thomas's character and the nature of his storytelling and the nature, in my opinion, of storytelling in general, which is that fiction blurs and nobody knows what the truth is. And within the movie itself, nobody knows what the truth is.

**Cineaste:** Why does Thomas always close his eyes when he tells a story?
**Alexie:** [Laughs.] That was in the book, but I don't know.

**Cineaste:** There is a literary tradition of blind seers, of course.
**Alexie:** I really don't know. The first time I wrote that story, he closed his eyes. I wrote, "Thomas closed his eyes." And it stayed.

**Cineaste:** For me, when I read that, it was as if he were trying to imagine it with such intensity that he had to close his eyes and move into another realm.
**Alexie:** It could be that! It just felt right, it just felt like something he would do.

**Cineaste:** We don't recall smoke signals as a motif in the book. Did you decide on the film's title?
**Alexie:** Yeah, I did. People keep asking me, "Why did Miramax change the title?" Well, Miramax didn't change the title, I did. In fact, I never wanted to call the movie, *This Is What It Means to Say Phoenix, Arizona*. That's the name of the short story. I love that title on the story, but it is *not* a cinematic title. There is an inverse proportional relationship between the length of movie titles and the success of the film. Very few long-titled films do well, because people forget the title.

Even though we were getting some very good Sundance coverage, people kept screwing up the movie title, and that would have killed the film. So, in looking for a title, we wanted something short and punchy, but also something that fit thematically. *Smoke Signals* fits for a number of reasons, for me. On the surface, it's a stereotypical title, you think of Indians in blankets on the plains sending smoke signals, so it brings up a stereotypical image that's vaguely humorous. But people will also instantly recognize that this is about Indians. Then, when you see the movie, you realize that, in a contemporary sense, smoke signals are about calls of distress, calls for help. That's really what this movie is about—Victor, Thomas, and everybody else calling for help. It's also about the theme of fire. The smoke that originates from the first fire in the movie is what causes these events, and the smoke from the second fire brings about the beginning of resolution. So I just thought *Smoke Signals* worked very poetically. It's something very memorable, and nobody is going to screw up that title!

**Cineaste:** Would you comment on the film's theme of the absent father and specifically on the ending of the film? How do you envision the future of your two young, fatherless protagonists?
**Alexie:** Well, I'm reminded of this quote from Gabriel García Márquez that my wife has up on the refrigerator. He says something like, "Men have been running the world for how many thousands of years, and look what we've done. It's about time we let women take over." So that theme is in my head, the idea that in Indian cultures in particular, men have lost all their traditional roles within society.

There are feminine and masculine roles within Indian society and, in many tribes, men and women played neither role, or went back and forth. But those traditional masculine roles—you know, hunter, warrior—they're all gone. I mean, driving a truck for the BIA is simply not going to fulfill your spiritual needs, like fishing for salmon or hunting for deer once did, so in some sense Indian men are much more lost and much more clueless than Indian women.

I think you'd find the same thing in every ethnic or racial community, that it's fathers who are missing. I was doing an interview yesterday, and it came to me that brown artists—African American, Chicano, Indian, and so on—write about fathers who physically leave and don't come back. White artists deal with fathers who leave emotionally, who sit in the chair in the living room but are gone. It's a theme that resonates. The actual physical presence of the father varies with ethnicity, I think, so the idea of a father leaving is nothing new for me. My father did leave to drink but he always came back. So for me it was a way of exploring that feeling of abandonment.

**Cineaste:** Is your vision of Indian society less dark in *Smoke Signals* than in *Lone Ranger*?

**Alexie:** Definitely. If you chart the course of my book, or my literary work, you're going to see that pattern. I always tease literary scholars who interview me, saying, "You know, you should use the title, 'Firewater World: The Idea of Recovery in Sherman Alexie's Fiction and Poetry,' because that's really what's happened." When I first started writing I was still drinking, so *Lone Ranger and Tonto* and the first book of poems, *The Business of Fancydancing*, are really soaked in alcohol. As I've been in recovery over the years and stayed sober, you'll see the work gradually freeing itself of alcoholism and going much deeper, exploring the emotional, sociological, and psychological reasons for any kind of addiction or dysfunctions within the community. I'm looking for the causes now, rather than the effects, and I think that's what *Smoke Signals* is about. *The Lone Ranger and Tonto* is about the effects of alcoholism on its characters, and I think the adaptation, *Smoke Signals*, is more about the causes of that behavior. It's more of a whole journey, you get there and you get back.

**Cineaste:** There's a stunning moment in the film when Victor tells the white police chief that he doesn't drink, that he's never drunk. It seemed a declaration of a break with his father and his father's past, trying to overcome that difficult social problem.

**Alexie:** Exactly, that he's going to be somebody different. In my books and poems, Victor's a drinker, an alcoholic, but in the movie he's never had a drop.

It's also a big break from my own work, so it's working on a couple of levels there. Not only the difference between my book Victor and my movie Victor, but, within the context of the story, it's also Victor's break away from his father, his creator, who is me.

**Cineaste:** Would you comment on the two young women driving their car in reverse?
**Alexie:** [Laughs.] Well, their names are Velma and Lucy!

**Cineaste:** To avoid copyright problems?
**Alexie:** It was an in-joke for me, playing around with the idea of a road movie. I love that movie, as an anti-road movie which deconstructs the whole macho road/buddy movie, so I wanted to put them in there as an homage to *Thelma & Louise*. It also has to do with the sense of time in the movie, when the past, present, and future are all the same, that circular sense of time which plays itself out in the seamless transitions from past to present. Within that circular sense of time, I also wanted to have this car driving in reverse. The phrase I always use is, "Sometimes to go forward you have to drive in reverse." So it's a visual metaphor for what we were doing.

It's also an Indian metaphor because our cars are always screwed up. There was a man who one summer drove his pickup all over the reservation in reverse because none of the forward gears worked. It's one of those moments that I think everybody can find amusing, but non-Indian audiences are going to say, "OK, this is funny, but what the hell's going on?," because there is no explanation for it. Indian audiences are really going to laugh, however, because they're going to completely understand it. I call those kinds of things Indian trapdoors, because an Indian will walk over them and fall in, but a non-Indian will keep on walking.

**Cineaste:** To get back to the music, we understand from the credits that you wrote the lyrics of five of the *Smoke Signals* songs, including "John Wayne's Teeth." Would you talk a bit about the film's use of music?
**Alexie:** As part of my obsessive-compulsive behavior, I guess, I had completely planned the whole movie. I knew exactly where three of the songs that I had written previously for Jim Boyd would fit in. Knowing the catalog of songs that Jim and I had written, when I was writing the screenplay I would be punching them in, knowing exactly where they would fit. I didn't want the music to be an afterthought, but an inherent and organic part of the film. Writing songs is another way of expressing ourselves. Just as I think screenplays are accessible poetry, I think songs are accessible poetry, and while I'm going to continue to write poetry

that nobody reads [laughs], that two thousand people read, I also want to express myself in poetic ways that will reach a much wider audience. For me, writing songs is a way to reach a different kind of audience. Using those songs in the film, however, is also a way of telling the story, of adding more layers to the story, as you see things on screen.

"A Million Miles Away," for instance, a song that plays over one of the flash-backs, was a way of doing that, of bridging the past and the present. The lyrics of that song, sung at the beginning of the journey, are not only about the distance between Phoenix, Arizona, and the Coeur d'Alene Indian reservation, but also about the distance between people. It's a sort of battered and bruised love song. The lyrics are completely atypical of a love song, with lines like, "Some people might think you're graceful, but I think you're brittle and bent," but it's still, "Let's get a car and drive it." It's about recognizing human frailty and being in love with a person despite their frailties, so the lyrics were always an integral part of the theme of the movie.

**Cineaste:** What was your input as a coproducer of the film?

**Alexie:** Oh, everything—casting, costumes, sets, editing. I was in the editing room, and a lot of the editing ideas are mine. It was in the editing room, in fact, that I decided I wanted to direct the next one. Editing was *fun*. The whole pro-cess of editing really made me appreciate editors and realize how overlooked and underrated they are in the filmmaking process. Editors are directors and screen-writers all over again. There were many scenes that worked as we shot them, but there were also scenes that did not work, and would not have worked without the skills of our editor. It was in the editing room that I learned more than I had at any other point during the film.

In particular, it made me realize the importance of storyboards, especially in independent film, where you don't have the money to make mistakes. I started reading all these books about storyboards, catching up on the scholarship about them. Then, looking at films by directors who storyboard and those who don't, I realized how wonderfully consistent the storyboarders are and how wildly incon-sistent the nonstoryboarders are. Even though the nonstoryboarders often have greater reputations, they have made some *terrible* films. Robert Altman, for ex-ample, has made classics and truly terrible films, films of such divergent qualities that it's awe-inspiring. A consistent storyboarder makes good films every time, I think.

Writing a new screenplay now, I'm very aware of editing possibilities, of tran-sitions, so I'm really writing the screenplay as a director, whereas I didn't write

*Smoke Signals* that way. I'm really conscious of scene transitions, but also about the possibilities of something not working, and trying to imagine other ways of telling this story within the editing room. So I'm editing visually, I'm doing storyboards as I'm writing, and trying to write as visually as possible.

**Cineaste:** In your opinion, what are the greatest challenges facing Native American societies in the U.S. today?

**Alexie:** The challenges to our sovereignty—artistically, politically, socially, economically. We are and always have been nations within this nation and any threats to that are dangerous. Not only in terms of the government trying to take away our sovereign rights to have casinos, to take the most crass example, but also in cultural appropriation, you know, with white people crawling into sweat lodges, and buying our religions.

**Cineaste:** Speaking of cultural issues, is mainstream U.S. popular culture an influence on your artistic creativity?

**Alexie:** I'm a thirty-one-year-old American, as well. I always tell people that the five primary influences in my life are my father, for his nontraditional Indian stories, my grandmother for her traditional Indian stories, Stephen King, John Steinbeck, and *The Brady Bunch*. That's who I am. I think a lot of Indian artists like to pretend that they're not influenced by pop culture or Western culture, but I am, and I'm happy to admit it. A lot of independent filmmakers would look down their nose at their own pop influences, or at my pop influences. It's a cultural currency. That's something that Tarantino has certainly benefited and learned from. In the best moments of his movies, he's talking about a common cultural currency, and the ways in which his characters talk about it really bring out their personalities.

**Cineaste:** U.S. popular culture as a lingua franca?

**Alexie:** Exactly, and, in the same way, I use that as a way to bridge the cultural distance between the characters in my movie and the non-Indian audience. It's a way for me, as the writer, to speak to the audience through my characters in a way that will give them something to hold onto as they're hearing and seeing something brand new.

**Cineaste:** There's a line in the film, and in your story, which is, "It's a good day to die." Do I recall that line from *Little Big Man*?

**Alexie:** Yeah, that's a *Little Big Man* reference. In every book and movie since then, it seems, the Indians always said that and I wanted to make fun of it. We used it twice in the movie, in fact. Once we said, "Sometimes it's a good day to die and sometimes it's a good day to play basketball," and another time, "Sometimes it's a good day to die and sometimes it's a good day to have breakfast." That notion has so little meaning in our lives that I wanted to make fun of it. It's never, ever, *ever*, a good day to die. There's always something better to do.

**Cineaste:** The film employs this sort of humor very often.
**Alexie:** I think humor is the most effective political tool out there, because people will listen to anything if they're laughing. The reason why someone like Rush Limbaugh is so popular is because he's damn funny. Even I—a dedicated liberal/communist/socialist kind of guy—listen to him once in a while, because you gotta know what the enemy's up to, but he makes me laugh in spite of myself. He'll be spouting this racist, homophobic, sexist, neanderthal stuff, and I'll be laughing, and thinking, "Oh God!" It's because he's funny that people respond to him. I think one thing that liberals have a decided lack of is a sense of humor. There's nothing worse than *earnest* emotion and I never want to be earnest. I always want to be on the edge of offending somebody, of challenging one notion or another, and never being comfortable not only with myself, or with my own politics or my character's politics, or their lives, but with everybody else's. Humor is really just about questioning the status quo, that's all it is.

# Tribal Visions

Kelley Blewster/1999

From *Biblio* 4.3 (1999): 22–29. Reprinted by permission of the interviewer.

*Thirty-two-year-old Sherman Alexie—Spokane/Coeur d'Alene poet, fiction writer, screenwriter for last summer's* Smoke Signals, *and, following the film's success, celebrity—has become for many the Representative American Indian. But his new-found visibility hasn't deterred him from freely brandishing a bitterly funny pen and tongue in the service of his pointed, poignant message.*

Sometimes, reading Sherman Alexie, you don't know whether to cry or laugh or feel insulted or feel ashamed. Sometimes when you finish one of his short stories or poems, you realize you've had a lump in your throat and the heat of tears behind your eyes from page one. Or you hear yourself laughing aloud and then realize with horror that what cracked you up was the image of a tribal cop kicking a dead Indian kid's head thirty yards. Or, reading Alexie's caricature of a pony-tailed professor of Native American literature who's a pathetic Indian-wannabe, you get it all of a sudden, if you're white, that whom he's poking fun at or spewing his anger at is *you.*

Or, at a Sherman Alexie reading, you join the person sitting next to you in chuckling and shaking your head in wise agreement over Alexie's comment, delivered with a grin, "Whites make movies about strange behaviors by white people that I don't understand. Y'all are all stalking each other or something." You knew in advance about the half-jesting jabs at white folks he makes when he's onstage, and you think you came prepared to laugh at your fellow whites because, well, that white guilt and those racial blunders and above all that century-old genocide and those broken treaties all belong to someone else ("I would never be so uncool/stupid/cruel"). But down deep, if you're paying attention, eventually you have to face the fact that you're laughing at yourself, and even then you let yourself remain a willing participant in the joke, because laughter salves the sting of Truth.

Sometimes it's more comfortable not to go where Sherman Alexie wants to lead you.

If you're white, and Alexie estimates that a large majority of his readers are, you understand that your race, the very pinkness of your Caucasian skin, will forever ban you from the world of the contemporary American Indian—his world—that he writes about. And so you get a flash of how it feels to be excluded because you don't belong to the group that at least momentarily has set the rules. If, that is, you let the feeling of being "the outsider" sink in, and if you take it to its next level: *Aha, so this is what it feels like to be the victim of prejudice.* This is what Alexie wants, and this is what too few critics and readers have granted him. Reviewers who were discomfited by stereotypical portrayals of whites in his novel *Indian Killer* (1996) tended to dismiss it. Other critics, and his reading audience in general, have tended to gush over him without subjecting his books, particularly his two novels, to the rigors of literary excellence and without closely examining the truths sent up by his depictions of racially charged issues—or, more precisely, without looking into themselves for vestiges of that racism (the more you wax disgusted over the world's injustice, the easier it is to keep assuming it's *out there* rather than *in here*).

On the other hand, maybe the fact that Alexie has become a star of sorts with all races (one young woman, when I mentioned his name, called him her "hero") is the main thing. Maybe having his message—the writings of a "cynical Indian," as he's called himself—devoured by a mass audience is a good enough place to start.

Sherman Alexie is as pleasant and courteous one-on-one as he is cocky in the spotlight. We met for dinner at a restaurant in Seattle, where he lives with his wife, Diane, of Hidatsa/Winnebago/Potawatomie descent, and their son, Joseph, almost two. Alexie's 6′ 2″ height and his shoulder blade–length wavy hair turn heads; his leisurely walk and his quick laugh suggest an easygoingness that veils a palpable intensity. I'm sure it's possible to have a shallow conversation with him—he's famous and therefore requires a public persona with a ready supply of quotable soundbites—but lighthearted chitchat is clearly not his preference, for in at least one way his conversational style resembles that of his onstage self: He loves to toss around potentially incendiary statements like he's wielding a flamethrower, then sit back with a smile and watch the fallout. Maybe it's partly to amuse himself, but mostly it seems a deliberate ploy to rattle people's cages. On Indian men married to white women: "A lot of these shaman guys are making money by selling their culture. An Indian woman would never let them get away with that." On one Sioux writer's definition of the word *warrior:* "But those

Sioux, they still think the war's on. They haven't quit fighting." On racial anger: "Take any brown person, from Bryant Gumbel to Colin Powell to the Chicano guy working at the restaurant—they've all wanted to kill a white person. All of us. I guarantee you." We were discussing the inspiration for Alexie's second and latest novel, *Indian Killer*. "You know when you're in college," he said, "when you've got that row of white guys in the back wearing baseball hats? The disruptive assholes? I would sit in class and in order even to be able to stay calm I would fantasize about murdering them and about how I would get away with it. I thought, 'Hmmm, that would make an interesting novel.' So that's where it came from—murder fantasies."

Set in Seattle, the story is about a serial murderer who scalps his victims and leaves owl feathers at his crime scenes. It's also about a tall, handsome young Indian man named John Smith, adopted at birth by white parents, who's slowly losing his grip on reality, in no small part, the book seems to indicate, because of the absence of a racial identity. Smith, a construction worker, "knew there was one white man who should die for all the lies that had been told to Indians." His loving and concerned but slightly pitiful and finally ineffectual adoptive parents have taken care throughout his life to expose him to Indian culture—attending powwows and the like. But since they don't know the particular tribe of their son's birth parents, they offer him a mishmash of native traditions—sort of a white person's typecast imaginings of what it must be like to be Indian. You get the feeling their attempts to be helpful in this vague way, though earnest, have done as much harm as good.

The novel portrays a city torn apart over a series of murders that most people believe were clearly committed by an Indian. It comes across as Alexie's definitive statement on race relations, and the picture it paints ain't pretty. The whites are either bigoted, narrow-minded, and violent—in thought if not in deed—or somewhat pathetic. Most of the Indians are only slightly more sympathetic, but they're certainly more complex and interesting. "The book is not called 'White People Who Are Good to Indians,'" Alexie told me, in a voice that said "get a clue." "It's about the ways in which Indians are culturally, psychologically, physically, and emotionally killed. Still." He laughed good-naturedly when I expressed my incredulity over one of the characters, a white professor who teaches a class on Native American literature with a curriculum made up mostly of white authors writing *about* Native Americans. "Oh, that happens all the time! It *still* happens all the time," he said. Then, slowly and emphatically: "Every single thing a white person in that book said was taken from a letter to me, from essays, from books, verbatim. I can footnote that novel. Not the same person said all those things, but they've all been said or written. I wanted to reverse the tension. And I wanted white readers to feel just as uncomfortable with it as I've felt my whole life with books written by white people about Indians." Such as? "Oh God, any Western, *any* Western."

On that level *Indian Killer* undoubtedly works. While reading it, the only way I could momentarily set aside my discomfort or distaste over the ugly or laughable caricatures of whites was by imagining myself in the place of an Indian reader coming across depictions of her race in a contemporary book by a white writer. *Lonesome Dove*, one of my favorite novels, leapt to mind. All the Indians in Larry McMurtry's masterpiece are bad to the bone—barely human—or, in the case of an impoverished band of Indians, they're to be pitied. Alexie agrees. "McMurtry plays Indians as psychopaths almost without fail. Great book, by the way, *Lonesome Dove*," he smiled. "Incredible book. But I can't think of a positive Indian in McMurtry's work. Not that he has to; that's not his job. But they're always psychopaths. And always physically scarred. Always."

Whatever the motives and logic behind McMurtry's Indian clichés—and it can be argued that he created them so for sound artistic reasons rather than trying to reflect How Indians Really Were—after reading *Indian Killer* I'll never again encounter the horrific exploits of *Lonesome Dove*'s Blue Duck and his outlaw cronies without experiencing at least a bit of awareness of what it must be like as a minority to see one's group portrayed unpleasantly in the art of the dominant culture. "That's why I wrote *Indian Killer*," Alexie said. "And people didn't get it. God, I mean all they talked about was, 'Oh, this is so filled with stereotypes.' But the reaction I was looking for was for people to feel uncomfortable. And so because they felt uncomfortable they dismissed the book, rather than accepting the fact that making them uncomfortable was the point of the book."

As literature *Indian Killer* is less successful. It feels like it wants to be a murder mystery, but it can't quite make up its mind. Alexie told me, "I tried to write a conventional thriller, I tried to write a book that would sell more copies, and I couldn't do it. I couldn't write a conventional mystery." It feels like it wants to be a character study, but it seems more like a catalogue of character *types*. You want to sink your teeth into it, but the distant treatment of the players keeps you at arm's length. Although you feel your throat catch for the tragic John Smith and you can sympathize with and even root for some of the other characters, you can't really love any of them because you don't sense the author really loves any of them. A conventional murder mystery doesn't engender these sorts of expectations, but

*Indian Killer* leaves you wanting. Having said all that, I couldn't put the book down. It's appalling and gripping and entertaining.

In truth, Sherman Alexie's literary output can't be circumscribed by a label focusing on its racial themes. An elegant little chapbook of love poems titled *Water Flowing Home* (1996) by itself belies such a description:

but I have salmon blood
from my mother and father

and always ignore barriers
and bridges, only follow
this simple and genetic map

that you have drawn
in my interior, this map
that always leads back

to that exact place
where you are
(from "Exact Drums")

Accessible, lyrical, heartfelt, these are the kind of poems that do what poetry's meant to do: evoke and recall emotion rather than simply play with the language. No, Alexie covers much, much richer terrain than just race relations; but it would be nearly impossible for readers to come away from most of his works without feeling more self-conscious about the color of their skin. Poems such as "Exact Drums" offer a moment of grace amidst the gravity of much of his subject matter—they are welcomed like the release of a pent-up breath.

Sherman Alexie's best work so far—a book that by itself would include him among the ranks of literary heavyweights—is *The Lone Ranger and Tonto Fistfight in Heaven* (1993), a collection of short stories. It also proves that if the substance of Alexie's message is weighty, his style often is anything but. He paints the joyful and the desperate moments of his characters' lives on the reservation in language that isn't funny so often as it is fanciful; perhaps seeing things through the whimsical lens of magical realism leavens the crueler affronts of life on an American Indian reservation—poverty, alcoholism, hunger, abusive schoolteachers, tubal ligation by deception.

Simon won the horseshoe pitch with a double-ringer that was so perfect we
all knew his grandchildren would still be telling the story, and Simon won the
storytelling contest when he told us the salmon used to swim so thick in the
Spokane River that an Indian could walk across the water on their backs.
    "You don't think Jesus Christ was walking on just faith?" he asked us all.
    Simon won the coyote contest when he told us that basketball should be our
new religion.
    He said, "A ball bouncing on hardwood sounds like a drum."
    He said, "An all-star jacket makes you one of the Shirt Wearers."
    Simon won the one-on-one basketball tournament with a jump shot from
one hundred years out.
    "Do you think it's any coincidence that basketball was invented just one
year after the Ghost Dancers fell at Wounded Knee?" he asked me and you.
    (from "The First Annual All-Indian Horseshoe Pitch and Barbecue")

In this book the writer draws characters you *can* love, even when they're doing
stupid or self-destructive things.
    For Alexie, humor—levity is a word that more consistently describes the
timbre of his literary voice—has always been the weapon of choice: the best defense during an at-times embattled childhood and now a way both in person and
on paper to discharge his message. Hydrocephalic as an infant—he's written that
he was "born with a skull that expanded on an hourly basis"—in Spokane, Washington, he underwent brain surgery before age six months. The doctors predicted
that he either wouldn't survive the operation or would come through with severe mental retardation. His father had a Catholic priest administer last rites; his
mother "snuck in a Protestant minister later to say a final prayer for me." Among
other health problems he suffered epileptic seizures till age seven, wet his bed
till age twelve. In and out of hospitals undergoing special therapies throughout
his early childhood, Alexie was exposed to much stimulation; instead of emerg-
ing from his health troubles mentally disabled, he learned to read by age three.
His first reading memory is of the Superman comic book his father brought him
from a pawn shop.
    His early traumas steeled him for a boyhood of wrenching poverty on the
Spokane Indian reservation (his mother is part Spokane, his father is full-blood
Coeur d'Alene). One of six siblings, Alexie as a teenager lost his older sister and
her husband to a mobile-home fire; house fires would later assume a major role
in many of his writings. Both his parents were practicing alcoholics. His mother
sobered up when he was seven and now works as a tribal drug and alcohol abuse

counselor. His father continued as a binge drinker, once a year or so disappearing for days. "Dad would never drink in the house. . . . He was always Mr. Mom," Alexie told me. "Mom did most of the working. . . . Dad read to me a lot and gave me books, and we played a lot." In recent years his father's deteriorating health has more or less forced sobriety on him.

Because he was delicate and because he was "weird," the young Alexie was bullied. "I'm still that frail kid. I still feel that, I still remember that," he said, then revealed the genesis of his dual faces of chutzpah and jocularity: "Now any hint of bullying toward me is met with severe arrogant force. That and humor." So the humor got him some kind of reward? "It was more like people can't run as fast when they're laughing," he quipped. "People like to laugh, and when you make them laugh they listen to you. That's how I get people to listen to me now. If I were saying the things I'm saying without a sense of humor, people would turn off right away. I mean I'm saying things people don't like for me to say. I'm saying very aggressive, controversial things, I suppose, about race and gender and sexuality. I'm way left [in my viewpoints], but if you say it funny, people listen. If you don't make 'em laugh, they'll walk away. I learned that at a young age." He added with a grin, "I'm still weird, but now I'm taller."

He spent a lot of time in the school library to avoid getting beat up. In "One Little Indian Boy," an autobiographical essay, he recalls, "I remember that Michael Sherwood, who has since died in a car wreck, sat on my chest and spat into my mouth for an hour. Michael wasn't some racist white guy. He was a Spokane Indian, one of my fellow tribal members." Alexie had read the entire reservation-school library by grade five. "Small library," he now comments offhandedly. In order to obtain the necessary credits for college that the reservation school couldn't provide, Alexie attended junior high and high school off the "rez," in the neighboring town of Reardan. He was one of the better players on the high-school basketball team—a squad of mostly white boys named the Reardan Indians—and received many of the traditional high-school accolades: team captain, class president, honor society, member of a championship debate team. About his tribal members' mixed attitudes toward his successes off the reservation then and now, Alexie said, "A lot of people were very proud of me and a lot are now. And a lot of people don't like it. A lot of people are so dysfunctional, to the point they believe that any Indian striving for success becomes white, that failure is an American Indian attribute. They've internalized the colonialism so much, they've internalized the stereotype so much, that they think any effort toward success is white."

Alexie attended Gonzaga University, a Jesuit college in Spokane, on scholarship;

took his first drink of alcohol; became a binge drunk; dropped out of college; and eventually enrolled at Washington State University, where he landed in a poetry-writing class taught by Alex Kuo. After reading the first assignment Alexie turned in, Kuo asked him what he was going to do with the rest of his life. "I told him he should be a writer," Kuo told me. So he spotted a natural talent? "Yes, but talent is really irrelevant. I've had maybe ten students with more 'talent' than Sherman. He had a dedication that other students with perhaps more 'talent' didn't have. . . . I spotted an intensity of language, a passion and an energy in his first few poems." Several of those poems ended up in Alexie's first book, the highly readable, critically successful *The Business of Fancydancing* (1992), a collection of poems, prose poems, and a few stories that came out after he'd published several pieces in journals such as the Brooklyn-based *Hanging Loose*, established himself as a popular performer of his own work at poetry readings around the town of Pullman (home of WSU), and sobered up.

Around this time, while Alexie was finding his early voice, his characters Victor and Thomas emerged. Like twins separated at birth who have evolved into a pair of not-quite-halves, these recurring players in Alexie's reservation world represent flip sides of each other—but it's a fidgety, rather reluctant coupling.

While Victor stood in line, he watched Thomas Builds-the-Fire standing near the magazine rack, talking to himself. Like he always did. Thomas was a storyteller that nobody wanted to listen to. That's like being a dentist in a town where everybody has false teeth.

Victor and Thomas Builds-the-Fire were the same age, had grown up and played in the dirt together. Ever since Victor could remember, it was Thomas who always had something to say.

Once, when they were seven years old, when Victor's father still lived with the family, Thomas closed his eyes and told Victor this story: "Your father's heart is weak. He is afraid of his own family. He is afraid of you. Late at night he sits in the dark. Watches the television until there's nothing but that white noise. Sometimes he feels like he wants to buy a motorcycle and ride away. He wants to run and hide. He doesn't want to be found."

Thomas Builds-the-Fire had known that Victor's father was going to leave, knew it before anyone. Now Victor stood in the Trading Post with a one-hundred-dollar check in his hand, wondering if Thomas knew that Victor's father was dead, if he knew what was going to happen next.

Just then Thomas looked at Victor, smiled, and walked over to him.

"Victor, I'm sorry about your father," Thomas said.

"How did you know about it?" Victor asked.

"I heard it on the wind. I heard it from the birds. I felt it in the sunlight. Also, your mother was just in here crying."

"Oh," Victor said and looked around the Trading Post. All the other Indians stared, surprised that Victor was even talking to Thomas. Nobody talked to Thomas anymore because he told the same damn stories over and over again. Victor was embarrassed, but he thought that Thomas might be able to help him. Victor felt a sudden need for tradition.

(from "This Is What It Means to Say Phoenix, Arizona," *The Lone Ranger and Tonto Fistfight in Heaven*)

Both characters appear in several books, and each changes in small ways from story to story, but their essences remain faithful and recognizable. Their differences—Victor's intemperance and cockiness against Thomas's quirky seriousness and gentle-heartedness—form the backdrop for the clash between tribal tradition and modernity in Alexie's irreverent, witty *Reservation Blues* (1995), a respectable first novel that was generally overpraised. Its quality is uneven, and it relies heavily on pop culture allusions to exhibit a certain cleverness, but it's a fun, poignant read, and as always with Alexie it frames the Indian-in-a-white-dominated-society issue in ways provocative and mostly new to a mainstream audience. The author agrees *Reservation Blues* is not his best work. He told one reporter he was "shocked" at its critical success and that he would grade it with a C-minus.

Alexie reaches full artistic range with his duo of uneasy counterparts in his screenplay for *Smoke Signals*, last summer's hit film that was the first movie ever written, co-produced, directed, and acted entirely by American Indians and which won two awards at the Sundance Film Festival. Besides acting as screenwriter Alexie co-produced the movie; Chris Eyre, a Cheyenne/Arapaho filmmaker from Oregon who graduated from New York University's film school, directed it. Loosely based on some of the stories from *The Lone Ranger and Tonto Fistfight in Heaven*, *Smoke Signals* on the surface is about a road trip Victor and Thomas take to recover Victor's dead father's ashes. It's also about growing up and reconciling oneself to one's parentage. But the movie achieves its potency in the tension between Victor and Thomas, who are drawn to each other even while they're repelled by one another. The attraction and the friction obviously arise from the fact that each embodies traits the other has disowned in himself; you just want to shake them and say, "Don't you see?" And they do partly get it in the end—after all, a Bildungsroman only rings true when the leading man (or men) attains at least a semblance of wholeness.

Although it's often risky to assume that art equals the autobiography of the artist, Alexie confirms he is the model for Thomas and Victor. "Thomas was in the very first short story I ever wrote ['Special Delivery,' from *The Business of Fancydancing*]," he told me. "I was having this debate with someone—just bantering—about what's more dangerous: a gun or the idea of a gun? I thought I'd write a short story to talk about it. So I asked myself, 'When would a situation like that happen?' And I thought, 'Oh, some Indian guy kidnapping somebody with the idea of a gun.' But who would do it? And I thought, 'Well, I'll do it.' But a weird me, a me who never left the rez. How eccentric would I be if I stayed? How would I have survived and adjusted? And that's how Thomas came to life. He's the me I'd be if I'd stayed."

Victor, Alexie continued, "came out of the drinking. I felt like he's me when I was drinking—that sort of angry, charming, charismatic asshole. He was there before Thomas—if not by name, then he was the voice of my early poems, because I was drinking when I was writing them. I think he was sort of the writerly persona I adopted. I was in love with his dysfunction . . . and as I sobered up I started remembering that guy. . . .

"You talk about characters in my novels being 3 percent of me or something; well, Thomas and Victor are very high percentages of me."

The exploits of Victor and Thomas provide a fair representation of much of Sherman Alexie's oeuvre so far—that is, his take on the balances every turn-of-the-millennium American Indian must strike for himself or herself. And his treatment of some of those themes feels familiar to non-Indians, too, especially in *Smoke Signals*, which in a voice-over quoting a poem by Dick Lourie poses the question, "How do we forgive our fathers?" But Alexie bristles when commentators call *Smoke Signals* or any of his work "universal"; in fact, he considers such a characterization racist. "When a white reviewer says *Smoke Signals* is universal," he explained, "what he's saying is that *white* people can get this and that *white* people are the judges of all that is universal, when white Americans constitute a tiny, minuscule percentage of the world's population. That statement is making the assumption that white stories are universal, that white culture is the template by which all other art is measured." True—maybe commentators who recognized "universality" in the necessity of forgiving one's father forgot they were speaking as members of an extensively psychoanalyzed generation of Westerners.

Currently, Alexie is working by turns on two new novels—*Al Capone's Bones*, about "the Mafia and Indians," and *Walk*, another road-trip story, about a kid who "ages from eight to eighteen on the road"—as well as on a book of short stories that "doesn't have a title yet." He's also begun a screenplay for *Indian Killer,* to be produced by ShadowCatcher Entertainment, the same company that made *Smoke Signals,* but he's "put that to the side right now" to undertake two other screenplay adaptations, including one of Timothy Truman's comic book *Scout,* about a Spokane soldier who has returned to the rez. The second, for Warner Brothers, is inspired by Norman Maclean's *Young Men and Fire* (1992), an award-winning book based on the true story of a 1949 wildfire in Montana that killed thirteen paratrooping firefighters. Alexie has expressed a desire to be invited to work on projects as Sherman Alexie the writer, not just as Sherman Alexie the American Indian writer—"everything I'm going to say is going to be directly influenced by my Indianness anyway"—and the Warner Brothers film satisfies that wish and goes farther. He was brought in "for both reasons: because I'm a good screenwriter but also because I bring something different to the table—an Indian sensibility, which is not present in Hollywood." And though Maclean's characters are white, some of them will be made into Indians in the movie. "Which is *great,*" said Alexie. "When has anyone ever changed a white character to an Indian?"

The busy young writer also is considering directing films, but the demands heaped on a director give him pause. "It consumes your life," he commented. "Do I want to spend all that time away from writing? I haven't decided yet."

Despite his successes in other art forms, Alexie has said he considers himself primarily a poet. His friend and former mentor Alex Kuo agrees, saying, "Sherman's poetry is much stronger than his fiction," and contrasts the pressures and frustrations of a popular fiction writer to those of a poet. For a fiction writer, Kuo observed, "Sales have to keep growing with each successive book. But every writer wants to be read, believes they have something to say. And for a book of poetry to sell even sixteen thousand copies is huge. So fiction is a temptation. I think Sherman Alexie's branching into movies is a part of that."

For all his invectives against the current state of race relations, for all his teasing of "white liberals," Alexie reveals in bits a compassion for people of any race grappling to understand and maybe change things. After describing excessive punishments exacted on him and other children in reservation schools, he acknowledges that "those situations are changing. A lot of the teachers coming into reservation schools now are crunchies [granola-loving hippie types]." He believes race relations will change, triggered mostly by a shift in demographics: "In twenty years more than half the country will have Spanish as their first language." He patiently explains to this white interviewer how his own tribal identity produces work very distinct from, say, a Sioux writer's. And he values artists' sharing their "tribal visions"—whether a Spokane/Coeur d'Alene tribal vision, a Lakota Sioux one, a white Southern one, an Irish Catholic one, or an African American one ("There are all kinds of tribes," he points out)—for the best reason: "To learn not to be afraid of each other."

Not all white readers of Sherman Alexie feel uncomfortable with his racial portrayals or see them as stereotypes. One acquaintance, who's read nearly all of Alexie's books and loves Native American literature in general, said, "All the whites in *Indian Killer* felt very real to me." His reaction is typical of one segment of Alexie's huge fan base. It seems you're either unsettled by his writing—in which case you can dismiss it or you can get at what it might be trying to say—or, like my acquaintance, you enthusiastically resonate with it. Although I disagree with such readers' often wholesale praise of Alexie's work, I envy their ready ability to easily relate to a view of the world as limned by someone of a different race. As a friend of mine has said, and as most of us doubtless have longed, "I wish we all were colorblind."

Sherman Alexie sees it differently. He says, "Good art is not universal. Good art is tribal." What he really wants you to understand is that as a thirty-two-year-old American Indian writer who grew up on a reservation in the Northwest, who is part of the TV generation and also schooled in the literary classics, who has a Catholic father and a Protestant mother, he has been just as influenced by the Western Civ tribal tradition as by the Spokane and Coeur d'Alene ones, just as shaped by pop culture as by reservation culture. "I'm the first practitioner of the Brady Bunch-school of Native American literature," he chuckled. "I'm a twenty-first-century Indian who believes in the twenty-first century."

# An Interview with Sherman Alexie

Joelle Fraser/2000

From the *Iowa Review* 30.3 (2000): 59–70. Reprinted by permission of the interviewer.

On a rare sunny Seattle day, Sherman Alexie's manager offered me my choice of soda or bottled water and gave me a tour of Alexie's three-room office, a good-looking rooftop space with a deck that overlooks the tony community of Bellevue. Some worlds may contrast more starkly with Alexie's boyhood home on the Coeur d'Alene Indian Reservation, but not many. [Editor's note: Alexie actually grew up in Wellpinit, on the Spokane Reservation in Washington State.]

Alexie arrived late, comfortable in cotton, hair pulled back in a loose ponytail. As we introduced ourselves his smile hid a sense of weary obligation—this poet, fiction writer, and filmmaker has many projects to promote. Though he became quite friendly after a few questions, at first his manner seemed to suggest, "Let's get to it."

**Joelle Fraser:** You're called "the future of American fiction" by the *New Yorker*.
**Sherman Alexie:** It's because they needed a brown guy. They had five of us I think. A guy asked me how do you feel about there being so few white men on the (1996) *Granta* list. I said there were eleven out of twenty: how could that be "few"? And sixteen overall were white! I got all sorts of grief for being on the *Granta* list by the way. Like I didn't belong on it—

**JF:** You only had *Reservation Blues* then. What about the response to the *New Yorker* list?
**SA:** Everybody's really happy with it.

**JF:** You've earned your place?
**SA:** Yeah, I guess. I'm an important brown guy now. (Laughs.) Being different helps. I'm not going to deny that it helps a lot. I mean the work has to be good, but the fact that I'm different makes it more attractive to magazines.

**JF:** So you grant that?
**SA:** Oh, yeah. I'm a firm believer in affirmative action—nobody unqualified ever

gets a job through affirmative action. Maybe less qualified, but not unqualified. Certainly I might get on lists or get opportunities because I'm different, because I'm Indian.

**JF:** And it doesn't bother you?
**SA:** No! Hell no! Reparation. (Laughs.) Nobody white is getting anything because they're white. It doesn't happen in the literary world, never, never once has a white guy gotten more because he's white. But then you have that cabal of New York writers, young good-looking New York literary boys, and they have their own sense of entitlement. I'm not anywhere near that stuff.

**JF:** How did people react to your story in the *New Yorker*, "The Toughest Indian in the World"?
**SA:** When I wrote it, I honestly didn't think about the reaction people would have to it. It's funny—it really brings up the homophobia in people. When a straight guy like me writes about a homoerotic experience in the first person with a narrator who is very similar to me—I could see people dying to ask me if it was autobiographical. They always ask in regard to everything else, but no one's asked me about that story. In the Seattle paper here, the critic called it a "graphic act of homosexuality" and I thought "graphic"? There's nothing graphic about it at all. It was three sentences. He talked about me being a "literary rabble-rouser" again.

**JF:** Someone else called you a similar name—the young rouser, the young something from Seattle—
**SA:** Oh, yeah—Larry McMurtry. Rambler. "The Young Rambler from Seattle." Yeah, I liked that one. It made me feel like I was in a bar brawl.

**JF:** You've said of writers who aren't Indian, like McMurtry, that they shouldn't write about Indians.
**SA:** Not exactly.

**JF:** Clarify that.
**SA:** At the beginning it was probably that but it's changed. People can write whatever they want—people accuse me of censorship when I say these things. But what I really want to say is that we should be talking about these books, written about Indians by non-Indians, honestly and accurately. I mean, they're outsider books. They're colonial books. Barbara Kingsolver's novels are colonial literature. Larry McMurtry's books are colonial literature. These are books by members of the privileged, of the powerful, writing about the culture that has been colonized.

This is no different than Nadine Gordimer, who's a colonial writer, and she would call herself that.

So I think this illusion of democracy in the country—it's the best country in the world—but this illusion allows artists to believe that it isn't a colony. When it still is. The United States and South Africa: the only difference is about fifty years, not even that much. And people forget that. So when McMurtry does what he does, he thinks he's being democratic, but he's actually being colonial. I wish we could talk about the literature in those terms, beyond the quality of it, but actually talking about in terms of "hey, this person doesn't know this—it's completely a work of imagination."

**JF:** How does this compare to, say, occupying the other gender?
**SA:** (Laughs.) Oh that's the same thing.

**JF:** You've done that, and written from a white person's view, too.
**SA:** Well, I know a lot more about being white—because I have to, I live in the white world. A white person doesn't live in the Indian world. I have to be white every day.

**JF:** What about your female characters?
**SA:** I'm not a woman. (Laughs.) Never was. I think often my characters, outside of Spokane Indian guys, are often a little bit thin because I have a difficult time getting into them and getting to know them. My white people often end up being sort of "cardboardy"—which is thematically all right—but it isn't necessarily my original purpose. I just get uncomfortable writing about them.

**JF:** Really. Is that something you're trying to develop and work on?
**SA:** Yeah, I'm trying to become a better writer. I think in the end I'll get closer to that. And about women's experience—I'm better than most male writers. They see the Madonna-whore—it's incredible: these progressive, liberal, intelligent, highly-educated men are writing complex, diverse, wonderful male characters in the same book where the female characters are like women in a 3 A.M. movie on Showtime.

**JF:** You've said having come from a matriarchal culture gives you more insight.
**SA:** I think it helps. And I give my stuff to the women around me. "Does this work?" I spend my whole life around women—I should know something. If I don't know it, I ask. It has to be a conscious effort. It's too easy to fall back on stereotypes and myths, and I think that's what most writers do about Indians and what most men do when they write about women.

**JF:** So you're conscious of it . . .

**SA:** I'm conscious of the fact that I mythologize. (Laughs.) I'm still a caveman. I just like to think of myself as a sensitive caveman.

**JF:** Going back to your growth as a writer, as you develop and gain facility— you're getting better technically, for example—do you fear that you'll lose some of that tension that comes from being a struggling new writer?

**SA:** My friend Donna, who helps me edit, we talk about this. When I first started, my grammar was atrocious, but she said that often people don't care when so-called "unprivileged people's" grammar is atrocious because it's part of the "voice." And they account for it in that way.

**JF:** In fact readers might think it's "appropriate."

**SA:** When in fact it's just bad grammar. It's the result of a poor education. But I'm better now. Most of my sentence fragments now are intentional. (Laughs.)

**JF:** What did your parents expect you to be?

**SA:** Oh, God. Alive. In their fondest hopes. I'm the first member of my family— that's extended—who's graduated from college. No one else has since. I was a very bright kid; I was a little prodigy in all sorts of ways. There were friends and family telling me I was going to be a doctor or a lawyer. Nobody predicted I would be doing this, including me.

**JF:** So you didn't have a sense of yourself as a writer until college?

**SA:** Right. I wrote and I loved reading, and brown guys—you're supposed to be Jesus, saving the world with law or medicine.

**JF:** And with writing can you save the world?

**SA:** You can do more than a doctor or a lawyer can. If I were a doctor nobody would be inviting me to talk to reservations. I'd be a different person. Writers can influence more people.

**JF:** Can poetry change the direction of society?

**SA:** I don't know. A lot of people are reading my poems and other people's poems because of me. This fifty-five-year-old white guy at a reading said, "I never got poems, I hated them, and then I read your book and liked them, and now I'm reading all sorts of poems." And that's great. If I can be a doorway . . .

**JF:** Paula Gunn Allen says of Native Americans, "We are the land." What do you think of that?

**SA:** I don't buy it. For one thing, environmentalism is a luxury. Just like being

a vegetarian is a luxury. When you have to worry about eating—you're not going to be worried about where the food's coming from, or who made your shoes.
Poverty, whether planned or not planned, is a way of making environmentalism
moot. Even this discussion is a luxury.

**JF:** This interview.

**SA:** You and me—doing this. Besides, Indians have no monopoly on environmentalism. That's one of the great myths. But we were subsistence livers. They're two
different things. Environmentalism is a conscious choice and subsistence is the
absence of choice. We had to use everything to survive. And now that we've been
assimilated and colonized and we have luxuries and excesses, we're just as wasteful as other people.

**JF:** But the myth persists with contemporary Indians.

**SA:** Part of it is that we had a land-based theology, but all theologies are land-
based. Christianity is land-based in its beginnings. I think in some ways Indians
embrace it because it's a cultural or racial self-esteem issue. We're trying to find
something positive that differentiates us from the dominant culture. And the
best way to do that—because the U.S. is so industrial and so wasteful—is to say,
"OK, we're environmentalists" and that separates us. When in fact, we're just a
part of the U.S. as well, and the wastefulness. The average everyday Indian—he's
not an environmentalist—he could give a shit. Just like the average white American. I grew up with my aunts and uncles and cousins throwing their cans out the
window.

**JF:** How does this tie in with literature?

**SA:** You throw in a couple of birds and four directions and corn pollen and it's
Native American literature, when it has nothing to do with the day-to-day lives
of Indians. I want my literature to concern the daily lives of Indians. I think most
Native American literature is so obsessed with nature that I don't think it has any
useful purpose. It has more to do with the lyric tradition of European Americans
than it does with indigenous cultures. So when an Indian writes a poem about a
tree, I think: "It's already been done!" And those white guys are going to do it better than you. Nobody can write about a tree like a white guy.

**JF:** Now why is that?

**SA:** I don't know. They've been doing it longer.

**JF:** I'd like to see what you'd write about a tree.

**SA:** I'm not even interested! I'm interested in people. I think most native literature is concerned with place because they tell us to be. That's the myth. I think it's detrimental. I think most Native American literature is unreadable by the vast majority of Native Americans.

**JF:** It's not reaching the people.
**SA:** If it's not tribal, if it's not accessible to Indians, then how can it be Native American literature? I think about it all the time. Tonight I'll look up from the reading and 95 percent of the people in the crowd will be white. There's something wrong with my not reaching Indians.

**JF:** But there's the ratio of whites to Indians.
**SA:** Yeah. But I factor that in and realize there still should be more Indians. I always think that. Generally speaking Indians don't read books. It's not a book culture. That's why I'm trying to make movies. Indians go to movies; Indians own VCRs.

**JF:** And maybe they'll read your books after.
**SA:** I'm trying to do that—sneak up on them.

**JF:** This is what your purpose is—to reach Indian people?
**SA:** It's selfish in the sense that we haven't had our Emily Dickinson or Walt Whitman; we haven't had our Shakespeare or Denis Johnson or James Wright. We haven't written a book that can compare to the best white novel. But they're out there. There's a kid out there, some boy or girl who will be that great writer, and hopefully they'll see what I do and get inspired by that.

**JF:** There are many celebrated Indian writers—
**SA:** But we haven't written anything even close to Faulkner or Hemingway or Jane Austen. Not yet. Of course, white people are about thirty, forty generations ahead in terms of writing. It'll happen. I meet young people all the time, email a lot of kids. The percentage of Indian kids doing some sort of artistic work is much higher than in the general population—painting, drawing, dancing, singing. The creation of art is still an everyday part of our culture, unlike the dominant culture, where art is sort of peripheral. It's not a big leap from a kid who dances to a kid who writes poems. It's the same impulse. It just needs a little push.

**JF:** What about writing programs, teaching? You don't teach college students, but do you have opinions on MFA programs, on artists' colonies?
**SA:** I think the summer stuff is just the place where writers go to get laid. You can't teach anything in a week or two.

**JF:** What about a writing program like Iowa?

**SA:** Yeah, that's fine. That's dedicated internship. But a summer thing? I've done two, both for friends. People do them because they need the money, and/or to get laid—because they will. Dedicated writers don't go—they're in MFA programs or they already have books. These people who attend the conferences and colonies are very privileged, mostly women, groupie types. They exist so ugly white guys get laid. (Laughs.)

**JF:** Ouch. You don't mind this going out?

**SA:** No! It's true! Only in rock music and the literary world do you see so many ugly white guys with beautiful women. That says a lot about the women, their character. They're attracted to more than surface.

**JF:** Will you ever get an academic position?

**SA:** I hope not. I don't want a real job of any variety. I don't want to have to get up in the morning, that's what it comes down to. Work is not the issue; I don't want the structure.

**JF:** Is it hard for you to switch hats, from poetry to screenplays to fiction? Some people might say you're trying to find your genre.

**SA:** It's all the same. It's just telling stories. It's not like I think about it separately.

**JF:** True, *Smoke Signals* is based on your poems and stories. And then there's your comedy . . .

**SA:** Yes—you've seen me read: it's funny. There's always been a stand-up element. Now I'm doing real stand-up, and it's amazing the freedom I got when I called it stand-up. I talked about things I would never talk about in a literary world. I can do anything I want, and I get the same amount of laughter when I do stand-up. What I hope to do is bring literary humor to my comedy fans instead of more dick jokes (although I tell my share of dick jokes)—and I want to bring more comedy to the poetry fans.

**JF:** Is there anyone else doing that?

**SA:** I don't know. A really good stand-up comic is a poet; it's about the use of language. It can be really poetic. And I like politically conscious comedy.

**JF:** Like whom?

**SA:** Bill Hicks, I don't know if you've ever heard of him.

**JF:** No.

SA: Well, you can have this one. (He gets a CD from a shelf.) And Chris Rock. Dennis Miller—smart as hell.

JF: So what's the future for you?
SA: I don't know. I know I'll keep writing poems. That's the constant. I don't know about novels. They're hard. It takes so much concentrated effort. When I'm writing a novel it's pretty much all I can do. I get bored. It takes months. I wrote *Res[ervation] Blues* in about four months, *Indian Killer* in about six. Movies do the same thing. *Smoke Signals* was fourteen months, and that's quick. It's all-encompassing. It feels like I'm going to end up writing poems, short stories, and screenplays. I'll continue to work for studios, honestly because it's enormous sums of money and I'll use one project to finance the other. Some people teach; I write screenplays. One's a lot more lucrative.

JF: What about memoir?
SA: In the end you are sort of responsible to the truth, and I like to lie. (Laughs.) I'm thirty-three, and as much as I talked about it, it doesn't matter whether you're twenty-five or forty-five, not a whole lot has gone on; the journey I'm on is pretty young. And I've rarely read a memoir that wasn't masturbatory. In a sense, you're always mythologizing your life; it's always an effort to make yourself epic. At least in fiction you can lie and sort of justify your delusion about your "epicness." But when you're writing a memoir, you're trying to make your life epic and it's not— nobody's life is. You know that book, *Drinking, A Love Story*? The whole time I'm thinking, "But you kept your job!"

JF: You've been sober for years, but in college, how did drinking affect your writing?
SA: I would wake up with stories on the typewriter and not remember writing them.

JF: Did your writing change when you got sober?
SA: I write less about alcohol, less and less and less. You're an addict—so of course you write about the thing you love most. I loved alcohol the most, loved it more than anybody or anything. That's what I wrote about. And it certainly accounted for some great writing. But it accounted for two or three years of good writing— it would never account for twenty years of good writing. I would have turned into Charles Bukowski. He wrote ten thousand poems and ten of them were great.

JF: Frost said a poem is a momentary stay against confusion. Do you feel like that's true?

SA: (Laughs.) That would mean that at some point in my life I didn't feel confused. He said that with more clarity than I've ever had. I'm trying to think— I was writing the other night, I wrote this poem called "One Stick Song," one I really like at the moment. It relates to the stick game, a gambling game. And I can tell you the story of that and we'll see what it means. I was at my uncle's wake. I don't know how other wakes work—

JF: Swedish wakes are wild, everyone's drunk.
SA: OK, there you go, similar. (Laughs.) It's a good time. Someone was talking about this song he'd sing—"one stick song." You see, you lose sticks in this gambling game, like chips or whatever. You're down to one stick. And you're going to lose if you lose it, so this is your most powerful song. You're desperate. But I hadn't heard the phrase "one stick song" in years, and as soon as I heard it I thought, oh my God, that's everything I've been doing. "One stick song" is a desperate celebration, a desperate attempt to save yourself: putting everything you have into one song. I looked around the room, thinking, "What are these people's one stick songs? What would it be—what is their one stick, what is the one thing they have left?"

JF: Was that poem meant to be an elegy for the uncle?
SA: It ended up being an elegy for all the family members I've lost.

JF: I just heard Mark Doty give a talk on the elegy, about how it can be applied not only to people but to any loss, and why it needs to both memorialize and make meaning of loss. To what extent do you think you're doing the work of the elegy?
SA: I recently wrote about a man from the reservation who drowned in a mud puddle. He was drunk, alone. How am I supposed to make meaning out of that? And yet I try. That's, in fact, what I'm here to do. You might say that now that man did not die alone.

JF: In your poem, "Capital Punishment," the refrain is "I am not a witness"—but it seems like you are.
SA: I guess a witness is all I am. I think, as a writer, you're pretty removed. As much as I talk about tribe or belonging—you don't, really. Writing is a very selfish, individualistic pursuit. So in that sense I'm a witness because I'm not participating.

JF: And literally, you're in Seattle and you're a witness on your old life on the reservation, on the other side of the state.

**SA:** Yes, I'm not there. And I'm not in the writing world; I'm outside a lot of circles.

**JF:** Whom do you connect with?
**SA:** With young people—one of the things I like to do is watch MTV, even though I don't like much of the music, I try to pay attention to what's in their lives.

**JF:** What's your take on TV?
**SA:** They've been screaming about the death of literacy for years, but I think TV is the Gutenberg press. I think TV is the only thing that keeps us vaguely in democracy even if it's in the hands of the corporate culture. If you're an artist, you write in your time. Moaning about the fact that maybe people read more books a hundred years ago—that's not true. I think the same percentage has always read.

**JF:** So you're not worried about the culture. You're not worried about video games—
**SA:** No. Not at all. (Laughs.)

**JF:** A lot of people are, it seems . . .
**SA:** People also thought Elvis Presley was the end of the world. (Laughs.)

**JF:** You do use a lot of pop cultural references in your work.
**SA:** It's the cultural currency. Superman means something different to me than it does to a white guy from Ames, Iowa, or New York City or L.A. It's a way for us to sit at the same table. I use pop culture like most poets use Latin. (Laughs.) They want to find out how smart they are—or, they think they're being "universal."

**JF:** You said once that universality is a misnomer, that it's really a Western sense of the word.
**SA:** Well, when people say universal they mean white people get it.

**JF:** What about *Smoke Signals'* universal themes of grief, and loss and coming to terms with death?
**SA:** That's an appropriate way to talk about it, saying universal themes. But some people call the whole work universal. That's wrong. And even if there are universal themes, it's within a very specific experience and character. And that's what made it good. It was promoted as the first feature film written, directed, and produced by Native Americans to ever receive distribution, and reviewers would fall all over themselves trying to discount that, saying, "That doesn't really matter. Who cares?" Of course it matters. It matters, and it's good, and it is what it is pre-

cisely because of that specificity. So "universal" is often a way to negate the particularity of a project, of an art. I hate that term; it's insulting. I don't want to be universal.

**JF:** But do you want to touch people who will say, "I've felt that too"?

**SA:** Yeah, but the thing is, people always told me their story. They didn't say, "This made me feel like a hundred other people." The creation is specific and the response is specific. Good art is specific. Godzilla is universal. A piece of shit like that plays all over the world. Then you know you got a problem.

**JF:** Along those lines, I'm wondering about a seeming paradox. You often say during readings and talks that you want to honor your culture's privacy, and yet your work is so public. It seems like you protect it and expose it at the same time. There's a tension created.

**SA:** Yes, of course there is. One of the ways I've dealt with it is that I don't write about anything sacred. I don't write about any ceremonies; I don't use any Indian songs.

**JF:** True. You mention sweat lodges but only obliquely. I'm thinking of the image of the old woman in the poem who emerges from the sweat lodge.

**SA:** Yes, I'm outside the sweat lodge. In *Reservation Blues* I'm in it and I realized I didn't like it. I approach my writing the same way I approach my life. It's what I've been taught and how I behave with regard to my spirituality.

**JF:** How do you draw the line as to what is off limits?

**SA:** My tribe drew that line for me a long time ago. It's not written down, but I know it. If you're Catholic you wouldn't tell anybody about the confessional. I feel a heavy personal responsibility, and I accept it, and I honor it. It's part of the beauty of my culture. I've been called fascist a couple of times, at panels. I've censored myself. I've written things that I have since known to be wrong.

**JF:** What kind of things . . . I guess you can't say.

**SA:** (Laughs.) All I can say is that I've written about cultural events inappropriately.

**JF:** How did you know?

**SA:** The people involved told me. After considering it, I realized they were right. In a few instances. Not every instance, but in a few. I can't take them out of what they're in, but I'm not going to republish them, or perform them in public, no anthologizing: they've died for me. There are Indian writers who write about things they aren't supposed to. They know. They'll pay for it. I'm a firm believer in what people call "karma." Even some of the writing I really admire, like Leslie Silko's *Ceremony*, steps on all sorts of sacred toes. I wouldn't go near that kind of writing. I'd be afraid of the repercussions. I write about a drunk in a bar, or a guy who plays basketball.

JF: So the only flak you get is from individuals who say, "I think you're making fun of me." Do you try to soothe things over?

SA: Some people are unsoothable. But I'm a nice enough guy, and I think people know that. If I weren't pissing people off, I wouldn't be doing my job. I just want to piss off the right people. I try not to pick on the people who have less power than I. It's one of the guidelines of my life. And if I have, then I feel badly about it. I try to make amends.

JF: You're only in your early thirties—and you have twelve books and two screenplays behind you. What was it like to have written so much so young and yet feel like you need to be a better writer? Do you feel like some work came out too soon?

SA: Everything, everything! *Reservation Blues*—ooh, ooh. I'm working on the screenplay now, and I see where I could be so much better. What I could have done. I can tell you what happened. In *Reservation Blues*, the original impulse was that I can't sing, and I wanted to write a novel about somebody who could. Everyone wants to be a rock star. You get to date supermodels (it's a joke!). With *Indian Killer* it was because I was sitting at Washington State with frat guys in the back row who I wanted to kill. And I would fantasize about murder.

JF: What were they doing that made you want to kill them?

SA: Just being white. Just drunk on their privilege, essentially. Showing up late, disrupting the class in all sorts of small ways that all added up to my thinking, "I want to kill them."

JF: So you write books about people you want to be.

SA: Umm. Do I want to be a murderer? (Laughs.) I don't think so, but we all want to kill somebody. It's fantasy. Well I guess then my next novel's about my love affair with Helen Hunt. (Laughs.)

JF: One of the things you said is that poetry equals anger and imagination. Do you feel like a lot of the power of your earlier work came from being a younger man full of passion and anger, and do you ever worry about that lessening as you get older and things get easier for you? That is, are you still angry, and has it changed if you are?

**SA:** I could respond to that in two ways: the richest black man in the country still has a hard time getting a taxi in New York at midnight. But for me, personal success or personal privilege—I have a tremendous amount of it now—I mean I have my own damned office. How many writers have that? Just to manage my life I had to hire somebody. And I'm rich. Not by Steve Forbes standards, but by Indian standards I'm the Indian Steve Forbes. I bought a TV last night because I wanted one for the office.

**JF:** Are you still amazed by that?

**SA:** Oh, yeah. I just laugh. When I had no money, and a great book came out, I couldn't get it. I had to wait. I love the idea that I have hardcover books here and at home that I haven't read yet. That's how I view that I'm rich. I have hardcover books I may never read. (Laughs.)

But even though I have success and privilege, my cousins don't. My tribe doesn't. I still get phone calls in the middle of the night—about deaths and car wrecks. I've lost uncles and cousins to violence or to slow deaths by neglect and abuse and poverty. I could try to walk away from that, to separate, but I don't. Every time I drive downtown Seattle I see dozens of homeless Indians. I would be callous beyond belief not to feel that, not to know I have cousins who are homeless in cities out there. So even if it's not happening to me directly, it's certainly happening to my family, and I have to pick up the phone. I'm incredibly privileged when I'm sitting at a typewriter, but once I get up and out of that role, I'm an Indian.

# American Literature:
# Interview with Sherman Alexie

Jessica Chapel/2000

From the *Atlantic Unbound*, originally posted online 1 June 2000. Reprinted by permission of the interviewer.

Since the publication in 1992 of his first poetry collection, *The Business of Fancy-dancing* (which was named a *New York Times* Notable Book of the Year), Sherman Alexie, a Spokane/Coeur d'Alene Indian, has made a name for himself as a prolific and deft writer of fiction as well as poetry. In addition to the several books of poetry he has published, Alexie has also produced two novels, *Reservation Blues* (1995) and *Indian Killer* (1996), and his first short-story collection, *The Lone Ranger and Tonto Fistfight in Heaven* (1993), inspired the well-received 1998 movie *Smoke Signals*, for which he wrote the screenplay.

Alexie's stories and poems explore the terrain of intimate relationships, contemporary American pop culture, and reservation life without falling into either sentimentality or cynicism. As in *The Lone Ranger and Tonto Fistfight in Heaven*, the stories in Alexie's new collection, *The Toughest Indian in the World*, blend irony and surreal situations adeptly, as when a white drifter holds up a pancake restaurant "demanding a dollar per customer and someone to love" and comes away with a young Spokane Indian man he nicknames "Salmon Boy," or when the actor John Wayne tells his children, "Oh, sons, you're just engaging in some harmless gender play." *Toughest Indian* unsettles as much as it amuses.

Alexie recently spoke with *Atlantic Unbound*'s Jessica Chapel.

**Jessica Chapel:** Up until now, the focus of your fiction has tended to be on reservation life and the relationships between fathers and sons. In your new collection of short stories, the focus seems to have shifted slightly—to the tensions between whites and Indians in intimate relationships, and urban Indians and Indians still on the reservation. The mood seems changed as well—hopeful, less angry. Do you consider these stories to be different than what you have written before, either in tone or theme?

**Sherman Alexie:** I was very much thinking about urban Indians as I worked on this collection. Sixty percent of all Indians live in urban areas, but nobody's writing about them. They're really an underrepresented population, and the ironic thing is very, very few of those we call Native American writers actually grew up on reservations, and yet most of their work is about reservations. As someone who grew up on a reservation, I'm tired of it. No, I'm exhausted.

I've been living in the city—Seattle—for five years. I live a very cosmopolitan life now. I've traveled the world and had dinner with movie stars. To pretend that I'm just a Rez boy is impossible. Certainly, I think this book has much more of an urban perspective.

**JC:** Unlike the other stories in the book, "The Sin Eaters," in which the U.S. government moves Indians to internment camps for medical experimentation, struck me as sinister and otherworldly. How did this story originate?

**SA:** I wrote that story around the time I wrote *Reservation Blues*, so it's actually several years old. In some sense, it's a failed novel—I started writing it as a novel but the tone was literally too dark and ominous to sustain for the length of an entire book. I don't think anybody could have made it through. I really liked its tone. I placed that story in the middle of the collection because it is so different from the others that it acts as a nice counterweight.

**JC:** You base many of your stories on the Spokane Reservation in Wellpinit, Washington, where you grew up. How have people on the reservation reacted to your work?

**SA:** There's been an effort to paint me as this negative figure on the reservation, but not because of my writing. The people who loved me when I was seven years old love my books, and the people who didn't like me when I was seven years old don't like my books. My writing career hasn't changed people's opinions of me. I was a controversial figure on my reservation when I was a kid. I was mouthy and opinionated and arrogant. Nothing has changed. The funny thing is, people loved the movie [*Smoke Signals*]. Even those who didn't like my books much loved the movie, so the power of film was certainly revealed in that.

**JC:** I've read that you are adapting *Reservation Blues* for film. Where does this project stand?

**SA:** It's with Miramax. We're close to getting a green light, very close. It's ambiguous, the movie business.

**JC:** You stated in a *Los Angeles Times* review of Ian Frazier's *On the Rez* that "Many Indians, myself among them, believe that the concept of tribal sovereignty should logically extend to culture and religion. . . ." What did you mean?

**SA:** That non-Indians should quit writing about us until we've established our voice—a completely voluntary moratorium. If non-Indians stop writing about us they'll have to publish us instead.

**JC:** Jonathan Miles, in a *Salon* article reacting to your review, took this argument as one that would exclude all outsiders from writing about another culture or group of people, whether that was women writing about men, or whites writing about Indians. "Such an approach would bind the typing fingers of even the most well-meaning outsiders . . . leaving a culture's stories firmly and exclusively in the hands of its tellers." Is this what you intend?
**SA:** I never said that. I was talking about Indians and our particular relationship to this country, which is one of broken treaties, the indigenous to the immigrant, and about sovereignty. No other ethnic group in this country is interested in the concept of sovereignty. I'm only talking about us. I never extended that argument anywhere.

Other people have tried to use that argument, and it's actually not logical. The real issue is that Indians' relationship to this country is still that of the colonized, so that when non-Indians write about us, it's colonial literature. And unless it's seen that way, there's a problem. What really bothered me about Ian Frazier's book is how everybody kept talking about it as some sort of special work, and it's not. It's a really ordinary book. There are flagrant inaccuracies. The galley had at least fifty historical errors. And I really had a problem with the point of view. What happens is that anybody can write these kinds of books about Indians, but the same does not hold true with any other group. Indians have so little political power, so little social and cultural power, that this happens to us all the time.

**JC:** Are Indians pressured by the marketplace to write certain kinds of stories?
**SA:** It's the corn-pollen, four directions, eagle-feathers school of Native literature. People are more interested in our spirituality than anything else. Certainly, I've never received that kind of pressure because I never wrote that kind of stuff, but there are a lot of people out there selling their spirituality.

**JC:** What expectations do you encounter from readers?
**SA:** It's so funny—because I'm a public Indian figure, people assume I have all these magical Indian powers, like I'm some sort of healer or shaman. That also extends to just being a writer in general—I think people assume that just because somebody's good with metaphors, he's a better human being. It's not true. I'm just better with metaphors than 99 percent of the population, and that doesn't make me magical, it just makes me fairly smart.

**JC:** In your experience, do white Americans have a different sense of history—both of events, and the significance of those events in contemporary culture—than American Indians?

**SA:** White Americans have a short memory. This country really hasn't entered puberty yet—white Americans' political thoughts are really young, and the culture is really young. The one general statement you can make about America is it's young, and wildly immature, and incredibly talented. Like some twelve-year-old kid who really pisses you off, because he's really good at everything and he knows it.

**JC:** What can be done to bring the U.S. from this immature point to maturity?

**SA:** I don't know. I'm one of those people who thinks that the world is getting better and better. I wouldn't want to be an Indian a hundred years ago—somebody would be shooting at me. I wouldn't want to be a woman forty years ago, and I wouldn't want to be a black person twenty-five years ago. I think the world is getting better, and it's getting better because of liberal social policies. I don't think there has ever been a conservative social policy that helped anybody, except those who enacted it. I don't believe in any -ism particularly, I believe in fighting conservatism. Conservatives didn't want women to vote, didn't want Indians to become citizens.

**JC:** Identity is a recurring theme in your work. Characters such as Junior in *Reservation Blues*, John Smith in *Indian Killer*, and the journalist in *The Toughest Indian in the World* struggle with their experience of what it means to be an Indian, what they are told it means to be an Indian, and how to present themselves as Indians both to whites and other Indians. Is this struggle or uncertainty endemic to the American Indian experience?

**SA:** It's endemic to everybody's experience. I think we're all struggling with our identity. Literature is all about the search for identity, regardless of the ethnicity. Southern, New Yorker, black, white, Asian, immigrant—everyone's trying to find a sense of belonging. In *The Toughest Indian*, the journalist's primary struggle is not ethnic identity, but his sexuality. I don't think he knows any of his identities. One of the points I was trying to make in that story is that being Indian is just part of who we are. I suppose the big difference in Indian literature is that Indians are indigenous to this country, so all non-Indian literature could be seen as immigrant literature. The search for immigrant identity is much different than the search for indigenous identity, so I suppose if you're indigenous to a place and you're still searching for your identity, that's pretty ironic.

# Hold Me Closer, Fancy Dancer:
## A Conversation with Sherman Alexie
Aileo Weinmann/2002

This interview originally appeared on the filmcritic.com website in conjunction with a review of Alexie's film *The Business of Fancydancing*. Reprinted by permission. Copyright © 2002 Filmcritic.com.

*The Business of Fancydancing*, like Sherman Alexie's writing, challenges audiences to negotiate multiple identities, to deal with an intersection of struggles. The film marks Alexie's debut as director, a role that he came to after wading through the frustrating process of trying to make a film through usual Hollywood channels. Filmcritic.com shares Alexie's unique perspective on how being "communistic leader" could be so much fun.

**filmcritic.com:** How was *The Business of Fancydancing* made, and how did that allow you to do what you wanted to with this project—things that you maybe weren't able to do before?

**Sherman Alexie:** Well, after *Smoke Signals* did so well for Miramax, I did a lot of work in Hollywood trying to get a movie made. I worked on my own projects, I did a lot of assignment writing on other people's ideas and none of it really came to anything. And I just got frustrated with that. Everybody goes out of their way in that town to say "No." And, frankly, nobody is really all that interested in Indians. So I stepped back and tried to figure out a way to make a movie. And the model of people making movies that appealed to me most—not just economically but aesthetically—was on digital. You know, with Lars von Trier and Thomas Vinterberg and all those Dogme guys . . . and I saw that an increasing number of American filmmakers were working on digital too. I just thought, "Well, I can do this. Somebody give me $12, I'll make a movie," and that's where it started from. So I took a video class at 911 Media Arts, a co-op here in Seattle, and it's there that I met Holly Taylor, who ended up being the [cinematographer] and editor. And most of the crew came from 911. They all had mostly documentary experience, and hadn't worked on a feature before, and so we all started off together. So it was quite the socialistic experience.

**filmcritic.com:** Why do you want to make movies?

**Alexie:** Of course part of it's just simple ego. It's fun. *(laughs)* I like the attention. But the biggest thing for me was with *Smoke Signals*—we screened it in Minneapolis at the University of Minnesota. This was I think a year and a half after its initial release. I was speaking at the university and they screened it while I was there. I just watched a little bit of it and the sound kept going out. It must have been an old print. I was getting really angry. But there were enough Indians in the crowd who had seen the movie enough times that they started filling in the dialogue. It was like the *Rocky Horror Indian Picture Show*, and it was stunning. You know, I'd never experienced that before. It's not like I could start reading a poem at a reading and everyone in the crowd starts reading it with me. It's not like I've written "Stairway to Heaven." But for a brief moment in Minneapolis, I felt like I had written "Stairway to Heaven," and that was where the sort of enormous cultural power of movies really hit me on a personal level. So it was a combination of those things. I love making movies because you become a long part of the history of moviemaking. I mean, I'm no Martin Scorsese or Woody Allen or any of those people, but I get to make movies. *(laughs)* And I get to write books. So it's joining an artistic tradition and creating an art form that I just love. I love to be part of the gang.

**filmcritic.com:** Wow, what a great moment that must have been.

**Alexie:** Oh, it was! You know, it's a great life I live and there are moments that transcend how much I love my life on a daily basis, and that one was just—when I'm on my deathbed and thinking of, you know, the five or six great moments in my life, that'll probably be one of them.

**filmcritic.com:** Talk about being a first-time director and what you learned in the course of making *The Business of Fancydancing*.

**Alexie:** Well, one of the reasons I was the director is because I'm not interested in being a director. *(laughs)* I hate the sort of cult that surrounds the idea of the director. I mean, it's a hard job and it's a difficult job, but it's not the only job on the set. So, I really wanted to create an atmosphere where everybody was sort of equal in the process. So by being the director, I got to, you know, be communistic leader. I guess in some sense I treated it like film school. I went in with a screenplay, but I went in with a screenplay that was very strange to begin with, very loosely connected. It was more of a series of scenes, images, and poems than a typical narrative, and on the set I allowed myself to be as free as possible. I would throw the script away, I would let the actors improvise. And, being a performer myself, I could improvise as the director, and give them new lines and interact with them in new ways, and create situations that hadn't been thought of in the screenplay. So I essentially tried to do everything I could think of to test myself, and to shoot every kind of scene imaginable. You know, I was never sure anybody would see this, so I didn't worry about it.

**filmcritic.com:** To try and remove yourself from having control over the process when it's something that is very important to you, which is adapting your first piece of published work into a story on film—it must have been an interesting struggle.

**Alexie:** Yeah, I'm just as arrogant as the next bastard. But I decided to take my arrogance the other way, right? "I'm going to be more selfless than anybody ever has." *(laughs)* So, you know, I inverted it. It's still just as arrogant, but people like you more. *(laughs)* It was so much fun, though. I guess I just tried to make it fun, and not destroy people's lives for the time period in which we were working. It can be so awful making films—eighteen-hour days, you know. I guess I tried to treat it like it wasn't that important, even though I was torn emotionally, because the work got pretty autobiographical. And I cried on the set, and other people cried and we got really close, but I guess—much like an actor's not supposed to think about the end result of the scene—I tried not to think of the end result of the scene, or a day, or the whole shoot. And that made it so much easier. I went in thinking, "this is never going to play anywhere," and that freed me. So now when anybody watches it or pays attention, it's great.

**filmcritic.com:** The struggle to be an Indian and be a celebrity—talk about how it's portrayed in the film and how it's been in your own life—the idea that success in white culture equals rejection in Indian culture, on the reservation.

**Alexie:** On a larger scale, every artist lives that life. You know, what is it in Isaiah? A prophet's always a stranger in his own land. Every artist, I think, goes through that. And for Indians, who come from tribal cultures, it's even more intense. In tribal cultures every story, every dance step, every move has an owner. The art has ownership. And you can't sing those songs or tell those stories unless you have explicit permission to tell them. There are a lot of social rules in an Indian tribe. You know, it's like an Edith Wharton novel on "the rez." But the Western Civ idea of art is, you know, sort of bulldozing your way through everything—that you have absolute freedom. And so that's a serious dichotomy, and there's always a clash; that being a member of a tribe and being an artist are often mutually exclusive things. And so I was interested in that conflict, always have been, I live it. So I wanted to make a movie about it—because nobody had. It's easy to make the movie people want to see. And it's harder to make the movie people weren't expecting. I tried to make one people wouldn't expect.

**filmcritic.com:** Seymour and Aristotle struggle in their college experience in very different ways. What were your own experiences at Gonzaga University and Washington State University like, and how did you make the transition?

**Alexie:** Well, I think I had both of their experiences. At Gonzaga, where I started, I think I was Aristotle: drunk and angry, and falling apart. I was always a high-functioning alcoholic in terms of grades; I got out of there with about a three-point. But I left, because I knew if I stayed there, I'd never finish. I was drinking too hard and was too angry, and ended up at Washington State, where I became more like Seymour: discovered writing, discovered a bunch of writer friends, really found my place, started writing, and found my future in that. So at one college I was Aristotle and at the other I was Seymour, and ended up graduating with honors from [WSU], so my college career was really schizophrenic.

**filmcritic.com:** Using alcohol and substance abuse is a major theme throughout this film and your work. Did leaving alcohol behind and going forward into writing come hand-in-hand for you?

**Alexie:** The night after I quit for the last time: you know when you make that decision, and I quit, the next day I got the acceptance letter from Hanging Loose Press for my first book of poems. So, I was like, "Oh!" So I believe in coincidence, but I also believe in interpreting coincidence exactly the way you want to interpret it. *(laughs)* So I think it was a wild coincidence—that I decided to let be magic. So since then, they've gone hand-in-hand, in good ways and bad ways. I mean, just as much as I was addicted to alcohol, I'm addicted to writing too, and it can be destructive in its own sort of way.

**filmcritic.com:** It must be a struggle to have that addictive personality and have a young son who needs so much attention as well.

**Alexie:** Oh, yeah, so there's a long history of good writers who are *bad* parents. I'm working my ass off so that he doesn't have to write a memoir about me later.

**filmcritic.com:** The concept of forgiveness—not just forgiving others, but forgiving oneself—seems really central to this movie. How did the concept of forgiveness shape the story?

**Alexie:** It's funny, I don't get talked about much in these terms, but I'm very Catholic: grew up Catholic, Catholic father, still am vaguely Catholic (I'm not very good at it anymore). So I think Catholicism and forgiveness and that aspect of Christianity is a really strong influence on me. And then once you place

Catholicism in the context of me being tribal and the ways in which the church
horrendously oppressed Indians, there is a serious amount of guilt. So, I think it's
a combination of guilt and irony and contradiction and forgiveness that mix up
together and become a dominant theme in everything I do. . . . And I didn't call it
Catholic in the movie, but I think it very much is. Seymour's conflict is very religious and very spiritual, and that's the way I approached it. Evan [Adams] and I
talked about that very much: that, in some ways, [Seymour]'s a pilgrim.

**filmcritic.com:** Homosexuality, the "other," and being Indian.
**Alexie:** As I've spent more time in urban situations and in the art world, I've
made more friends who are gay. So it's a huge part of my life. My best friend is a
lesbian. So part of it is just that my work is starting to reflect the way in which
I live my life. I mean I haven't lived on the reservation in eighteen years, so my
work is finally catching up to the diverse urban life in which I live. But artistically, I'm fascinated by the concept of tribes. And Evan and I, again, when I was
writing this movie, had a conversation about tribes: the idea of Indian tribes, and
the idea that gay people are a tribe. And we started talking about social rules, and
the way interactions happen, and the way you behave, and the uniforms you wear,
and the signifiers, and the ways in which [Seymour] can jump back and forth between the worlds. That sometimes he feels a lot more Indian than gay, and vice-
versa. That he's never really fully one or the other, but he certainly—depending
on the situation—feels more like one than the other. And so that was just in my
head when I started writing. The idea of what happens when you switch tribes
like that. Where are your allegiances? And, especially when you think about being gay—gay people being universally hated around the world—then you're really
leaving your tribe in all sorts of ways. And so I guess I upped the dramatic impact: not only moving to the city, not only being a writer, but also being gay. You
know, he's leaving his tribe physically, and culturally, and spiritually, and sexually. Part of me writing about gay people in this movie was a larger social effort.
I knew a lot of Indians will see this movie, and there's *a lot* of homophobes in the
Indian world, so I wanted to slap them in the face a bit.

**filmcritic.com:** How do you decide which poems to put in the movie?
**Alexie:** Oh, man, you know it's funny. By and large, the ones I put in were the
ones that—in my performing them—have gotten the largest audience reaction.
But, in Evan's performance of them—which is vastly different than mine—they
became very different poems. So, in some sense, it didn't really matter which
poems I picked, because Evan made them his own, and would've made any of
them his own, and I could not have predicted what they would have become. That

was the great part: I mean I picked them for specific reasons—I wanted this one to be funny, I wanted this one to be sad, I wanted this one to be redemptive, really concrete ideas—and in the context of the film, and the context of Evan's performance, they became something else entirely. So, looking back, I thought, "Oh, it's funny you didn't know that." In the screenplay, you know its turns, but I felt so possessive of the poems, I thought I knew them better than anybody else did. But you realize everything you create is always of its own, and that's what happened to the poems. I'm not sure I'll ever be able to read them aloud again.

**filmcritic.com:** What are you working on now?

**Alexie:** A book of short stories that will be out in the spring (it doesn't have a title yet). A book of poems that will probably be out next fall. I just signed on to do a biography of Jimi Hendrix—a very non-traditional biography . . . and I'm doing some assignment work in Hollywood, raising money, so I can finance the next film. So, you know, I'm sure you'll probably see my punch-lines in a really bad romantic comedy coming to a theater near you *(laughs)* . . . I'm not telling you what I'm writing. When there are good movies that come out, I'll tell you. When they're not, and my name didn't get involved in the credits, I'm not telling a soul.

**filmcritic.com:** So how long before we might hear about a "good movie" of yours?

**Alexie:** *(Laughs)* Well, I'm really hopeful for this one with HBO. I can't talk about it, but keep watching for HBO news. I've really got my fingers and toes—I'm crossing everything.

# Sherman Alexie in Conversation with Williams Cole

Williams Cole/2002

From the *Brooklyn Rail*, Winter 2003. Reprinted by permission.

Sherman Alexie grew up on the Spokane Indian Reservation in Wellpinit, Washington, and is the author of eight books of poetry (published by Brooklyn's Hanging Loose Press) and several novels and collections of short fiction. He also co-wrote the screenplay for the award-winning film *Smoke Signals* (Miramax) and recently directed a feature film, *The Business of Fancydancing*. Among his many awards are a Hemingway Foundation/PEN Award, the Lila Wallace-*Reader's Digest* Award and an award from the National Endowment for the Arts. He was also named by *Granta* magazine as one of the 20 Best American Novelists under 40 and by the *New Yorker* as one of the 20 Writers for the 21st Century. He is a three-time world heavyweight poetry slam champion.

Alexie lives with his wife and two children in Seattle, Washington. Williams Cole, a Contributing Editor for the *Rail*, spoke to him via telephone in November.

**Williams Cole (Rail):** Do you think New Yorkers in general know much about Native Americans, as compared to those living in the U.S. West?
**Sherman Alexie:** I don't know what New Yorkers know about Indians. I know that people think I'm Puerto Rican in New York (laughs). I know we disappear in New York. I mean, many other places . . . you go out to Mississippi, for example, and Indians have real political power. Or you go into certain states where Indians are the majority and we're the ones who send representatives to Congress. Tom Daschle is in Congress because of Indians. The big political issue in a place like New York is our invisibility. If you want to start talking about what would be good in New York, I'd say it's that Indians would start having a presence, especially because in such a liberal area that would really benefit us. If we had more of a presence it would probably help all the other Indians nationwide. So I guess the first issue is to make sure that Indians are a visible and active part of the culture there. But that might be impossible. No one's an active, visible culture there. Everyone is so blended. I mean, I get spoken to in a hundred different languages

in Manhattan because I'm seen as something different . . . but I know what something I am.

**Rail:** But New York is a media capital in the country. Why do you think that network news and other major media don't seem by and large to cover Native American issues?

**Alexie:** When they do, they always cover the ninety-seven Lakota Sioux living in a shack on Pine Ridge reservation. That story comes up about every two years, they do poor Lakotas or, you know, they do the wise grandfather segment. They are only vaguely covering the fact that this astronaut currently going up is one-eighth Chickasaw. The first astronaut with American Indian heritage is going up. I don't know how connected he is with that tribe. They are certainly playing him now as I would if I was part of that tribe, I'd say "yeah, I grew up with him!" But it's those issues, the idea of twenty-first-century Indians as lawyers and doctors and engineers and architects—you know, I live in a white collar Indian world now. And you don't see any representations of white collar Indians in any kind of media—journalism or movies or books or magazines. It's just simply not a part of the discussion. Even Indian-created art and media is about the same images, the elders, the spiritual visions; it's never really about the ordinary ways in which we live our lives.

**Rail:** Why do you think that is?

**Alexie:** Well, money is made by appealing to the largest audience possible, and when you appeal to a large audience you appeal to the lowest common denominator, the easiest images, the non-challenging images, the expected images. The wise Indian image is a proven commodity, a valuable commodity. And it's also flattering and self-flattering. Especially in movies, commercials too. I always sort of laugh when people talk about the "environmental Indians." You ever been to a rez? There's a whole lot of tin cans on the road.

**Rail:** How much room do you think there is in the commercial publishing world for Indian writers in general?

**Alexie:** They have room for about seven of us (laughs). There is not a whole lot of room, but I guess there's not a whole lot of room for anyone. But someone like Tony Hillerman, who writes good mysteries but works with expected images, has sold many books. Any one of his books has probably sold more copies than all of us other Indian writers put together.

**Rail:** So there's usually one commercially chosen writer that is also marketed heavily?

**Alexie:** Yes, also because he's easy to market. Tony Hillerman's books don't really question any assumptions about Indians, they work within those assumptions. And so, are they enjoyable? Sure. But they sell well because they don't question anything. And the more questions a piece of art contains, the less likely it is to sell well. And that's going to happen, that's natural. But the sad part is that this process excludes people from the very communities that are underrepresented. So it always ends up that Tony Hillerman ends up representing all of us. It's not his fault. It's that the media is not interested in the alternatives.

**Rail:** I read a quote of yours that said you want to write books that challenge and offend rather than works that are solely entertainment. I can relate to that. But how can you survive commercially and still maintain this goal?

**Alexie:** I'm always going to sell 50-75,000 copies of my books, which gives me a great living. But I'm certainly never going to be Stephen King or John Grisham or even Philip Roth. I'm never going to have that kind of career. I'm always going to only exist as a very successful literary writer. And I don't think there's ever going to be that kind of commercial breakthrough for me. Number one, this is because I'm writing about Indians and most of the reading audience is white. And, number two, because I write politically.

**Rail:** Do you feel, then, that you've max'd in terms of commercial literary success? That you've gone as far as you can as someone who writes politically?

**Alexie:** I hope I haven't max'd in terms of sales. I would love to sell more books and I would love to reach a wider audience. I'm not truly going to be happy until every single human being on the planet reads something I've written.

**Rail:** How about if a big publisher said that they were going to quadruple the publicity budget for your books because they were convinced it would be a success . . .

**Alexie:** I've had those offers and I've turned them down.

**Rail:** Why, because they came with strings attached?

**Alexie:** Well, there were no obvious strings attached but . . . (laughs). For me, it was always a question of people figuring that I have a chance at that huge breakthrough, that I could have a *Lovely Bones*, Alice Sebold's best-selling book, that this could happen for me. But, you know, in all the effort to push that, what if it didn't happen? Then I become the guy who failed. So, I've always been very careful with the size of my advances and the size of my publicity budget. So have my press and my literary agent been as well. We've always been very realistic about my place in the literary world. We're always prepared for a book to break out, but it doesn't mean we are counting on it. And we don't assume it. So I guess I go through this career with realistic assumptions. And if something great and un-expected happens, we're prepared to deal with it but we're not creating entire plans for it.

**Rail:** So in the literary world most of the reading population, one can assume, is middle- to upper-middle-class whites, and then on the other side you have the super-commercial reading public . . .

**Alexie:** Well, the reading literary public are white, middle-class and upper-class college-educated women. That's who my readers are. I mean, I do a reading at a bookstore and 70 percent of the crowd will be white women. So, that makes me happy.

**Rail:** Why?

**Alexie:** I mean, I prefer the company of women. And all my agents, managers, accountants . . . everyone that works around me are women. So, my entire support structure is made up of women. That's fine with me. But, so, in the end to break out I would have to start appealing to more men (laughs). And I certainly don't want to do that.

**Rail:** Do you do readings at reservations around the country?

**Alexie:** I've been everywhere. From rich white schools in Manhattan to poor schools on reservations. I figure the only way to get myself into certain audiences is to go myself and so I try to diversify my audiences. If they're not coming to me I'm going to try to get to them.

**Rail:** I want to ask you how you ended up hooking up with Bob Hershon and Hanging Loose Press, a small Brooklyn-based press.

**Alexie:** Yeah, how did I end up with a Jewish editor in Brooklyn! In my first poetry class in college one of my first assignments was to research literary maga-zines and submit poems. The teacher was not only interested in the artistic pro-cess but also the process of becoming a writer so he was teaching us that you could write your whole life but if you want to start getting an audience there's a whole other process you have to know about and deal with. So, it was very utili-tarian as well. I still don't know why the Washington State University library had the complete *Hanging Loose*—every issue of the magazine back to the first one that was, coincidentally, published in October of 1966, the year I was born, when it was still really hanging loose and came in an envelope, loose leaf. And I read it through—back then it was about sixty issues. And I loved it. It's funny because they had published one other Indian writer, Wilma McDaniel; most of her work actually has to do with her Dust Bowl Okie roots more than it does her Cherokee roots.

But most of *Hanging Loose*'s work is naturally northeast-based and a lot of it, probably half of it, is New York City–based. Which all makes sense. But the work just appealed to me. It had a kind of conversational, humorous poems that seemed to be the kind of stuff I was writing. Without even knowing who Frank O'Hara was at that point, I ended up writing like Frank O'Hara (laughs). And once I saw the magazine and saw Bob Hershon's work and the editor's work too which really appealed to me. But especially Bob's which is just hilarious. I'd really been trying to find a way to reconcile my humor with poetry. You know, you're not supposed to write funny poems. It's like illegal. I think it's banned in forty-three states, the funny poem. So, I felt really at home there, just reading the magazine. And once I started sending in poems, and they accepted me, because I was writing stuff they liked. And, of course it mattered that I was an Indian kid from Washington state, and that they were four guys from the northeast, but there was some place in the middle where we found a lot to talk about.

**Rail:** And you stuck with them when your popularity grew.
**Alexie:** Oh, sure. Hanging Loose publishes my poems and Atlantic Grove is my fiction publisher. Two independent houses. My paperbacks have gone to major houses but I still publish with the two small houses I started with. It's loyalty and it's also that I am much less of a commodity that way. You have to control that. It would have been easy to become something reprehensible. I've seen other Indians and other Indian-esque people do it. Where they become this sort of mascot. Someone like William Least Heat Moon. Who, you know, that's not his name (laughs). His name is William Trowbridge.

**Rail:** So you found it important early on to control your placement and identity?
**Alexie:** Yeah, I was very self-aware and self-conscious of maintaining some integrity and not letting money become the motivating factor.

**Rail:** Are you still writing that book about how the United States would be now if the British had won the Revolutionary War?
**Alexie:** (laughs) Yeah, I finished that novel and it was awful. I've got three awful novels in my trunk. Actually, it's not a trunk anymore. I've got three awful novels on Zip disks, the twenty-first-century trunk in the attic. In my will, everything unpublished in my lifetime will be published after I'm dead.

**Rail:** In that novel, though, how did you conceive the place of Indians in America? Was there a difference under the British?

**Alexie:** Well, the parallel, the thing I built on was that in Canada Indian people, they call themselves First Nation up there, have a much more visible presence in the national media. There are national newscasters who are Indian. Indian actors get to play in national touring companies. There was an Indian up there for a while who was doing Hamlet for a national touring company. There are still all sorts of political problems but they are much more visible and have much more power. So I just translated that to here, into the United States. That what would happen if Geronimo and Crazy Horse and Sitting Bull and Chief Joseph all were given more power, how would that affect contemporary life? What would be going on now? So in the novel we are much more a part of the world. In the novel our political power matches black American political power. So we had that kind of visibility in the media, that kind of power. So we had our own Jesse Jacksons and Michael Jordans and Colin Powells and actors and Condoleeza Rice and our own liberals and conservatives. And we were also much more diverse, so we had more voice and more opinion and much larger visibility in the book and then how that would affect national policies. But, in that manuscript I just wasn't up to par yet. I mean I'll try again when I get older and smarter, if I do get smarter.

**Rail:** Do you think there's a distinct sentiment among the Indians you know regarding the Bush administration?

**Alexie:** Well, the thing is that poor people anywhere don't care. They're worrying about eating. So, political activism is really a luxury. I think most people are worried about getting to work on time. I think that is reflected in the Indian world. I think something people don't know about Indians at all is how fundamentalist Indians can be. You can't really tell the political difference between a reservation Indian and a small farm town white guy. It's a very conservative mindset: pro-gun, pro-military, pro-life, pro-capital punishment. So, Indians in a weird way live these incredibly conservative lives with incredibly conservative values but vote for Democrats because it's the Democrats who try to help us. We live ironic and contradictory lives.

**Rail:** But doesn't learning the real history of America politicize Indians?

**Alexie:** The thing I always say is that the difference between being poor and privileged is that poor people become politically aware at a much earlier age. And the poorer you are the more political you become at an earlier age. For me, it was growing up on a reservation and being surrounded by politics and lies and the results of lying politicians and failed policies. My first political thought came when I was six standing in line for government food and I realized, "Wait, I'm only in this line because I'm Indian." You turn on the TV and you see commercials for eighty kinds of butter, and yet I'm standing in line to get one kind of butter that says "butter" on it. So, we're aware of that. But, honestly, there's never been a difference between political administrations in regard to Indians. You know the "D" or the "R" or the "I" after their names have never really changed how many lies politicians tell us.

**Rail:** To wrap up, if you could say one thing to someone reading this right now about what they should be aware of or look for regarding Native American issues, what would you say?
**Alexie:** Well, what came to my head right there was the parallel to Nazi Germany. We are the first line of defense. We are the weakest, the most easily affected by policy. So, once you hear about Indians getting their ass kicked by the government and government policies, other people will be getting their ass kicked up the line. So whatever happens to us and however we are treated is eventually going to be how you're treated. So every group should be vitally interested in protecting our interests because we're the privates, we're the foot soldiers on the front lines.

# Voice of the New Tribes

Duncan Campbell/2002

*A native American, Sherman Alexie was raised on a reservation, where his family still live. Taught by Jesuits, he became a songwriter, comedian, poet, and film-maker and was hailed as one of the best young American novelists. His work subverts ideas of the nobly suffering Indian and often presents the hard reality of urban life.*

In *Reservation Blues*, the first novel by the native American writer Sherman Alexie, one of the main characters explains that "when any Indian shows the slightest hint of talent in any direction, the rest of the tribe starts expecting Jesus."

While the rest of the tribe on the Spokane reservation in Washington state may have had slightly more modest expectations, they can hardly have anticipated that the talented if somewhat sickly and eccentric Alexie child would become a bestselling novelist, fellowship-winning poet, prize-winning short-story writer, stand-up comedian, recorded songwriter and independent film director by the time he was thirty-five. Alexie has achieved all that and more, even becoming surely the first native American ever to have been physically embraced by a serving president of the United States (Bill Clinton) and told, "Sherman—you're fucking funny!"

He has been hailed as the "Richard Wright of the American Indians," denounced as being "septic with unappeasable anger" by *Time* magazine and become the joint winner in 2001 with Richard Ford of the Malamud short story prize. *Granta* and the *New Yorker* have both placed him on lists of best young American writers.

The son of a Coeur d'Alene native American father and a Spokane native American mother, Alexie was born hydrocephalic and was not expected to survive a brain operation in infancy. One of six brothers and sisters, he grew up on a reservation of 1,100 people, where most of his family still live. His father held a string of blue-collar jobs, such as logging and truck driving, albeit often curtailed by alcoholism, and his mother worked on the reservation as an addiction and youth counsellor. Taught to read by his father by the age of three, Alexie eventually left the reservation for an outside high school where he and its mascot were

the only native Americans, but where a better education was available. By now
a healthy and athletic six footer, he became a basketball star; he still plays three
times a week.

His early literary influences were traditional. "It was 99 percent white: Steinbeck, Faulkner, Hemingway, Emily Dickinson, Stephen King, Walt Whitman, the
kind of literary education any Indian kid can get at a very bad public reservation
school," says Alexie, sitting in his small office in Seattle, where he now lives. "Part
of my education was through my dad, who loved genre fiction—Mickey Spillane,
Zane Grey—and the JFK assassination books. I was the youngest JFK conspiracy
buff in the world: a five-year-old 'rez' kid re-enacting Dealey Plaza with my Lego."

The notion that native American literature might exist was not addressed.
"Indians are poor so our culture is poor American culture—television and *National Enquirer* and movies. It wasn't until I got to college that anyone showed me
anything written by an Indian."

The native American writers he now admires remained unknown to him until
he was in his twenties: Adrian Louis, Leslie Silko, Joy Harjo, Simon Ortiz, James
Welch. "I didn't know until I was twenty-one of Leslie Silko's *Ceremony*, which
is probably *the* book of native American literature." (Alexie refers to himself as
an Indian and says, only half in jest, that he only uses the term native American,
which he considers a guilty liberal expression, in "mixed company.")

Having spent much time with doctors as a child, he planned a medical career
and specialised at school in science and maths. But after two years at the Jesuit
Gonzaga University in Spokane and three fainting spells in human anatomy class
he changed course. He eventually graduated in American studies from Washington State University in Pullman, one of the 7 percent of native Americans to
graduate from college, less than half the national average.

If doctors were an early influence, so were Catholic priests. They feature
heavily in his work, from the dashing and romantic Father Arnold in his first
novel, *Reservation Blues*, to the huge and strange Father Duncan in *Indian Killer*,
his darkest and most controversial work.

"I love Jesuits. They are the rock 'n' roll stars of the Catholic church. I love
their mysticism, their social and economic politics. I love their poetic streak and
their rebelliousness." He still attends church, irregularly. He says that Washington,
where he lives, "is the least church-going state in the country. Part of the reason [I
attend irregularly] is that I get recognised at church and it can hardly be a sacred
experience when people are whispering about you. But I still am heavily Catholic-
and Christian-influenced."

After finishing his studies, he worked briefly as an administrator on an educational exchange programme before becoming a full-time writer. He was first published in 1992 by the Brooklyn-based literary magazine, *Hanging Loose*. Bob Hershon, one of the magazine's editors, who spotted Alexie's work and published his first poem, "Distances," says, "he just submitted some poems. But we soon started thinking—this kid is really good. Since then he has gone from being a promising young writer to being a phenomenon. He really is one of a kind."

Alexie has since written two novels and twelve collections of poems and short stories. He has also been the world heavyweight poetry bout champion, where you have to pluck a word from a hat and create a new poem, three times running at the Taos poetry festival in New Mexico. He has also worked as a stand-up comedian. In his writing, the native American characters are not particularly stoic or noble or tragic, as they have often been portrayed in twentieth-century American literature. They may be gay intellectuals or thwarted basketball players, middle-class journalists or elderly movie extras, boozy rock musicians or alienated construction workers, or reservation girls whose cars only go in reverse because all the other gears are broken.

One of his short stories, "Dear John Wayne," describes a fantasy affair the actor had with a Navajo film extra. In the story, Wayne, whom Alexie portrays as a thoughtful feminist, tells his sons: "I often close my eyes and try to put myself into a woman's shoes. I try to think like a woman. I try to embrace the feminine in myself. Do you know what I mean?" "No," said the boys.

*Reservation Blues*, his first full-length novel, told the bitter-sweet tale of a dysfunctional native American band called Coyote Springs, stumbling their way from bar-room to record company and back again, along with a side story that involves the blues musician Robert Johnson and a talking guitar. His second novel, *Indian Killer*, is about a native American boy taken at birth against his mother's wishes for adoption by a white family in Seattle. Later, the boy abducts a white child and there is a series of violent murders. The book received many laudatory reviews. One critic enthused: "Not since Richard Wright's *Native Son* has a novel by a minority writer so devastatingly indicted an entire society and laid bare with merciless candour the racial hatred festering at the centre of it." But it also attracted, from *Time* magazine, the judgment that Alexie was "septic with his own unappeasable anger."

He laughs. "The gall of *Time*! I got a T-shirt with the quote on it. I loved the reaction. In some masochistic way, I love the really violent reviews more than the good reviews. I worried about being manipulative, especially when I wasn't a parent then. But there was an Indian kid being kidnapped and a white kid being kidnapped. Everyone failed to see any ambiguity. It's sold by far the least of all my

books. Indians didn't like it. It was the book that was hardest to write, that gave
me the most nightmares, that still, to this day, troubles me the most because I
can't even get a grasp on it. It's the only one I re-read. I think a book that disturbs
me that much is the one I probably care the most about."

Scott Malcomson, who wrote the recent *One Drop of Blood, the American Mis-
adventure of Race*, is one of Alexie's admirers: "The weird thing, in a way, is that
he has become such a popular Indian writer, yet he doesn't play the traditional
Indian roles—the spiritually superior role, or the nobly damned plains warrior.
He is so true to himself, especially when he's changing his mind, that he offends
a lot of people." Malcomson says he thinks the closest literary parallel is with the
Latino writer Richard Rodriguez: "They are both tremendously funny and observant narcissists, exacting and intimate in their prose. They have a profound interest in looking at ugly things. Neither was ever interested in selling positive images, as far as I know."

Within the native American world, Alexie inspires both great affection and
resentful dismay, with critics objecting to his unflattering portrayal of native
American society. Musician Jim Boyd, the forty-six-year-old winner of last year's
Nammy (the native American music award) for his CD, *AlterNatives*, met Alexie
ten years ago at a folk festival and has collaborated with him since. "People know
exactly what he stands for and they either love him or hate him for it," says Boyd.
"On the reservation, we have our little secrets. Sherman has gone against that and
sometimes the truth hurts. A lot of things he writes about just weren't out there
before. But a lot of the things he talked about needed to be said. I really admire
him for that. And because he does everything—he writes novels and songs and
poems and he's a comedian—he's an inspiration, especially for kids."

Perhaps the most familiar images of native Americans are cinematic. Alexie
has tried to redress the balance by writing screenplays for *Smoke Signals* and *The
Business of Fancydancing*, which he also directed. Elvis Mitchell, in the *New York
Times*, described *Smoke Signals* as "a show-offy exercise in suffering." But Evan
Adams, who acted in both films, argues that "Sherman has managed to almost
single-handedly dismantle the popular and populist image of the American Indian.
He's given us a voice."

Alexie has ambivalent feelings about westerns such as John Ford's *The Search-
ers* (1956), which he describes as "probably the most anti-Indian movie," but re-
serves his most damning criticism for last year's *Windtalkers*, directed by John
Woo, which was based on the true story of native Americans in the second world
war who used their language to communicate commands that the Japanese could

not decode. It starred Nicolas Cage. Alexie says, "I don't think there's ever been such a failure of imagination going from the idea to what ended up on screen."

He now lives in Madrona Valley in Seattle, a gentrified area in what was once a mainly black neighbourhood known as the Central District. In his short story collection, *The Lone Ranger and Tonto Fistfight in Heaven* in 1993, he wrote that "Indians can reside in the city but never live there." But he no longer believes that. "You believe things at the time you write them. I believed that then!" He laughs.

"I was much more fundamental then. What changed me was September 11: I am now desperately trying to let go of the idea of being right, the idea of making decisions based on imaginary tribes. The terrorists were flying planes into the buildings because they thought they were right and they had special knowledge, and we continue to react. And we will be going to war in Iraq soon because we think we have special knowledge—and we don't. We are making these decisions not based on any moral or ethical choice, but simply on the basis of power and money and ancient traditions that are full of shit, so I am increasingly suspicious of the word 'tradition,' whether in political or literary terms."

While over 60 percent of native Americans now live in urban areas, very little of their literature deals with this experience. *The Toughest Indian in the World*, his collection of short stories, was almost exclusively urban and white collar. "I want to be a white-collar American Indian writer because that's what I am now."

Alexie is conscious that he has a voice few native Americans possess, at a time when attention is focused on them as it has not been for years. The growth of casinos, which are now permitted on their land, has created a bubble of money which has made some powerful politically. It has led, too, to a growth in the number of people claiming native American blood, now 2.6 [million], up from 1.8 [million] only a decade ago, although still less than 1 percent of the nation.

"I have enormous cultural power now and it's all out of proportion to the number of books I actually sell," he says. "Because of my ethnicity, my age, the times we live in, I have power." But he is angry at what he sees as the hypocrisy around him. "The arrogance of this country to have a Holocaust museum, to point out the genocidal sins of another culture is amazing. [American general] Philip Sheridan, who was the Colin Powell of his day, said, 'We should kill Indian children because nits make lice.' President Andrew Jackson said, 'Let's kill the Indians.'"

There is much in Alexie's writing about sex and, in particular, sex between white people and native Americans. In *The Business of Fancydancing*, his collection of poems and stories, he writes that "Indians are an endangered species."

Alexie met his wife, Diane, at an academic camp for native American children where she was working as a site coordinator and he was the judge in a writing competition. They each made a conscious decision to marry a fellow native American. Does he expect his two young sons will follow suit? "Of course, we would prefer it. But the only thing I can be assured of is that they will probably partner with people who like books. Maybe that's the new tribe."

He says he has always argued that non-Indian artists doing Indian work should certainly enjoy success, "but I think, for instance, Tony Hillerman's work [mystery novels set around reservations] should be classified as what it is—colonial literature. . . . I think there's an arrogance amongst white Americans about their relationship to the oppressed people that prevents them from seeing themselves as coming from a position of privilege."

A theme that runs through Alexie's work is alcoholism, not least because there was much of it in the family. Many theories have been advanced as to why alcoholism has done such damage to native Americans; they are more than three times more likely to die of cirrhosis of the liver than white people, four times more likely to die in an alcohol-related accident and three times more likely to be murdered or commit suicide.

"The two groups of people I have been around who drink the most are poor whites and poor Indians. Often the definition of what alcoholic is depends on how much you are paying for your drinks. I think it's a combination of poverty and despair, but the way we so willingly fell into it, and still do in such large numbers, makes me think there must be something inside our culture that made us so willing to fall apart that way."

Alexie himself gave up drinking eleven years ago. "I think far fewer people are drinking themselves to death. I used to call it the symptom of a disease called poverty and political oppression and believed that if you dealt with the oppression people wouldn't need to drink, but I don't think that's true any more. I think the one thing you have to do before anything else is sober up."

When President Clinton was still in the White House in 1998, he invited Alexie and a small group of others to take part in a televised "Dialogue on Race" forum. "He said, 'Sherman, before I was president, the only thing I knew about Indians was that my grandmother was part Cherokee.'"

"Later on, I was asked if Indians were part of the national dialogue on race. I said, 'No, the only time white folks talk to me about Indians is when they tell me their grandmothers were part Cherokee.' As the show wore on, I thought 'Oh, my God, I gave the president shit—the president!' Afterwards I was scared and tried to hide—and he came across to me and grabbed me by the shoulder and leaned in close to me and said, 'Sherman, you're fucking funny!'"

Alexie mainly votes Democrat, or for a candidate of the left. He says, "My family, like most Indians, were socially conservative. We give our money to Democrats because they protect us, but we live very Republican lives—pro-gun, pro-death penalty, pro-life, homophobic, racist. The average rez Indian is more racist towards black people than the average small-town white person."

His parents, brothers, and twin sisters are still on the reservation, most of them having worked for the casino or in the reservation administration. His sisters are considering opening a beauty parlour there. One brother is about to start college for the first time at thirty-eight, to Alexie's delight. An older sister died in a mobile-home fire, an event that is a viscerally haunting theme throughout his writing. In his poetry collection, *First Indian on the Moon*, he writes:

Fire
follows my family
each spark
each flame
a soldier
in the US Cavalry

He visits every month. "The people who hate me there now are the people who hated me when I was seven. . . . In any small town, eccentricity is viewed as suspicious. In a tribally-controlled small town, eccentricities are viewed with much more suspicion."

Although his family life is a frequent subject of his writing, his folks are proud of his achievements. "I have done some heavy-duty stuff about my family, and it can be very painful. But if I give a reading in Spokane near my rez, my mom, dad, and all my siblings will be in the third row and they'll laugh along and cry along with stories about them."

In 1996, *Granta* included Alexie in its Best of Young American Novelists issue, along with Jonathan Franzen, among others. *Granta* editor Ian Jack, who was one of the judges, made the decision on the basis of *Reservation Blues.* "I can't speak for my fellow jurists, but I suspect that they, like me, liked his work because it had something to tell us. Native American life, life on the reservation, is a pretty under-described experience. I knew nothing about it. OK, I could have read nonfiction about it but I suspect it would mainly, if not entirely, have been by non-Indians, if I can use that word. Fiction, if it's any good, should persuade you of individual and inner lives. Alexie's book wasn't sanctimonious or pious or a piece of political pleading—it introduced you to characters who were native American and made them as complex and odd as everyone else. The charge might then be that we picked him for non-literary reasons. To which I'd say: (a) he is a good writer—inventive, vivid; (b) it isn't impure or unliterary to like or admire novels because they bring you news—Zola down a coal mine, Dickens in a slum, Tom Wolfe in Wall Street. Alexie told me about things I hadn't thought of before, this must also be true of many people in the U.S.A."

So who will write the Great Native American Novel? "It won't be me," says Alexie. "It will be the next generation, some amazingly gifted Indian kid out there now is getting bombarded with images and with possibilities and will write Portrait of An Indian as a Young Man—or Woman, will write our Moby Indian. I can't wait."

He still writes and lives at a driven pace as though making up for generations of indifference and indignity. In the spring a new collection of short stories will be published in the U.S., in the autumn a new collection of poems and a biography of Jimi Hendrix. There is also a memoir which will trace his own family from a much-decorated grandfather who died in the second world war in Okinawa through to his own sunny young Seattle sons.

"I'm a narcissist, as all artists and writers are, but how can you be of service? Looking at what's available in the native American world, no one has written that multi-generational epic, no one has really talked about the changes in our lives. My mother's mother sat on the knee of Chief Joseph [the Nez Percé leader who surrendered in 1877 saying "I will fight no more forever"]. She went from Chief Joseph to space shuttles before she died and no one's really talked about that in the Indian world."

# Redeemers

Matt Dellinger/2003

*Sherman Alexie's story "What You Pawn I Will Redeem" appears this week in the magazine and here online (see Fiction). Alexie has written several novels and the screenplays for the films* Smoke Signals *and last year's* The Business of Fancy-dancing, *the latter of which he also directed. His new collection of short stories,* Ten Little Indians, *will be published this June by Grove Press. Alexie spoke with the* New Yorker's *Matt Dellinger about his Native American heritage, the challenges of film-making, and the dangers of tribalism.*

**Matt Dellinger**: The main object in your story, the pawned item, is the powwow-dance regalia of the narrator's grandmother. The narrator spends twenty-four hours trying to raise the money to buy it back. The powwow dance is also at the center of the movie you wrote and directed, *The Business of Fancydancing.* Tell me about the significance of Native American dancing, and of the regalia.

**Sherman Alexie:** Well, I think most people would recognize powwow dancing, Indian dancing, in a generic sort of way. But I don't think they necessarily think about its cultural or religious or spiritual applications. And the power any particular outfit would have, and its meanings, the way the colors of a powwow outfit can reflect the family's philosophies and history, much the same way a coat of arms can in other cultures. Fancydancing is a pretty modern interpretation. In the years immediately following the Second World War, veterans came back and needed a new way to express themselves, so fancydancing came to the forefront in Oklahoma and in the Midwest back then, and it was really just sort of a contemporary reinterpretation of traditional powwow dancing. Also, in the twentieth century Indian tribes were becoming more assimilated. Fancydancing became an amalgamation of cultural influences, tribal influences.

**MD:** Are dances passed down through families?

**SA:** Well, there's a difference between powwow dancing and tribal dancing. Tribe ceremonies are very private, and are passed down from person to person very specifically. Powwow dancing is much more pan-Indian, much more public, so there are still some sacred elements to it, but it's also much more commercial, much more entertainment driven as well. It's a combination of things.

**MD:** Would the regalia have been used in one or the other?
**SA:** In both. Both in a sacred and in a public way.

**MD:** The narrator's relationship to his culture in this story is sort of tenuous but strong at the same time. . . .
**SA:** A distant love affair, yeah.

**MD:** And the way he carries out his quest for the money is both very sincere and haphazard.
**SA:** Oh, I think it's completely sincere. And utterly random and misguided and romantic and stupid and alcoholic. This story is also, in some sense, I think, a response to my work in Hollywood, where the heroic quest—every movie has to be about a heroic quest—is always so pure. Hollywood is all about purity. And, in a time of war, everything is stark contrasts: this side is pure, and that side is pure. So I guess I wanted a very ordinary protagonist, an ordinary hero, and that was what was interesting to me in writing this—the idea about some stumblebum trying to do something amazing.

**MD:** Are you trying to convey anything about the Indian condition in general?
**SA:** The first thought in my head is, well, yeah, we are stumblebums trying to do something amazing. Last night, I was reading Richard Rodriguez's *Brown*, and he was talking about Indians, and the language—the fundamentalism and essentialism—and fake and real purity of Indians, and how even today we remain unassimilable. In some sense, this guy just refuses to belong.

**MD:** I don't think anyone would say that you romanticize Indian culture.
**SA:** No. That would be the worst thing I could ever be accused of. You know, because as Indians we've been so stereotyped and maligned and oppressed and abused, in acts and deed, in action and word, we seek literature that cheers us in some way, that acts as some sort of antidote, rather than an examination of us, and an interrogation of us. I mean, Indians don't necessarily want to be interrogated by our own art, we want to be cheered. I think a lot of Indians want Indian artists to be cultural cheerleaders rather than cultural investigators. I'll leave it up to mainstream journalists to do that. It's much the same way that this country right now wants our artists and our journalists to be cheerleaders. And in terms of our American identity I think mainstream journalists are.

**MD:** Do you think that being investigative ultimately helps in some way?

**SA:** Well, I think the worst part about tribalism is its tendency to fundamentalize, and if I can fight fundamentalism in any of its forms I'm happy.

**MD:** You wrote a column recently in the *Stranger* that talked about the antiwar movement, which you're involved in, and about the irony you saw in America's freedom fighting. You quoted Hugo of St. Victor.

**SA:** Yes, about the perfect man. "The tender soul has fixed his love on one spot in the world; the strong man has extended his love to all places; the perfect man has extinguished his." The idea of being countryless and tribeless is the ideal. And, in my pessimistic, cynical way, I took it to mean that you always have to be interrogating—everything you believe, yourself, all of your backgrounds, every tribe you belong to officially or unofficially. In this particular instance, I'm just as interested in the fate of the Iraqis as I am in the Americans'.

**MD:** Do you participate in powwows at all?

**SA:** No. You know, in some sense, early on I was tribeless, or at least pushing toward a tribeless sense, and this morning I was talking to my wife—she's Hidatsa Indian—after reading an op-ed in the New Mexico paper, and I said, "Well, tribal influence—my tribe is just one influence, and probably not the largest one now." I mean, liberals get accused more than conservatives of being focussed on identity politics, but there's nothing that screams identity politics more than calling somebody anti-American. So this war is all about identity politics.

**MD:** The protagonist in your story, a homeless Indian, wanders around the city and meets homeless members of the Aleut tribe waiting on the bench for their boat, which never comes. Is their dedication to their tribe meant to feel sweet?

**SA:** Ah. No, I think it's tender nostalgia, and also doomed. Nostalgia is always doomed and dooming.

**MD:** Reservation Indians sometimes get stereotyped as self-defeating, in the way they live their lives and regarding the choices they make, and even, some people would say, in their adherence to their own culture.

**SA:** Well, first of all, I would argue that reservation Indians are much more assimilated into American society than people would assume, or believe, depending on the reservation. A majority are very assimilated, and, aside from particular cultural things and ceremonies, there's not a whole lot of cultural difference between poor white people and Indians. Indian culture is, by and large, pop culture. In other ways, I think it can be seen from the outside as self-defeating, and the end result might be self-defeating, but I think a lot of Indians view their separation and their refusal to belong as an open act of defiance. So, even as they might go down in flames, they're proud of themselves. They're cultural kamikazes in some sense. And I think the narrator of the story in some sense is a cultural kamikaze.

**MD:** But he's ultimately rewarded for it.
**SA:** He's still homeless. I mean, he's got the regalia, but what the hell is he going to do with it? It was interesting to me when I read the story again this morning—I'm always puzzled by myself. Like, what the hell does that mean? But the end, in my head, I saw it being filmed. And I thought, That's a huge triumph, him dancing in the streets with the outfit. But, as with any triumph in any movie, when it says "The End" you have to think, Well, what happened to them after that?

**MD:** He may very well go and pawn it again.
**SA:** Exactly. I thought the sequel to the story would be "What I Redeemed I'm Going to Pawn."

**MD:** Who are your fans, mostly?
**SA:** College-educated, middle-class white women is the largest group by far.

**MD:** Why do you think that is?
**SA:** I think they're the most educated, most curious, interesting group of people in the country. I think that white women are more apt to read laterally. So I think there's some strong identification for women, and their political and social positions, and minorities. I think that the political power of, let's say, the average Indian man and a white woman are pretty equal. Of course, the percentage of Indians in the crowd is always going to be larger than for other writers. Depending on the area, ten or twenty percent will be Indians, but most of the rest will be white women.

**MD:** You also do slam poetry. How does that audience differ?
**SA:** It's still pretty much the same. The typical slam audience isn't necessarily my audience. When I participate in that sort of event, my book audience carries over. I think that, by and large, in the slam world book poets like me are probably viewed with more suspicion.

**MD:** You don't have the street cred?
**SA:** Right. I do horrible things like write in meter.

**MD:** Did you find it difficult to write a screenplay from your own work?
**SA:** Well, the difficulty in writing screenplays is not my approach to them, it's everybody else's interpretation of what a movie is supposed to be. In the literary

world, creativity and originality are a plus. And then in the movie world everything gets crammed into formulas, even in the so-called independent world. If
you look at the fifty or sixty independent movies that enjoyed mass release last
year, you're still going to be looking at three-act structures. And happy endings.

**MD:** Could you write a movie like that?
**SA:** I've tried. I'm miserable at it. I script-doctor in Hollywood and I work on
projects, and I think people hire me to read good screenplays they know are never
going to make it. I rewrite them, or I originate them, and the projects never get
made, and I always fail. Often the reason projects fail is that I bring something
strange to them. And it's funny, because I love movies. All movies. I just have been
unable to combine my literary sense and screenplay structure into a fully winning
formula yet. And I don't know that I'll ever be able to.

**MD:** In your writing, do you feel a responsibility to be a social commentator?
**SA:** I was talking this morning with a writer friend, David James Duncan, about
that, and about how we wish in some sense we could be alone in our studies
working at our art. I mean, that's our natural tendency—to be hermits. But we
keep getting called out. I don't volunteer.

**MD:** You do write columns for newspapers.
**SA:** Yes. I've just started that, and reluctantly. I'm really nervous about it. Certainly, I hope it's something I'll get better at, but it's not a strength right now. I've
got moments. The *Stranger* asked me to write a couple of things, and as we were
doing it I kept thinking that one of the reasons conservatives dominate media
right now is that binary thinking plays well. Liberals are so damn nervous and so
damn conflicted, and live in the gray, and that doesn't play well. So I'm going to
try to see if I can be a binary liberal, to be as funny and combative and aggressive
as the conservative writers are.

**MD:** When you're writing fiction or films, how much do you consciously think
about making a social comment?
**SA:** I think it finds its way in, regardless. Often when I'm at my worst is when I'm
consciously trying to make a statement.

**MD:** What about other Indian writers?
**SA:** There's Simon Ortiz. He does it in such a low-key way. I think Susan Power's
*The Grass Dancer* was very subtle. She's Standing Rock Sioux.

**MD:** What about white people writing about Indians? Have you read anything good?

**SA:** I like Tom Spanbauer. *The Man Who Fell in Love with the Moon* is incredible. I think Craig Lesley's books are good. I like the mysteries by Dana Stabenow—the Kate Shugak mysteries. I think her politics end up being more about a woman's politics, which is great that another identity takes precedence, that it's a white woman writing about an Indian woman and that the woman part comes out stronger, so that the Indian politics sort of interweave, and the environmentalism sort of interweaves. I think the main character, Kate, would identify herself primarily as a woman, and her interactions are with a wide variety of people.

**MD:** You made a point in one of your *Stranger* columns about the irony of Native Americans fighting in the Army. I've seen some powwows, and at them the honoring of veterans seems to almost eclipse everything else.
**SA:** Everything else. Oh, God. Yeah. I hate it. My next book is all about that. It's called "Inventing My Grandfather." My grandfather died on Okinawa in the Second World War, and his wife died three months later, leaving my father and his sister orphans. So I was raised by a war orphan who joined the Army himself, between Korea and Vietnam. I was always stunned by that. The Museum of Tolerance, in Los Angeles, asked me to be part of a genealogy exhibit. The genealogist did much more research on my grandfather. I discovered that he was a war hero. He won nine medals. I ended up on *Oprah* in January promoting the exhibit. Oprah surprised the hell out of me and had this brigadier general come out and present me with the medals I thought were going to take years to get reissued. And there were actually twelve of them. So I was on TV, on a black woman's television show, an Indian getting twelve medals from a Special Forces brigadier general. It was bizarre. What a country. Great country. I'd had the idea of a book in mind before that, and since then, and in a time of war, I've been writing a lot of stuff. My father died a month ago. So the book is about all those connections—about war and warriors, and honoring war among Indians, and essentially how you go from grandfather war hero to grandson Commie pinko pacifist, in two uneasy steps.

**MD:** So it's a personal history?
**SA:** Yeah. It's about the idea of Native American violence and American violence. And the idea of man and men and manhood. And the way it works in the Indian world versus the rest of American culture. For Indians right now my general thought is that there is this huge inferiority complex: we desperately want to belong. And what better way to prove you belong than to go to war for this country? A volunteer army is staffed by poor people. So maybe the whole thing we've been talking about today—this idea of keeping distance and being unassimilable and

all that—maybe that's all bullshit. I left the reservation. And I encourage every-body else to leave. My wife said this morning, "Nothing wrong with leaving the ghetto."

**MD:** Do you feel you've snubbed your culture?
**SA:** You know, I believe the American culture is so infused and so assimilated and so combined that all of us contribute to it. Being a part of it confirms all of us. And my entrance into the mainstream has changed the mainstream—forgive the immodesty—but I think my career has totally altered many people's ideas of what an Indian can do and can be. Especially other Indians.

**MD:** Do you mean the pure facts of your success? Not the work itself?
**SA:** Yeah. Not the work itself. My success, my cultural power, my influence.

**MD:** Do you do readings and things on reservations? Visit schools?
**SA:** Yeah. And, you know, the next generation—there's going to be nine of me. That's what you hope.

# Seriously Sherman: Seattle's Favorite Pissed Off Poet Talks about Truth, Terror, Tradition, and What's So Great about America Anyway?
Timothy Harris/2003

From *Real Change News* May 29–June 11, 2003. Reprinted by permission. The interviewer, Timothy Harris, is the Executive Director of Real Change.

Award-winning author Sherman Alexie has never been one to sit still for long. Over the past decade, this thirty-six-year-old Coeur d'Alene Indian from Spokane has established himself as a major literary voice through his poetry, novels, short stories, and movies. His new book of short stories, *Ten Little Indians*, will be released by Grove/Atlantic in June. It contains "What You Pawn I will Redeem," a story recently published in the *New Yorker* that features a *Real Change* vendor as the central character. Alexie is currently working on two biographies, one on guitar-phenomenon Jimi Hendrix, and the other on his own grandfather, a highly decorated World War II veteran.

Alexie is a passionate, funny, politically committed personality who challenges the certitudes of both right and left, arriving at a politics that transcends easy definition. In this interview, Sherman discusses his own success, politics, and identity, and tells us why, after everything, America is still a great country.

**Real Change:** First of all, I'd like your opinion on something that comes up a lot these days. George Bush: Do you think he's as dumb as he looks?
**Sherman Alexie:** I don't think he's dumb. I think he has probably slightly above-average intelligence. But that's hardly a qualification for President of the United States and the Most Powerful Man in the World. I think compared to the average middle-manager, the average CPA, the average lawyer, Dubya fits in well, but compared to Clinton or 90 percent of the men and women in the Senate, Dubya is far less intelligent.

In the words of his own former chief speechwriter, David Frum, Dubya is "uncurious." So it's not so much a matter of his intelligence as his intellectual ambition.

**RC:** What do you think got him where he is?

**Alexie:** (Laughs) Luck. The other day I was arguing with somebody, one of my gym friends and a conservative, and he was talking about Dubya's accomplishment. And I said, "He hasn't really done that much. I mean, if your father's President of the United States, and you become President of the United States, you haven't really done much. To match my father all I would have had to do is have spotty blue-collar employment for forty years. So he didn't rise above his father. He didn't become a priest, or a poet. He didn't branch out into anything new or exciting. He's daddy's son.

**RC:** He went into the family business.

**Alexie:** Yeah, exactly. They just needed a figurehead. I mean, there are conservative politicians I respect and admire, even if I don't agree with their politics necessarily. And then there are those conservative politicians, and liberals too, who completely exist as figureheads, as symbols. Reagan was a symbol. A powerful symbol, but he had nothing to do with his policies. Part of it was due to his Alzheimer's, I'm sure, but he never served on boards. He never was the intellectual they call to speak on this or that policy. It's the same thing with Dubya. After he's done, it's eight and done, and he'll exist merely as a symbol.

**RC:** You've said that recent events have made you suspicious of tradition, and that you are trying to let go of "the idea of being right." What are some of the questions that the American response to September 11th has raised for you?

**Alexie:** The idea of responding as a tribe. Immediately, that day, I was suspicious when the word heroes started popping up. That made the victims into symbols and not human beings.

I do a comedy bit about it: don't you think that, out of all the people who died, there was at least *one* major asshole? At least one major asshole? Don't you think, of all the people who died, there's one whose kids are quietly celebrating? Don't you think there's at least one murderer in the bunch who got away with it? A rapist, a child abuser, or a pedophile? But instead, they were immediate icons, and that's dangerous.

We canonized them immediately, just as asshole terrorists are canonized by their tribes. Nobody's responding individually or asking, "Why did this happen and what can we do to prevent it from happening again?" Instead it was "What can my country do? What can my tribe do? How can I defend it?"

War is all about the idea of tribes and defending your country, so I've been trying to let go of the idea of basing my politics on the good of a small group. I've become less and less Indian-centric as the years have gone on. After September 11th,

I barely talk about it. I talk about poor people; I talk about disadvantaged people, and that sort of covers everything I need to cover. It becomes not about race, region, or country, but about a particular group of people sharing the same circumstances. I talk about the universal condition of the poor, and thinking and talking about it that way helps eliminate the negativity of tribalism. That's been my response: to see people by their power or lack thereof, rather than the color of their skin.

**RC:** It's the double-edged sword of identity politics.

**Alexie:** Yeah. Exactly. That's why liberals are losing elections. We've gone over to that completely. We're marching for ourselves, and no one's really extending. We're not basing our policies on also changing the lives of people who don't agree with us.

**RC:** Your last book of short stories, *The Toughest Indian in the World*, was mostly about professionally successful urban Indians, which makes sense since it's pretty much what you've become; you've taken on that frame of reference. You're one of those rare people who've been able to transcend the limitations of their class, and I'm wondering how that feels for you: if you've become comfortable with who you are now, or if you still feel like a visitor?

**Alexie:** Well, I'm happy. What did Mae West say: "I've been rich and poor. Rich is better." My own variation on that is, "Money doesn't solve all your problems, but it solves most of them, and gives you a fighting chance at the rest." Anybody who says poverty is ennobling is full of shit. It's debilitating and demoralizing and destructive. So, regardless of my emotional feelings, my self-esteem and etcetera, the fact that I have money and comfort is only a plus.

On the emotional side, there's a lot of guilt. You grow up poor and then get this kind of power and privilege, and of course you're going to feel guilty. There were kids I grew up with who were ambitious and intelligent, and for various reasons, most often not of their own design, didn't have the kind of success I did, so I think about that. I see them when I go home to the rez, and they have admiration and rage and hatred and love for me. So, I'm skilled, and I'm lucky. And sometimes I feel much more lucky than skilled. Some mornings I wake up thinking I don't deserve it. Other mornings I wake up and think, "Yes, I do."

I wouldn't be doing what I do if I wasn't already half-crazy anyway. The thought of being half-crazy and successful makes me crazier, I think. Personality-wise, with my particular handbag of disorders, I'm not much different from a lot of people on the street. I'm just well enough to manage.

**RC:** But you must be fairly driven. It seems like you always have six projects going. You're insanely busy.

Alexie: Yeah, but I have to be. I'm obsessive—it's the obsessive-compulsive disorder (laughs). If I'm not writing a book, I'm taking a shower. I'm washing my hands if I'm not writing a poem, so I try to write the poem. The impulse is to wash my hands, but I use that energy to write a poem.

RC: You're working on a Hendrix biography. Do you feel any particular connection to Jimi?

Alexie: Well, being from the Northwest, and into the music, but my big connection was my sister who died when I was fourteen and was a huge fan of his music and the psychedelic rock of that era. She got pregnant at Altamont and was hanging around Berkeley. She was an Indian Hippie, big time. I really admired and envied the life she was living at that time.

Looking back, it was random and chaotic and emotionally devastating, but back then it seemed romantic, so I'm writing the biography with two eyes. There's the romantic side—and, I don't want to sound like a neo-con, but I also talk about the destruction it caused, not only for the individual, but also for the culture and the country. I'm a liberal with a healthy respect for self-discipline. I believe self-discipline is directly connected to self-esteem. We've heard all the liberal, artistic takes on Hendrix. I want to do the liberal Dale Carnegie take on him.

RC: When you wrote the screenplay for *Smoke Signals*, your strategy was to create a very accessible film that would resonate with mainstream audiences. *The Business of Fancydancing*, really, was anything but. It's much more thematically ambitious; it's much more challenging. It was kind of an art house film.

Alexie: It was so arty the art houses didn't want it.

RC: So, what led you there?

Alexie: Rebellion. As much as I like *Smoke Signals*—I love it in some ways, and I certainly love what it's done for my career—it's not really consistent with my art. And maybe some part of it is poverty guilt.

RC: So, "Now that I've done something successful, I need to do something that will be completely marginal and flop?"

Alexie: Yeah, exactly (laughs). To prove that I don't belong. *Fancydancing* was this really mentally ill blast of insecurity. I mean, that's what my wife said.

RC: I find my wife is usually right.

Alexie: Yeah, I know. She said, "Make *Smoke Signals* again. People love it. It's a good movie." And I might. But it seemed important to me to make a statement about who I am and what I do and my ambition. I think it's really interesting, and

I think it's really flawed in many ways, but I also think it has something to say. So I like to think of it as this noble experiment, and a sign of things to come. This is where I'm going. This is what I want to do. It's an economic failure, but in the end we only spent a couple hundred thousand dollars, which is a lot of money but it's not a lot of money for a movie. And we're gradually making it back. By the time the video and DVD play out, we will break even.

RC: Do you still have plans to do a movie around *Indian Killer*?
Alexie: Evan Adams, who was in *Smoke Signals* and *Fancydancing*, is writing and directing that. I gave it over to him. I just sort of lost the fire for it. So it's his project. I don't even know what they're doing. I stepped away completely.

RC: I read somewhere that *Indian Killer* is the book you've written that you still feel like you haven't come to terms with.
Alexie: Yeah, I don't know where it came from. I remember writing it. I was so angry. My career was really blasting off then, so there was that sort of heady rush and people's questions, and the responsibility of being an artist and a spokesperson for my race. And I just lost it. It was a huge binge.

RC: It was on overstock at University Bookstore so I sent copies to relatives, and I think it freaked them out. They didn't know what to make of it.
Alexie: Nobody does. Nobody will go near it. I mean, my poetry books sold more than that. I think it was a sort of a statement. *Indian Killer* was my *Fancydancing* at that point in my life.

RC: One critic has compared you to Latino writer Richard Rodriguez, saying you both have "a profound interest in looking at ugly things." Do you think that's true?
Alexie: (Laughs) Whoa! Who said that?

RC: I dunno. It's on your website.
Alexie: Is it? I don't even look.

RC: It's in a long review from some London paper. I think it was the *Guardian*.
Alexie: Wow! It's probably true. No one ever praises, you know, the lyric beauty. No one ever says, "We need someone to write about a tree! Call Sherman Alexie!" Yeah, I would agree with that. Hopefully I find some beauty inside the ugly stuff. Not very often. Generally I'm a pessimist. Generally I'm cynical and disillusioned. So . . .

RC: You know, there's something really fascinating about a train wreck.
Alexie: Yeah, and I guess that's what I do. I watch the human train wreck. I always

think it's funny when people accuse me of being a liberal romantic, or a liberal dreamer. That's hardly true. I think human beings are by and large despicable. And I think the world is by and large an awful place. So my liberalism is certainly not based in romanticism. I don't think anything we do is going to change a damn thing.

**RC:** So that leads me directly to my next question.
**Alexie:** Uh huh?

**RC:** Can you name three redeeming things about the human race?
**Alexie:** The first thing that pops into my head is the last one minute of any college basketball game. Then, iambic pentameter. Who would have thought you could write like your heart beats? And, uh, antibiotics.

**RC:** There's a level of honesty in your work that pisses some people off. An example would be "What You Pawn I Will Redeem." In this story, Jackson Squared comes into Real Change and talks his way into fifty free papers, but after an hour he tosses them in the trash because, when it comes right down to it, he'd really rather be drinking. Then he rolls his passed-out friend for his last buck-fifty. It has the ring of truth, but why is this a useful sort of truth-telling?
**Alexie:** Part of that story for me was to be sure that in representing a homeless man, I show all of him. I mean, he's not homeless by accident; it's going to be part of who he is to always fuck up. No matter how true and honest his ambitions, his actions are always going to trip him up. So, that was the point there, to be sure I didn't romanticize him. He wasn't some downtrodden oppressed man stumbling through the streets. Here was a guy fully participating in his own destruction.

Homeless people don't need to be romanticized and they don't need to be vilified—there's plenty of both—what they need is to be humanized. And to humanize somebody you show everything. Everything. The best of who they are and the worst of who they are.

Hate happens when we romanticize and vilify. As soon as we humanize people, it's really hard to go to war against them. You start identifying yourself with their strengths and weaknesses.

That story's had such an amazing response because I wrote it in a way that people can identify with this homeless guy. I didn't want to demonize anybody around the homeless guy either. Like the Korean convenience store guy, who could easily be vilified; the cop, the pawnshop owner. To take everybody out of the realm of symbol and make them human beings. All these people in the end are basically decent. I think people are responding to that, especially in this time, where everything is in the language of hate and war. Here was this story that spoke the language of individualization and decency.

**RC:** Last question. What gives you hope?
**Alexie:** (Sighs) It's the little things. First, that my sons are incredibly comfortable. That I live in a country that enables somebody like me to transcend class and race, all those categories, to become, simply, a success. Now it's up to them. There's nothing holding them back. No poverty. No addiction. They're at the same starting line as everybody else. They're not a hundred yards back. And that gives me hope, for them.

Worldwide? Countrywide? Art. Books. Poems. When I get letters from people who disagree with me but say interesting things. I get much more hate mail, but when I get respect mail from someone who disagrees it gives me hope.

That I could wake up and drive here in twenty minutes to have breakfast with you. In a lot of places in the world you can't do that. I'm so happy I live here. I don't like anti-Americanism. I think right-wing Republicans often refuse to see the bad, but liberals often refuse to see what's great.

Antibiotics. Doctors, nurses. We complain about our healthcare system but look at what SARS and AIDS is doing in the rest of the world. My children's pediatrician. Immunization. That gives me hope.

**RC:** Yeah. Bill Gates is wiping out diarrhea in Africa.
**Alexie:** There you go! Yeah. Bill Gates gives me hope. There's an example of somebody having an awakening. Eddie Vedder impaling Dubya's mask on a mike-stand. That gives me hope. I'm happy for Oprah Winfrey. I'm happy for Michael Jordan. I'm happy to see so many people transcend race and class. Richard Rodriguez. He and I can look at ugly things together and get a lot of respect for it.

One of the great things for me is *Real Change*: the interactions I have almost everyday in this city with people selling it. I give them whatever I have in my pocket—whether it's $10, $20, or $50, I'll give them whatever's in my pocket for the newspaper. You sneak up on the vendors, I think; they don't realize they're part of the capitalist system. I mean, if you can stand on a corner and sell *Real Change*, then you can sell anything. You could have any job, because that's a tough gig. It's the interaction: looking at the nametag, then calling people by their name, looking them in the eye. You know: seeing them. That gives me hope.

# A Conversation with
# Sherman Alexie by Diane Thiel

Diane Thiel/2004

From *Crossroads: The Journal of the Poetry Society of America* 61 (2004): 4–7.
Reprinted by permission of the interviewer.

**Diane Thiel:** Can you say a bit about working in different genres in your writing, and often crossing genres in a single book? A signature element in your books seems to be a fusion of forms. One wonders while reading: "Is this a poem or short story?" What distinctions do you see between genres? Do you think some distinctions are rather artificial? Has your relationship with the different forms changed at all in the evolution of your work?

**Sherman Alexie:** I suppose, as an Indian living in the U.S., I'm used to crossing real and imaginary boundaries, and have, in fact, enjoyed a richer and crazier and more magical life precisely because I have fearlessly and fearfully crossed all sorts of those barriers. I guess I approach my poetry the same way I have approached every other thing in my life. I just don't like being told what to do. I write whatever feels and sounds right to me. At the beginning of my career, I wrote free verse with some formal influences, but I have lately been writing more formal verse with free verse influences. I don't feel the need to spend all my time living on either the free verse or the formal reservation. I want it all; hunger is my crime.

**DT:** And what about the fusion of poetry and story in your work, in *The Business of Fancydancing: Stories and Poems*, and in *One Stick Song* in particular. Could you tell me a bit more about crossing those barriers? Not many writers defy the genres, and I'm curious about your decision to collect the stories and poems together as you have. And also about your path towards the novels and screenplays. Did you feel you needed a larger or different kind of canvas to tell certain stories?

**SA:** The original decision to include poems and stories in the first collection, *The Business of Fancydancing*, was made by the Hanging Loose Press editors. I was only twenty-three years old when that book was accepted for publication, and didn't really know how to put a book together (I still don't know how!), so it was really an editorial decision. I guess those Hanging Loose guys understood my work was a blend of poetry and fiction, and since I was such a baby writer then, I think that fusion is just natural, maybe even reflexive. I have to work hard now to make a poem completely identifiable as a poem, and not as a hybrid. Of course, I still love hybrids. I'm a hybrid. So I think it was the Hanging Loose editors who helped me define myself as a poet. They're still my poetry publishers, and I'm very curious what they'll do with my next book, which will be mostly formal poems. I think my path toward novels and screenplays was, number one, the simple effort to make more money so I could be a full-time writer. But heck, I haven't published a novel in seven years, so I'm not sure I can be described as a novelist. I think I'm a poet with short story inclinations. And since screenplays and movies are poetic in structure and intent, I find that I'm much more comfortable writing screenplays than I am writing novels. I am currently working on my first nonfiction, a big book about four generations of Indian men in my family, and our relationship with war, and I've broken it down into fiction, nonfiction project, and poetry, so I'm really looking for a hybrid work here. In some sense, I feel this new book is a summation of all my themes until now. After this book, I think I'll be looking in some radical new directions.

**DT:** Could you speak a bit about converting literature for the screen? What are the different demands of the work in print and the work on the screen? What is your process? What useful advice have you received along the way? Was there any "advice" that you instinctively did not agree with?

**SA:** Although I have written two produced movies, and worked on screenplays for a half-dozen unproduced flicks, I still haven't figured out what works or what doesn't. I don't think the audiences for movies are nearly as forgiving or ambitious as the audiences for poetry or fiction. Ninety-nine percent of all movies ever made, from the most independent to the most capital driven, from the crappy ones to the classics, are identical in structure. If poets worked like film-makers, we'd all be writing sonnets, only sonnets, and nothing else! Just try to make a movie out of "The Wasteland" or *Portrait of the Artist as a Young Man*. I want to make movies that are much more like poems, so I'll be making them myself for extremely low budgets. The best advice I've ever received: "Sherman, quit wasting your time in Hollywood!" Of course, I have completely ignored that advice.

**DT:** In *First Indian on the Moon*, the poem "The Alcoholic Love Poems" ends with the lines "All I said was 'When I used to drink, you're exactly the kind of Indian I loved to get drunk with.' Oh all my life in the past tense." How does the recognition of "past tense" in this poem affect your writing? Do you often feel as if you are writing about past selves, past injuries? Can you discuss how past meets present in your work?

SA: In my dictionary, "Indian" and "nostalgic" are synonyms. As colonized people, I think we're always looking to the past for some real and imaginary sense of purity and authenticity. But I hate my nostalgia. I think I'm pop-culture obsessed because I hope it's an antidote for the disease of nostalgia. So I think the past and present are always duking it out in my work. The Lone Ranger and Tonto will always be fistfighting.

DT: The title poem of your first book, *The Business of Fancydancing*, is a sestina, and I notice that an interest in using the various forms of poetry has persisted in your body of work. Who were your early influences of "formal" poetry? Why did you feel drawn to it? What do you think are some of the possibilities using form provides?

SA: Although I would certainly be defined as a free verse poet, I have always worked in traditional and invented forms. Though I've never recognized it before, the fact that the title poem of my first book is a sestina says a lot about my varied ambitions. My earliest interest in formalism came from individual poems rather than certain poets. Marvell's "To His Coy Mistress," Roethke's "My Papa's Waltz," Gwendolyn Brooks' "We Real Cool," and Langston Hughes' "A Dream Deferred" are poems that come to mind as early formal poems I admired. Speaking both seriously and facetiously, I think I've spent my whole career rewriting "My Papa's Waltz" with an Indian twist. Lately, as I've been writing much more formally—with end rhyme, a tenuous dance with meter, and explicit form—I've discovered that in writing toward that end rhyme, that accented or unaccented syllable, or that stanza break, I am constantly surprising myself with new ideas, new vocabulary, and new ways of looking at the world. The conscious use of form seems to have freed my subconscious.

DT: That's exactly how I feel about using form—that it has the power to free the subconscious. I've actually thought about Roethke's poem when reading your work. For me, too, it was one of the poems that startled me into poetry early on. It's an interesting poem to teach because of the range of reaction to it. Some—those who focus on the waltz and the horseplay—feel the tone to be much lighter. Others—those who concentrate more on the whiskey on his breath, the way the child "hung on like death," and the ear scraping a buckle—feel that it's much darker. I think that the tug of the two different tones creates the true charge in the poem.

SA: I think the poem is incredibly sad and violent, and its sadness and violence is underscored by its gentle rhymes and rhythms. It's Mother Goose on acid, maybe. I think that its gentle music is a form of denial about the terror contained in the poem, or maybe it's the way kids think, huh? My dad wasn't violent, but he would leave us to go drinking, and would sometimes be gone for a few weeks. He was completely undependable and unpredictable. My wife's father was a scary and unpredictable alcoholic, charming and funny one moment, violent and caustic the next. So Roethke's poem, I think, is all about the unpredictability of the alcoholic father.

**DT:** I find the way the personal fuses with the political a very evocative element in your work. The love poem, for instance, is often simultaneously a political poem. Sometimes this is suggestive, but other times it is quite direct, even in the very title—as in "Seven Love Songs Which Include the Collected History of the United States of America." Could you discuss this fusion and how it evolved in your work?

**SA:** I've stated in other places that Indians are politicized from birth. I was five or six years old, standing in line to get free government food on the reservation, when I had my first political thought: "Hey, I'm in this line because I'm an Indian!" Of course, I was having a great time in that line with my very funny and highly verbose siblings and parents. I would guess my family, pound for pound, is one of the funniest in the world! So I was taught to fuse the political and the artistic, the poem and the punchline. It seems to me it is just as much nature as nurture. In terms of love, I was involved in a longterm love affair with a white woman, and our races and our political positions were always a subject of discussion and dissent. I am never, not even in my most intimate moments, completely free of my tribe.

**DT:** The poet Michael S. Harper (with whom I studied years ago) has a book entitled, *History Is Your Own Heartbeat.* I've always been particularly interested in exploring history in a poem, but doing so via a very personal current. Was it a conscious choice for you—to take on all that history in your work, or did it just slowly become your subject matter? What writers influenced you, in the way the personal and the historical mesh?

**SA:** Generally speaking, I think Indians have a much longer memory than white Americans. Or perhaps we Indians hold more passionate grudges! But I think my work has been more autobiographical than historical. So maybe I've been a personal historian. A poet-memoirist. In the link between personal and world history, I think other Native American poets have influenced me most—Simon Ortiz, Adrian C. Louis, Joy Harjo, Leslie Silko, just to name a few, who are constantly aware of history. In Ortiz's book-length poem, *From Sand Creek,* he weaves his personal history with the history of genocide in the U.S., and creates a stunning brand of confessional poetry. Simon seems to be confessing in a royal voice, with a tribal "we" and not a narcissistic "I." I hope that's what I'm doing with my poems.

**DT:** I've been thinking as we talk that perhaps the reason you're drawn to form in poetry might have something to do with your attraction to repetition and re-frains. Many of your poems employ a kind of elliptical repetition. In your chap-book, *Water Flowing Home*, for instance, I feel the poem "This Woman Speaks" has an elliptical quality:

> This woman speaks, this
> woman, who loves me, speaks
>
> to another woman, her
> mother, this daughter
>
> speaks to her mother . . .

Could you comment on your use of repetition and the cultural aspects of this?
**SA:** In my tribe, and in the Native American world, in general, repetition is sacred. All of our songs go on for hours, "This Indian will be coming around the moun-tain when he comes, when he comes, when he comes . . ." So I think repetition ap-peals to me on that level, and it also appeals to me on a simple musical level. I want my poems to sound like tribal songs, and with repetition, I can sometimes make English sound like Salish. I also think that in terms of spirituality and prayer repetition can sound a note of desperation. Think of Hopkins, "Pitched past pain . . ." God can feel so far away. So we sinful slobs have to keep screaming until God pays attention.

**DT:** When I heard you read in New Mexico, I was struck by the performative as-pect. I know you've been involved in a number of poetry slams and have held the title of Heavyweight Poetry Champion (or something like that). Do you think of a poem as something meant to be performed, and what are the different ways you've developed to make a poem come alive in the air?
**SA:** Storytellers were telling stories long before they had the means to record them or write them down, so I think performance is primal. I know it feels primal to me. When I'm really doing well on stage, I feel almost as crazy and wonderful as I do when I'm writing the stuff. As a storyteller, I also feel a responsibility to my audience. I want them to feel as strongly about the work as I do. I want them to know how much I both love and hate it. If a poem is funny, I want to hear the laughter. If it's sad, I want to hear the tears.

**DT:** How did your "stand-up" readings develop? Was it something you always did, or did it develop as a kind of backlash to the often dry humorless readings that can be a part of the literary world? Would you consider yourself an extrovert? Or do you just don that persona when you are performing?

**SA:** Most of the readings I've been to are so damn boring! We've got a lot of competition out there in the world. I have to be at least as good as Eminem or I'm dead! In my personal life, I'm an introvert. I spend most of my time alone, with my thoughts for company, and much prefer a book and a bathtub to any gathering of messy human beings. As a public performer, I "act." It's a strange thing. I become a slightly larger and more exaggerated version of myself.

**DT:** I hear a great deal of humor in your fiction and drama (and in your performances), but it's often more subtle in your poetry. How do you feel about humor in poetry, in general?

**SA:** I think my poems are very funny, but readers are not trained to laugh at poems. And I think funny poems are seriously devalued in the poetry world. I'd love to edit an anthology of humorous poems that are serious and great by any standard. I'd call it "Funny Poems." I think Auden is hilarious. I think Lucille Clifton is very funny. And Frost is to my mind an incredibly bitter Bob Newhart.

**DT:** There are many references to the dream world in your work, even when it's not explicitly a dream being explored. "Dead Letter Office," for instance, begins with a very believable occurrence—receiving a letter written in your native tongue that needs translating—but as the poem goes on, the experience feels increasingly surreal, and you traipse after the translator, "Big Mom" for years, "holding some brief letter from the past." I chose that poem as an example because it's not directly about a dream, and yet it feels decidedly like one.

**SA:** I was hydrocephalic at birth, had serious brain surgery at six months of age, and had epileptic seizures and was on serious sedatives until age seven, so I certainly have a more scarred and ragged brain than most. I don't know how to speak of it medically, but I'm sure my brain damage gives me all sorts of visions! I've always been nightmare-prone and insomniac, so sleep and the lack of sleep, and dreams and nightmares have always been my primary obsession. I was taking phenobarbital before I went to kindergarten, so I was probably destined to be a poet, enit?

# A World of Story-Smoke:
# A Conversation with Sherman Alexie

Åse Nygren/2004

This interview first appeared in *MELUS: Journal of the Society for the Study of the MultiEthnic Literature of the United States* 30.4 (Winter 2005): 149–69, and is reprinted by permission of the journal. The interview was conducted by Åse Nygren in Alexie's office and home in Seattle in September 2004.

Songwriter, filmmaker, comedian, and writer of prose and poetry, Sherman Alexie grew up on the Spokane Indian Reservation in Wellpinit, Washington, about fifty miles northwest of Spokane. The reservation (approximately 1,100 Spokane Tribal members live there), where the effects of what Alexie chooses to call an "on-going colonialism" still assert its painful presence, is central in Alexie's fiction, *The Lone Ranger and Tonto Fistfight in Heaven* (1993) and *Reservation Blues* (1995). Presented as a demarcated space of suffering, Alexie's fictional reservation is a place where his characters are tormented by collective memories of a genocidal past, of cavalry-approved hangings, massacres, and smallpox-infected blankets. It is a haunted place where "faint voices . . . echo[] all over" (*Reservation Blues* 46) and where "dreams . . . [a]re murdered . . . the bones buried quickly just inches below the surface, all waiting to break through the foundations of those government houses built by the Department of Housing and Urban Development" (*Reservation Blues* 7). Although some of Alexie's characters leave the reservation and enter the urban space in his second novel, *Indian Killer* (1996), the experience of growing up, as Alexie puts it in the interview, "firmly within borders," continues to affect the characters' lives, especially their emotional lives.

Inevitably when dealing with ethnic literature, it is impossible not to be self-conscious of one's own position. As a European white female scholar, I felt compelled to raise questions of perspective, including those of nationality, ethnicity, and gender. Within this context of self-reflection, the interview touches upon issues such as the desire for a "pure" or authentic American Indian identity and the critical demand for the genre "American Indian literature."

One of the most intriguing aspects of Alexie's fiction is his use of the comic. Although the subject matters in Alexie's fiction are morally and ethically engaging, the same texts are often ironic, satiric, and full of humor. As the characters in a caricature-like manner stagger across the reservation, between drinking the next beer and cracking the next joke, the reader is often invited to laugh along with them, even at them. Alexie's artistic vision thus mixes humor and suffering in a manner that for me resembles what Roberto Benigni does in his film *Life Is Beautiful* or Art Spiegelman in his graphic novels, *Maus: A Survivor's Tale*. Such a comparison becomes all the more justified in the light of one of Alexie's most provocative comments in the interview, his parallel between the Indian and the Jewish Holocausts.

Alexie's texts can be considered trauma narratives, and the interview explores his views on trauma and the thematization of suffering. Although trauma does silence, and suffering does exist without expression in language and without metaphysics, the moment pain is transformed into suffering, it is also transferred into language. This enables the traumatized person to remember, work through, and mourn the lost object. Given the inarticulateness of many of Alexie's characters, I also suggest that Alexie's narratives call attention to the inherent difficulties of representing suffering. The characters are muted by the traumas of hatred and chaos, loss and grief, danger and fear, and cannot—except in a few rare cases— articulate their suffering. Instead, they tend to resort to self-destructive behavior, including violence and substance abuse. Thus, while Alexie's narratives demonstrate the need to give suffering a language, they also call attention to the inherent unsharability of suffering. In the interview with Alexie, I was particularly interested in his views on trauma and his thematization of suffering.

While in Alexie's early fiction, the reservation is a geographical space of borders and confinement, in his more recent fiction, *The Toughest Indian in the World* (2000) and *Ten Little Indians* (2003), the reservation changes its ontology and becomes a mental and emotional territory. In the interview below, Alexie says that this ontological change is a result of his own "expanded world-view." During the course of his writing career, Alexie explains, he has moved from what he calls a "fundamental" world-view which earlier made him "so focused on Indian identity that [he] didn't look at the details," to what he hopes will be "the triumph of the ordinary." His writing has thus shifted in emphasis from angry protests to evocations of love and empathy.

**Åse Nygren:** What are some of the inspirations and motivations behind your writing? Are they autobiographical, political, or historical?
**Sherman Alexie:** Like we were saying just before we turned the tape on, people in Scandinavia don't really know about Indian writers or know that there even are

Indian writers. I didn't know either. Even though I was growing up on a reservation, and going to reservation schools, I had never really been shown Indian literature before. So it wasn't even a possibility growing up. I loved reading but I
hadn't thought of a career as a writer. I hadn't thought about books as a career
in any form. I took a class in creative writing because I couldn't handle human
anatomy lab and it was the only class that fit my schedule. This was the first time
anyone had shown me contemporary poetry. The most contemporary poem I had
read before was "The Waste Land." I had no idea you could write about NOW. I
read Allen Ginsberg's "Howl" for the first time. Even Langston Hughes felt new to
me. And I fell in love with it immediately. Over night, I knew I was going to be a
writer.

**ÅN:** Were there any Indian writers on the reading list for the poetry class you
took?
**SA:** The poetry teacher gave me a book called *Songs from This Earth on Turtle's
Back*, an anthology on Native literature by Joseph Bruchac. Before I read that
book I had no idea that you could write about Indian life with powwows, ceremonies, broken down cars, cheap motels; all this stuff that was my life as I was growing up on the reservation. I remember in particular one line by Adrian Louis, a
Paiute poet: "Adrian, I'm in the reservation of my mind!" It captured for me the
way I felt about myself, at least then. It was nothing I'd ever had before. I thought
to myself: I want to write like this! So that's where it began. The beginning was
accidental. But I got very serious about it quickly. I went through the college library looking at poetry journals trying to figure out what was going on in the
world, trying to catch up, essentially, for a lifetime of not reading.

**ÅN:** Did you read all different kinds of poetry, or did you focus on works by
American Indians?
**SA:** Any poetry. Anything and everything. I pulled books off the shelves randomly because I liked the title, or the cover, or the author photo. I read hundreds
of poems over a year or so to catch up. As I sat there in the poetry stacks in the
library a whole new world opened to me. Before, I had always thought that I was
a freak in the way I saw and felt about the world. As I started reading the works of
all these poets I realized that I, at least, wasn't the only freak! [Laughs] I think we
belong to a lot of tribes; culturally, ethnically, and racially. I'm a poet and this is
the world in which I belong.

**ÅN:** So your ambitions and motivations weren't political to begin with?
**SA:** No. My writing was very personal and autobiographical. I was simply finding

out who I was and who I wanted to be. As I started writing, I became more political, much because of people's reactions to me. I was writing against so many ideas of what I was supposed to be writing. So even though much of my early work deals with alcohol and alcoholism because of personal experiences, I got a lot of criticism because alcoholism is such a loaded topic for Indians. People thought I was writing about stereotypes, but more than anything I was writing about my own life. As an Indian, you don't have the luxury of being called an autobiographical writer often. You end up writing for the whole race. At the beginning of my career I was twenty-one years old, and I didn't have any defense against that. So I became political because people viewed me politically. I got political to fight people's ideas about me. It is only in the last few years that my politics has found a way into my work that feels natural. Part of the reason is because you grow older. The way I think about it is that I used to spend more time looking inside myself, looking internally. Now I look at more of the world and a wider range of people.

**ÅN:** Ethnic literatures have a powerful social role in shaping ethnic identity and in making ethnic groups visible, thus filling an important political function. With the rise of ethnic literatures, there has been in criticism a tendency to link literature written by writers of a certain ethnic descent with a specific group of people, and thus with a specific ethnic experience. Is this a classification that you are comfortable with?
**SA:** I think it's lazy scholarship. For instance, Gerald Vizenor and I have nothing in common in terms of what we write about, how we write, and how we look at the world. There'd be no reason to link us other than our ethnicity. He has much more in common with experimental writing, like William Gass's *In the Heart of the Heart of the Country*.

I guess the problem is not that I'm labeled as a Native American writer, but that writers like John Updike and Jonathan Franzen aren't labeled as White American writers. They are simply assumed to be the norm, and everybody else is judged in reaction to them.

**ÅN:** But even though the term "Indian" is a limitation in some ways, couldn't it work as a door opener in other ways?
**SA:** Yes, it is good in some ways. The good thing is that there are so few of us that I'm automatically exotic. It makes me different automatically. We live in a capitalistic society and it's all about competition. In the world of writing, I have an edge because I'm an Indian. If I was a white guy writer, I'd be just another white guy writer.

**ÅN:** Do you think that these labels—African American literature, American Indian literature etc.—are useful in promoting a specific group of writers?

**SA:** Economically, I think this type of labeling helps because it focuses the market. But in terms of criticism I don't think it does. Such labels are often used by critics to diminish the works, or by supporters to promote it. There are people who love Native literature, for instance, just because Indians write it. They don't really view it critically. On the other hand, some critics think that we have careers or success just because of our ethnicity. You end up being pushed by two sides: Loved only because you're an Indian, or hated because you're an Indian!

**ÅN:** In discussions on American Indian literature, some critics claim that one of the characteristic features of American Indian literature is often a certain dose of sentimentality. What critics mean by this is that references to the Indian beliefs and spirituality—the four directions, Father Sky, Mother Earth, corn pollen, etc.—are somehow always already charged with sentimentality. In your fiction, you seem to refuse this sentimentality through various means, for example, through your use of irony. I would like to hear your reaction to such a categorizing of American Indian literature and how you work against it in your fiction.

**SA:** I'm not sure if sentimentality is the right word. But I would agree that there is a lot of nostalgia. Like any colonized people, Indians look to the precolonial times as being better just because we weren't colonized. There is a certain tendency there of nostalgia as a disease. Because our identity has been so fractured, and because we've been subject to so much oppression and relocation—our tribes dissipated, many destroyed—the concept of a pure Indian identity is really strong in Indian literature. For instance, very few of the top thirty or forty Native writers publishing now grew up on the reservation, and yet most Native literature is about the reservation. So there is a nostalgia for purity: a time when we were all together and when our identity was sure, and when our lives were better.

**ÅN:** It's an understandable nostalgia in one sense.

**SA:** Yes. And there is great writing coming out of that nostalgia. I would say that bad Native writing is sentimental, and there is plenty of it. But writers like Scott Momaday, James Welch, and Simon Ortiz are not sentimental.

**ÅN:** In an interview by Swiss scholar Hartwig Isernhagen, American Indian writers Gerald Vizenor and Scott Momaday, and First Nations writer Jeanette Armstrong were all asked the question, "How do you address the question of violence in your works?" Is there, in your opinion, a central narration of violence in Indian literature?

**SA:** Well, yes, I think so. After all, we come out of genocide, and our entire history is filled with murder and war. Perhaps violence is not the right word, though. But there is definitely a lot of humiliation in Native literature. We write about being humiliated a lot. And that takes physical forms, emotional forms, and mental forms. I think Native literature is the literature of humiliation and shame.

**ÅN:** How important is tribal specificity to your own writing? Is it the Spokane Tribe or a more generic concept of "Indianness" that is of interest to you?
**SA:** To me, there are a few things going on. I'm very aware of my Spokaneness. I grew up on the Spokane Indian reservation, and my tribe heavily influences my personality and the ways in which I see the world. But there is also a strong Northwest identity. Because we spend so much time interacting now, I think Indian identity is more regional than it is tribal. Navajos and Apaches are going to have a lot more in common with each other than they would have with the Spokane. I strongly identify with salmon people, and so I get along with the tribes on this side. The way in which they talk and act feels close to home.

**ÅN:** One important concern among American Indian writers has been the question of how one deals with a painful past, such as the one shared by the Indian peoples of the United States, without falling into the trap of victimization. How important is this issue for you when you write your fiction?
**SA:** I write autobiographically, so when you talk about surviving pain and trauma and getting out of it—I did, I have! But the people I know have not. So what do I do in my literature? Do I portray the Indian world as I see it? And I do see it as doomed, and that you have to get lucky to escape that. Should I write the literature of hope no matter how I feel? No! I'm not hopeful. So how do you avoid victimization? We can't. We are victims.

**ÅN:** Vizenor is very adamant when it comes to this question. I spoke with him in 2002 and what he seems to want to avoid more than anything else is victimization, something which is reflected in terms that he uses in his literature, like, for instance, "survivance."
**SA:** Survival is a low hope. I don't want just survival, or "survivance." I want triumph! But you don't get it. That's the thing. You don't get it. Also, our story is not worse than anybody else's.

**ÅN:** How do you mean?
**SA:** Pain is relative. For instance, in the last movie I made I worked with a woman who grew up very wealthy, very privileged economically, but she had lived through such hell in her family that it made my life seem sweet and gentle. So

I try not to measure people's pain. I mean, if I'd throw a rock randomly right now I'd hit someone whose life is worse than mine ever was. Nothing in my life can measure up to the kids in that school [in Beslan]. Nothing! Nothing! And nothing in my life can measure up to losing somebody in the World Trade towers. Everybody's pain is important.

**ÅN:** I find the concept of "collective trauma" particularly useful concerning the suffering that many of your characters are experiencing. Many of them suffer from not only personal losses and grievances—absent fathers, poverty, unemployment, alcoholism, etc.—but also from a cultural loss and a collective trauma, which include experiences of racism and stereotyping. Their losses and grievances affect their behavior and their lives on many levels. In my view, your fiction explores how such trauma both damages and creates community and identity alike. Both identity and community are, of course, condemned to ongoing dysfunction. Do you think that suffering is part of what constitutes Indianness? Perhaps in a somewhat comparable way by which we have come to associate African American identity with slavery, or Jewish identity with the Holocaust? If so, how does this relation differ from, e.g., the relation between African Americans and suffering, or Jews and suffering?

**SA:** Yes! The phrase I've also used is "blood memory." I think the strongest parallel in my mind has always been the Jewish people and the Holocaust. Certainly, their oppression has been constant for 1,900 years longer, but the fact is that you cannot separate our identity from our pain. At some point it becomes primarily our identity. The whole idea of authenticity—"How Indian are you?"—is the most direct result of the fact that we don't know what an American Indian identity is. There is no measure anymore. There is no way of knowing, except perhaps through our pain. And so, we're lost. We're always wandering.

**ÅN:** Like the lost tribes of Israel?

**SA:** Yes. It's so amazing that the indigenous people of the United States have become the most immigrant group. The process is slowly changing. My generation and the next generation—we are immigrants! I am an immigrant into the United States, and now my children are fully assimilated.

**ÅN:** A scholar by the name of Kai Erikson has put a social dimension into the term "trauma." He talks about "traumatized communities" in the sense of damages to the tissues that hold human groups together as well as to the dominant spirit of a group, which is a fitting concept when we talk about "collective trauma" or "blood memory."

**SA:** Yes it is. Some day they're going to find it, but I feel that it is true that pain is carried in the DNA. And because it is carried in the DNA, pain can mutate through generations. One of the most obvious proofs for that is child abuse. Kids who get abused so often grow up and become abusers.

**ÅN:** Many of your characters—Victor and Junior in *The Lone Ranger* and *Reservation Blues*, John Smith in *Indian Killer*, Harlan in *Ten Little Indians*, to mention a few—are struggling with their experiences of what it means to be an Indian, and what they are told it means to be an Indian. At times, they seem at a loss as to what Indian identity really IS. Is their struggle linked with the fact that Indian identity has often been reduced to stereotype? In other words, do you think that the long-term reduction of the Indian to stereotype in American culture has resulted in a collective crisis of identity for many Indians today?

**SA:** Yes, certainly, because you can never measure up to a stereotype. You can never be as strong as a stereotypical warrior, as godly as a stereotypical shaman, or as drunk as a drunken Indian. You can never measure up to extremes. So you're always going to feel less than the image, whether it's positive or negative. One of the real dangers is that other Indians have taken many stereotypes as a reality, as a way to measure each other and ourselves. Take Harlan Atwater, for instance. Because he was adopted out, and because he grew up this way or that way, he would be viewed by other Indians as not being Indian. White people wouldn't see him as Indian and now Indians don't see him as Indian. Indians have accepted stereotypes just as much as non-Indians have. We believe them too. I think that many Indians have watched too much television! [Laughs]

**ÅN:** In a sense, of course, the search for identity is endemic for everyone, isn't it? Aren't we all searching for a sense of belonging?

**SA:** Yes, I guess that's a good way to put it. The search for identity is not special.

**ÅN:** But for Indians, that search has been complicated by, for instance, the stereotype?

**SA:** Well, we have no economic, political, or social power. We have no power to change our lives. We are powerless.

**ÅN:** Is that one of the reasons why, although images of Jews and Blacks displaying exaggerated ethnic features—such as big noses and lips—have been forbidden in the U.S. decades ago, racist images of Indians continue to flourish? The image of the Indian mascot is only one example here. Does the answer lie in what you have just touched upon, that Indians are powerlessness?

**SA:** Yes. We have no power to change the stereotypes. We have no allies. No other group is joining with us to fight those things. The romantic idea is that if people are feeling a lot of pain you'd wish that people would empathize more. I wish that was true.

**ÅN:** Of course feminism as a movement encounters similar problems.
**SA:** Yes. It's the whole idea of the human range of empathy. Honestly, I think that people who can't empathize with the mascot or with feminism, for instance, are not so far removed from a criminal. The inability to understand why something might be offensive is a form of sociopathy.

**ÅN:** Although the subject matters in your texts are morally and ethically engaging, the same texts are often ironic, satiric, and full of humor. I read your ironic and satiric re-thinking, even de-familiarization, of a painful past, in alignment with writer Art Spiegelman and filmmaker Roberto Benigni. Spiegelman's two books in cartoon form, entitled *Maus: A Survivor's Tale I and II*, and Benigni's film *Life Is Beautiful* both deal with the Jewish Holocaust in the comic mode, and have, consequently, shocked readers/viewers out of any lingering sense of familiarity with the historic events described. Would you like your books to have a similar effect on your readers? What are some of the gains? Dangers?
**SA:** Well, I'm a big fan of graphic novels. I like their immediacy. Automatically when you look at a graphic novel, or when you look at a cartoon, there is always an ironical, satirical edge and an underlying humor. So yes, I aim to be funny, and I aim for my humor to be very political. But I think more along the lines of political stand-up comedians like Richard Pryor and Lenny Bruce than I do about other writers.

**ÅN:** What might be some of the gains and dangers?
**SA:** Dangers? Playing to the audience. Reacting completely to the audience rather than generating it from yourself, so that you're reflexive and you're performing rather than dealing with something on an emotional level. I think I have a tendency in my work to lapse into performance mode. Rather than something out of my heart, it ends up being something on the surface designed for effect. One of the great things is that through that immediacy of performance and humor you can reach people who otherwise might not be listening. I think being funny breaks down barriers between people. I can get up in front of any crowd, and if I make them laugh first, I can say almost anything to them.

**ÅN:** In "The Search Engine" (from *Ten Little Indians*), the Indian student Corliss is reading a book by (the somewhat amateurish) Indian writer Harlan Atwater. You write that "Harlan Atwater was making fun of being Indian, of the essential sadness of being Indian, and so maybe he was saying Indians aren't sad at all" (7). In "The Approximate Size of my Favorite Tumor" (from *The Lone Ranger and Tonto Fistfight in Heaven*), we can read about the Indian man who is dying of cancer, but who still manages to joke about his situation: "Still, you have to realize that laughter saved Norma and me from pain, too. Humor was an antiseptic that cleaned the deepest of personal wounds" (164). My third example is taken from your novel *Indian Killer*, where you write that among Indians "laughter [is] a ceremony used to drive away personal and collective demons" (21). What is the function of humor, then? Do you mean to suggest that humor can be transformative and liberating?

SA: [Laughs] When I write it, I believe it! I don't know if it works in real life. Making fun of things or being satirical doesn't make me feel better about things. It's a tool that enables me to talk about anything. I don't know if it necessarily changes things, or changes anybody who is listening to me. It makes dialogue possible, but I don't think it makes change possible.

ÅN: Are you ever afraid that the comical element will subvert attention from the gravitas of your writing?

SA: Yes, it happens all the time. People assume that you're not being serious because you're being funny. By and large I figure that people who say those sort of things aren't funny. And being funny is just how I am. I can't just stop . . . [Laughs]. But it's also a personal defense, of course. When I don't want to talk about something, or when I'm uncomfortable. It's not all good, humor, but it's always serious.

ÅN: Your parodic intertextuality and ironic re-thinking of historic events are commonly seen as markers of postmodernity. What do you think the term "postmodernism" promises, or does not promise, with respect to your fiction? Can we understand your works of fiction better by aligning them with postmodernist ideas?

SA: Again, it's a generic label. I don't think the term "postmodernism" says anything more about my work than the term "Native American" does. It's just a label. My idea of postmodern will always be the language poets or Andy Warhol—that sort of more intellectual and less emotional work. That's how I look upon postmodernism, as more of an intellectual enterprise. And that's not me.

ÅN: Alternate responses to a loss of the past and of a communal feeling among your characters are *repeating* or *re-membering*, in Toni Morrison's idea of the latter. This is particularly true about your first three works of fiction—*The Lone*

*Ranger, Reservation Blues,* and *Indian Killer.* While re-membering is a painful process, which brings back personal and collective horrors, it may also have
a healing and freeing effect once memory is properly re-visited and worked-
through. The character of Thomas Builds-the-Fire is actively, almost obsessively,
re-membering a painful past, and is described as "the self-proclaimed storyteller of the Spokane tribe": "Thomas repeated stories constantly. All the other
Indians on the reservation heard those stories so often that the words crept into
dreams. . . . Thomas Builds-the-Fire's stories climbed into your clothes like sand,
gave you itches that could not be scratched. If you repeated even a sentence from
one of those stories, your throat was never the same again. Those stories hung
in your clothes and hair like smoke, and no amount of laundry soap or sham-
poo washed them out. Victor and Junior often tried to beat those stories out of
Thomas, tied him down and taped his mouth shut. . . . But none of that stopped
Thomas, who talked and talked." Have you taken on a similar role of a storyteller?
If so, for whom are you telling, and re-telling, your stories?
**SA:** [Laughs] Do you mean I'm irritating? Well, demographically speaking, most
of the fiction in this country is bought by middle class, college-educated white
women. So that's who I'm writing for. That's who's getting my stories in their hair
like smoke. If you go to my readings, that's who's there. At the beginning I had
ambitions about a specific audience, but now I write for pretty much everybody. I
want everybody! And I'm not waiting for people to come to my stories, I'm going
to them. I want the whole world to smell like story-smoke, my story-smoke! So
in that sense I'm like Thomas. Thomas is really obsessed about making sure that
people hear him, but his world-view is tiny in terms of his audience. My world-
view was small in the beginning, too. Now, it has expanded.

**ÅN:** According to some, man is a fiction-making animal, one that is defined by
fantasies and fiction. Peter Brooks, for instance, sees the narrative impulse as an
attempt to cope with the human facts of our existence in the body and in time,
that is, with death. Silence, as equivalent to death, is what must be avoided in
order to "remain in the world." I am curious to hear some of your thoughts on
such existential claims as to the function of literature.
**SA:** That's a very serious way to put it, I guess. I think what that definition is
missing is the element of play. Even animals play, even animals create fiction.
Narrative is play and we all practice that. I think that's more of what it is.

**ÅN:** That's a postmodern idea, narrative as play.
**SA:** Is it? Well, I guess I am a postmodern writer then. [Laughs] But the play

could be very serious. The thing is: I love telling stories. I'm not in agony when I'm telling stories. I'm not serious. Most of the time I'm pretty excited!

**ÅN:** I suppose that Brooks's theorizing on the narrative drive doesn't exclude the question of play. What he is talking about is that narrative drive we have, the desire to create plots out of our lives.
**SA:** Well, yes. I would agree with him on that. When I'm really in the groove, everything disappears. The whole world just fades away and it's just me and the story. I do know that that's when I feel closest to God, whatever God is. That's when I feel like I'm praying. I never feel spiritual anywhere, except in the presence of my own stories.

**ÅN:** In trauma literature, the storytelling impulse is generally seen as an attempt not only to work-through a painful past but also a necessary means to break through the silence imposed by trauma. In my own work, I conceive of silent suffering as the endurance of pain over time, while complaint, or conscious suffering, should be understood as the beginning of narrative. If attended to by another's anticipation and empathy, the silence imposed by trauma can be broken through. In your view, could an imaginary reader—any reader that the writer has in mind when writing his/her text—fulfill the function of a "witness" who attends emphatically to the text's complaint (through an act of engagement and remembering)?
**SA:** The ideal reader would do that. But as the reader takes the story or witnesses it, doesn't he or she use it to witness their own lives? I don't think the readers jump across the text to the author very much, except in a very generic way. An ideal reader would, but real readers don't. I wish I had an ideal reader!

**ÅN:** Do you have an ideal reader in mind when you write?
**SA:** I gave up predicting what readers will do, or wanting a certain reaction. It's just impossible to know. That's a serious control issue if you think you know what your readers are going to do. I like to think of myself as the ideal reader. Not necessarily of any individual texts, but I love everything, and I approach everything with excitement and love. I'm a reading addict. I love books, comics, magazines—everything! So I guess an ideal reader for me would be less about a specific reaction to the work than a way in which they approach it. I just want passion!

**ÅN:** In my own work, I contend that traumatic inarticulateness is typically accompanied by an inherent need to break the silence imposed on the traumatized victim. The silence of trauma, I argue, is broken out of necessity, since a trauma unrelieved will typically lead to neurosis or pathology, i.e., illness or violence.

To witness, or to endure such suffering, would be deeply disturbing to say the least. Would you say that your characters in this sense simply suffer their pain in time? Or do some of them transform their pain into suffering? Does your fiction, in a sense, give them the right to suffer? Does it assign their suffering an ethical (metaphysical) value?

SA: Oh, God. Huge question!

ÅN: Because in your first three works of fiction in particular, there is a lot of suffering . . .

SA: Oh, yes. It's terrible! I myself as a person have gotten out of that, and my characters have gotten out of it in a way. I was suffering with the characters earlier when I was writing. What they felt, I felt. Because the work was so auto-biographical, it was like reliving it again. In a therapeutic sense, I guess you could say that. That also happens in therapy. You talk about it, you say it!

ÅN: Like Freud's idea of the "talking cure"?

SA: Yes. I've done play-acting, reenacting, taking the voices of all the people. . . . The thing is, that when you're in therapy doing this crap you do the exact same crap you do as a writer. So I don't know that it helps writers. Because the thing that fucked you up in the first place is what you're doing again. As for the characters—I make them suffer! I specifically designed them to be suffering. John Smith, for instance, there's no redemption there; there's no healing, there's no talking cure. For a lot of the characters there's no cure. All there is, is suffering. The whole point of their identity is suffering. What keeps coming back to me is that when I think about Indians all I think about is suffering. My first measure on any Indian is pain.

ÅN: In an earlier interview, you have stated that if there is one thing you would like to achieve as a writer it would be to contribute to the building of an American Indian Holocaust museum. In the poem, "The Game Between the Jews and the Indians Is Tied Going into the Bottom of the Ninth Inning," you draw a par-allel between the experience of the Jewish people and the Indians: "So, now, when you touch me / my skin, will you think / of Sand Creek, Wounded Knee? / And what will I remember / when your skin is next to mine / Auschwitz, Buchen-wald?" And in the poem, "Inside Dachau," you also draw a parallel between the Jewish Holocaust and the centuries of colonization that Indians in the present day U.S. have been subjected to: "We are the sons / and daughters of the walk-ing dead. We have lost everyone. / What do we indigenous people want from our country? / We stand over mass graves. Our collective grief makes us numb. / We

are waiting for the construction of our museum." In your opinion, is the term "holocaust" applicable when describing the effects of five centuries of colonization on the Indian peoples of what is today the U.S.? Are genocides comparable?
SA: Yes, I think genocides are comparable. The difference is that this country did what they planned to do. Hitler didn't get to finish it. He didn't get to accomplish it.

ÅN: What about the risk of de-historicizing unique experiences of oppression, then? There are, for instance, varying views in academia as to whether you can use the term "holocaust" or not, with regards to other events than the Jewish Holocaust, which is considered a unique event by many. Demographer Russell Thornton does, however, refer to what happened in this country as "The American Indian Holocaust."
SA: I call it that. It's a political move to call it that. It's rebellious. I'm sure it could be interpreted as anti-Semitic in a way of claiming ownership of somebody else's word. But I call it that to draw direct parallels in a way that people don't want to. People outside of this country will tend to view what happened here as genocide. But you will not get people to admit that here. It's a very exclusivist view. People will not even own to the fact that they live in a colony. That it's still a colony. They won't even accept that term, let alone the idea of genocide. So it's very much a political move on my part to call it a Holocaust. I realize the term was generated to mean something specific, but I want it to mean more. They had the same ambitions, and the end result is the same. So yes, I want what happened here to receive the same sort of sacred respect that what happened in Germany does. I want our dead to be honored.

ÅN: Are genocides comparable?
SA: It's not necessarily a comparison. I'm not measuring the size. One death is too many. But I think other people measure the value of lives differently. Some deaths are more important. And I think they're all important. I want them all to be acknowledged. I think we end up measuring them by their success rate rather than the philosophy that started it. We talk about the genocide itself rather than the genocidal impulse. And it's easy to become a Nazi.

ÅN: The focus and mood has slightly shifted in your two latest books, *The Toughest Indian in the World* and *Ten Little Indians*. Rather than exploring the terrain of reservation life where anger times imagination is the ascribed method for survival, your characters have entered the urban scene where they continually negotiate between their Indian identity, their "American" identity (whatever that is), and other identities based on, for example, sexuality, class, and generation. While many of your characters in your earlier works seem to be denied subjectivity, or character, and have been assigned, as it were, to such mental reservations as stereotypes, it seems that your "new" characters are beginning to claim, and attain, subjectivity. In that capacity, many of them seem to be exploring the inner and intimate landscape of love—searching for love, holding on to love, falling in love, failing love, etc. There are portraits of loving fathers and husbands, ethnically mixed marriages, one of them lesbian, where your characters "lov[e] each other across the distance," and then there is, of course, Seymour who goes on a nonviolent killing spree in search of love. You have said that when you read the line "I'm in the reservation of my mind" from a poem by Paiute poet Adrian Louis you knew that you wanted to be a writer. How would you say that Louis's concept of "the reservation of my mind" relates to the characters I have referred to, let us call them love-seeking? Do your "new" characters so to speak alter how you relate to Louis's concept of a "mental reservation"?

**SA:** As an Indian the idea of the reservation is always there. You grow up firmly within borders. As you grow up as an Indian, you know mathematically for certain your ethnicity. I'm 13/16 Indian. Everything is assigned and valued and placed. When I was born, I had a social security number and a tribal identification number. So I think my new characters carry that idea of borders into their love lives and into their new lives. Even if they can be successful, the idea of borders goes beyond their ethnicity and into their personal decisions, and they limit themselves in other ways. Love for me has always been political. It has always been informed by the reservation, and it still is. I guess some of my characters are trying to get away from that.

**ÅN:** Love is very much in focus in your two last books, *The Toughest Indian in the World* and *Ten Little Indians*.

**SA:** Yes. I've been married for ten years, more than a quarter of my life now. And the changes in my life have been dramatic. My house is 1,300 square feet. This [where we are sitting] is my floor. But I grew up poor! So to survive I had to assign a certain set of values for myself, when it came to measuring any emotion. I was so rigid that I had to set up a way of survival that was really mercenary, and narcissistic. My characters go through similar things. Once you get to a place where you have financial success or security, when you don't have to worry about the light bill or food, and you still have all those mercenary narcissistic feelings, what do you do? What do you do when survival is assured? Then it really gets complicated. Worrying about racism is easy! Easy! Dealing with racism is easy, compared with dealing with being in love.

**ÅN:** Love is tough. It's hard work.

**SA:** Yes, it is. And it's the stuff I go through, and that I see now. I couldn't see all this stuff before. I was fundamental. I was so focused on Indian identity I didn't look at the details. So having children, having friends, my life diversifying—all that has changed me. When you talk about love, part of what I write is simply fantasy fulfillment. Part of it is simply alternative worlds—taking an emotion and going somewhere with it. So back again to the play. I'm no longer a reservation Indian. I don't want to be extraordinary anymore, or exotic.

**ÅN:** Just ordinary?

**SA:** Yes, just ordinary. Low bar again. I want to be the triumph of the ordinary!

## Works Cited

Alexie, Sherman. *First Indian on the Moon.* New York: Hanging Loose, 1993.

———. *Indian Killer.* New York: Warner, 1996.

———. *The Lone Ranger and Tonto Fistfight in Heaven.* New York: Harper Perennial, 1994.

———. *Reservation Blues.* New York: Warner, 1995.

———. *The Summer of Black Widows.* New York: Hanging Loose, 1996.

———. *Ten Little Indians.* New York: Grove, 2003.

———. *The Toughest Indian in the World.* New York: Atlantic Monthly, 2000.

Brooks, Peter. "Freud's Masterplot: A Model for Narrative." *Reading for the Plot.* New York: Knopf, 1984. 90–112.

———. *Psychoanalysis and Storytelling.* Oxford: Blackwell, 1994.

Erikson, Kai. "Notes on Trauma and Community." *Trauma: Explorations in Memory.* Ed. Cathy Caruth. Baltimore MD: Johns Hopkins UP, 1995. 183–99.

LaCapra, Dominick. *Writing History, Writing Trauma.* Baltimore MD: Johns Hopkins UP, 2001.

*Life Is Beautiful.* Dir. Roberto Benigni. Miramax, 1998.

Spiegelman, Art. *Maus I: A Survivor's Tale: My Father Bleeds History.* London: Pantheon, 1986.

———. *Maus II: A Survivor's Tale: And Here My Troubles Began.* London: Pantheon, 1992.

Thornton, Russell. *American Indian Holocaust and Survival: A Population History Since 1492.* Norman: U of Oklahoma P, 1987.

# Reservation to Riches:
# A Conversation with Sherman Alexie

Lorena Allam/2006

"Reservation to Riches: A Conversation with Sherman Alexie," produced by Lorena Allam, first broadcast on ABC Radio National's *Awaye* program, 16 June 2006, is reproduced by permission of the Australian Broadcasting Corporation and ABC Online. © 2006 ABC. All rights reserved. Further program information on *Awaye* can be found at http://www.abc.net.au/rn/awaye/. The interviewer, Lorena Allam, is from the Gamilaroi and Yawalaraay peoples of northwest New South Wales. The original radio interview has been transcribed by Nancy Peterson.

**Sherman Alexie:** Hello my name is Sherman Alexie. I'm an American. I'm Spokane-Coeur d'Alene Indian. I grew up on the Spokane Indian Reservation in Washington state. I'm a writer, filmmaker, jet-lagged traveler.

**Lorena Allam:** Well, what made you decide to come all the way to Australia?
**SA:** Well, it's always a dream. Australia and New Zealand really figure large in the fantasy life of Americans. Ever since I was little, platypi and kangaroos and wallabies, all of that, really formed this dream place for me, so I've always wanted to come here because of that. And the Sydney Festival has been asking me for a number of years, but I didn't want to travel this far alone, so we waited until my youngest son, who's four now, was old enough to handle the trip.

**LA:** I'm interested that you say we figured prominently in your imagination because a lot of Americans come to Australia and they don't know a lot about us, and they certainly don't know a lot about aboriginal people. Did you know about us?
**SA:** Yeah, the politics, the similarities. We're very similar in terms of the percentage of the population we are, similar in the genocidal history, in the continuing political exclusion and oppression, and the infighting and all the pain and agony. So certainly all that I knew about, and then the magical, the wonderful nature of the culture as well—the positive aspects. I knew there were a lot of similarities. When I was little I remember there was this traveling group of Australian aboriginals who ended up on my reservation, and they sang songs and played the . . .

**LA:** Didgeridoo.

**SA:** You know it's a haunting instrument. I saw a guy playing it down on the wharf yesterday. So the culture, the politics—I knew that the life was similar for aboriginals here and aboriginals in the United States.

**LA:** There are a lot of aboriginal writers here especially who say you are a big influence of theirs. Were you aware of that, the reach of your work?

**SA:** I had no idea about that—this is a long ways away. I've met individual Australians, aboriginals, who have talked about their work, and I know the effect has been the same as it was for people in the United States, where I was writing about really ordinary lives. Most of the Native American writers in the United States are academics, college professors, who sort of write out of *that* worldview, and I'm a guy from the reservation, certainly not an academic. So I think that everyday way of writing really appealed to a lot of people in the United States, and so it doesn't surprise me that it happened here. It makes me happy.

**LA:** Well, one of the things about your writing is it's about Indian people's inner lives, their relationships with each other, their relationships to their history and their children, and all those things. It's not written for a non-Indian audience predominantly. Is that fair to say?

**SA:** Well, that ends up being who the audience is. I don't know about in Australia, but the audience for literary fiction in the United States is college-educated white women. That's who reads books, and that's the people most willing to read outside themselves. But I have a huge Native audience in a way that other Native writers don't because my subject matter is very pop culture oriented and sort of middle-class, lower-class based. So I think that's probably the appeal.

**LA:** But also don't you think your writing sounds like the people?

**SA:** I sound like us. I get that rez accent going, you can hear the accent sort of seeping through the pages. All of a sudden, everybody's going, "Yeah, I know that guy."

**LA:** And the way you describe how people live with this everyday trauma of people who drink, and violence, unhappiness, and all those things. But they are almost like a backdrop to their lives—it's so integrated into their lives. It's not victimhood that you're writing about.

**SA:** You get so used to it, you don't even notice. So it's more accepting, I guess. Eccentricity is more tolerated—you know, that's just Junior, that's just Arnold, that's just the way they are—and you don't notice as much I guess. The humor in the books is what really makes them sound and appeal more to Indians because we're funny. I guess on the base of great pain you have to be funny—the two funniest groups of people I've ever been around are Native Americans and Jewish folks, so I guess there's something inherently funny about genocide.

**LA:** It's true of us too. If you sit around with a group of black fellows we'll laugh—that's what we love to do—and we'll crack jokes about all kinds of things. What I think people love about your books is that those jokes are in your books, they're not just in our lives. Very few people are brave enough to kind of tell it like it is in that way.

**SA:** You get in trouble. Sure, when I do write like I do, I do get a lot of grief from other Native writers and Native academics and Native people that I'm airing dirty laundry or that I'm portraying us in negative ways or that I'm dealing in stereotypes. No, I'm not. The idea of the drunken Indian is not a stereotype—it's a damp reality. I just try to write what I see and what I know. Now I write about urban Indians mostly. Something like 70 percent of Native Americans live in urban areas, and the urban Native life has not been written about at all—very few books deal exclusively with an urban life—so that's where I'm focusing now.

**LA:** What are some of the labels that people try and pin on you—angry?
**SA:** Angry—a few years ago *Time* magazine reviewed one of my books and said I was "septic with my own unappeasable fury."

**LA:** That sounds like a medical condition!
**SA:** I know, it was amazing. So I went and got a t-shirt, and on the front it says "septic," and on the back it says, "with my own unappeasable fury." I love that one. You know I go to readings sometimes where people will raise their hands and ask questions like, "Do you hate white people?" How do you respond to that? "Well, not *all* of them."

Funny thing is I get the anger label, but I also get the funny label in a condescending way as in, "Oh, he's funny. He's not serious—he's funny." I get that clown thing, so I guess if you combine those things I'm an angry clown. That's my Indian name, actually. [Laughter.]

**LA:** There are recurring characters in your books—there's Thomas, and there's Victor and Junior, and so on. They are kind of family groups that recur a lot in your stories. Why do they keep coming back?
**SA:** Part of it is is the models I had in writing, like Louise Erdrich, whose characters reappear in her books over and over again—in the Native world like her, and then also William Faulkner, Sherwood Anderson. Some of my favorite books growing up were those books that contained characters who reappeared in the

writer's work over and over, so part of it is a literary history. But also part of it is tribal, in the sense that these are my people. And I have a natural instinct to "tribe up" in whatever I do. In literature I just feel more comfortable when writing about people I know, even though they're not real—I mean, I know they're not real, don't worry about me—but they return, and that just feels like an old song.

**LA:** Do people assume that there's autobiography in everything you write?
**SA:** I used to deny all that stuff, especially in my first book, which came out in the States in 1993, *The Lone Ranger and Tonto Fistfight in Heaven,* a book of short stories. I reread the book last year—we reissued it in a new edition—and I reread it for the first time in years and I thought, "This is a memoir. This is a family memoir. This is completely stolen from my own life." Yeah, I mean they accuse me of that, but they're correct in their accusations.

**LA:** At least you're stealing your own story, right? I mean, there's a huge industry of appropriation of indigenous culture symbols, whether they're from literature or visual art. That's our big problem in Australia—the appropriation of our visual arts. And you've had that experience yourself.
**SA:** Ah—Nasdijj.

**LA:** You want to tell people about that story?
**SA:** There was this "native" writer, and I put the term "native" in quotes, named "Nasdijj." It was in the summer of '97 or '98, I picked up *Esquire* magazine, which is a literary men's magazine (put "literary" in quotes as well), and there was a memoir, a short essay, in there from this writer named Nasdijj, who was writing about his raising an adopted Navajo son with a seizure disorder named Tommy Nothing Fancy. As I read the essay, I thought, "This guy sounds like me." The sort of rhythm of his sentences, the use of repetition, the sort of sly sense of humor, the irony—I thought, this guy sounds like me, who is this guy? And I was flattered in the first couple of pages. But as it went on, I started reading sort of paraphrases of my work and lines and paragraphs—it wasn't plagiarism but it was very exact *homage.* And I thought, well I don't know this guy.

I'm sure in the Australian world it's small—you know that whole six degrees of separation, that's for everybody else; for Natives it's two, and it comes down to "I know somebody who slept with you." The idea that there would be this "native" writer appearing in *Esquire* that I didn't know or didn't know of was fakey and suspicious. Anyways, I went through this whole process of finding out who he was and, with Navajo writers' help, breaking down all the inconsistencies in Navajo-ness in his stuff. He ends up being a fraud, he gets revealed. Even though all of us Native writers all along had said he was a fraud, it took a white guy, a great guy writing for the *LA Weekly*, to unmask him completely. It was a big hub-bub for a while, and I had an essay in *Time* about it, but it faded, it went away, and it will happen again.

**LA:** It must have made you angry at the time to have your own life story kind of stolen.
**SA:** It made me feel undervalued or unrecognized. But it also verges into my own ego, my own arrogance, and all that. It was uncomfortable. I do have a pretty epic life story—reservation Indian kid grows up to be internationally published writer, filmmaker—it's huge.

**LA:** Indian reservation kid with life-threatening illness . . .
**SA:** . . . illnesses and brain surgery at six months of age, and raised by parents who didn't graduate from high school, who had an outhouse until I was seven. And then to have that story mimicked, that biography mimicked, by a fraud and then to have that fraud win awards, and get celebrated for doing, talking, and being who I already was. I had already appeared in the pages of *Esquire*, and been cele-brated and won awards for the story six years earlier, and somehow or another *Esquire* had forgotten about me. I felt disappeared. It made me think of Ralph Ellison's great book, *Invisible Man*. Despite all the fame and success I've had, it re-minded me that I'm still just an Indian.

**LA:** You mentioned your childhood, this fairly amazing story that you have. Do you want to tell people what it was like? You were hydrocephalic?
**SA:** Hydrocephalic—which means I was born with too much cerebral spinal fluid, and it was crushing my brain. So they had to dig holes in my head, drain the fluid, and install shunts to drain off the fluid. Most hydrocephalics keep the shunts for the rest of their lives. They took mine out. So I'm a shunt-less hydrocephalic— which I put in my personal ad; it attracted a lot of women too. You know, single Indian male in search of *other* shunt-less hydrocephalics. [Laughter.]

But brain damage affected me in all sorts of weird ways—seizures until I was seven. I was on phenobarbital from age one—a serious sedative, so I was a junkie in diapers—which is a good thing to give to a Native American who comes from a family of addicts, anyway, to make sure they get hooked on phenobarbital.

**LA:** Yeah, let's just cut out the first ten years and go straight to . . .
**SA:** . . . just cut to the chase, get right to the addiction. I grew up in a family of alcoholics—my mother, my father, my brother, sisters, aunts, uncles, cousins, family dog, spiders roaming around the house with whiskey. I grew up in that

environment, but I was so sick and the treatment was so new that I actually got amazing medical care. And I think part of it was that I was a Native American, and it wasn't that important, so they could do whatever they wanted. I was a beautiful guinea pig, and it worked.

**LA:** But you learnt to read at an early age.
**SA:** Yeah, but that wasn't because I'm some amazing genius or prodigy, but because they put books in front of me. They had me doing all this therapy—physical, occupational, mental therapy—because they thought I was going to be severely mentally disabled because of the surgery. I was a test case, so they really put me through all these extensive academic things as a kid, as a baby. They were flying me to Seattle, flying me to all these venues to train me, in essence. I'm sort of the American medical establishment's indigenous Frankenstein monster.

**LA:** I was going to say that there's a science fiction novel in there.
**SA:** So they built me. The difference between me and my peers on the reservation is that I had early childhood education.

**LA:** You took yourself off the reservation to go to high school.
**SA:** I always knew I was leaving. My mom always teased me—she still teases me, "You were born with a suitcase." I always dreamed of leaving the rez, as you do, I'm sure it's the same here. I wanted my walkabout to keep going, to keep walking—no "about," just "walk"—"about" implies you're coming back. [Laughter.] I wanted to become a pediatrician. Like most really sick kids, I got obsessed with my caregivers. A lot of really sick kids dream of becoming a pediatrician. I knew I couldn't become that on the reservation, but I couldn't get up the courage to leave. My reservation is 98 percent Indian, and 90 percent of that is Spokane Indian. We did a family tree in sixth grade, and everybody was related, including the teacher. The only white people I knew had lived on the reservation for generations, so they had become Indian by osmosis. On the first day of seventh grade, I sat down in the classroom, and I opened up my math book, and my mom's name was written in it—my mom's maiden name. It was my mom's seventh-grade math book I was looking at, and I knew I had to leave. It took another year of courage, and then I went to the white border town to school, where I was the only Indian except for the mascot.

It was there I learned the concept that you can belong to many tribes at the same time. I ended up getting very lucky: I ended up with a peer group of white kids who were obsessive, compulsive workaholics, who had their own dreams of leaving a little town. We all really connected in that way; we all were on our way to something bigger from our little towns. And whether it was Indian or white didn't matter as much as the desire to get out. All these smart, amazing white kids really accepted me.

**LA:** From there you went to university?
**SA:** Gonzaga University in Spokane, Washington—a Jesuit university. I'm Catholic by choice and by force. I went to a Catholic university and started drinking. I didn't drink on the reservation; I didn't start drinking until I got to college. I sort of kept it together for eighteen years, and I got to college and fell apart pretty quickly. I still managed to go to class and get decent grades, but I was killing myself. So for the next six years, I went to school and drank. I transferred to a public university, drinking, but all I did was buy less expensive booze.

**LA:** What made you stop drinking then?
**SA:** A number of factors. Number one: I didn't want to die. It all came down to one night in particular. After ruining my then-girlfriend's birthday party, I drove drunk. I barely remember it. But at some point during the night, I must have realized I was being stupid, so I stopped and went home. The next morning there's a knock on the door, and it's the police. They ask me about a 1965 Malibu registered in my name: "Do you know it's been stolen?" And I said, "Oh no," and I had no idea what they were talking about. They said, "Somebody stole your car and left it running out in the middle of the Palouse Highway." So twelve miles from the college town, apparently I had stopped the car, got out and walked home—and left the car running in the middle of the road. That was the point where I thought, "Ok, I think it might be time to get sober."

I don't necessarily believe in magic, but I believe in interpreting coincidence exactly the way you want to. That morning, when I checked the mail, the acceptance for my first book of poems was in the box, *The Business of Fancydancing.* A small press in Brooklyn, New York, said "we will be happy to publish your book," and I thought, "Ah—message, message."

**LA:** You've written poetry, prose, novels, screenplays, music. You're doing some comedy as well, stand-up comedy?
**SA:** That was sort of an accident. When people describe me as funny, my siblings and my mother just laugh because to them I was the morose guy living in the basement. Now people think, "Oh, your brother's so funny"—but they would think, "No, he's not. He's depressed." [Laughter.] But as I did performances and readings, I was funny. Sometimes I try *not* to be funny, and I can't help it—it's just the standard mode of operation, especially if I'm uncomfortable.

**LA:** People say it's a distancing technique as well.
**SA:** It's a sign of serious dysfunction, an inability to commit and connect with other human beings.

**LA:** But it also means the opposite: it means you get people to laugh, you're in the door of their mind.
**SA:** I'd have to pay you eighty dollars an hour if we keep talking this way. [Laughter.]

**LA:** So what's left to do on your list? Of all the things that you've written, what's next?
**SA:** A stage play. I made a tiny little movie called *The Business of Fancydancing* that nobody saw—rightfully so, it's not very good—that we're turning into a stage play at a local theater company. A friend of mine saw it, and she realized that it fails as a movie because it's supposed to be a play. We are working at adapting it for the stage; it will be a musical, a musical set at an Indian funeral. So it will be a happy-go-lucky, doo-wop sort of thing.

**LA:** What's your favorite thing to write? What's your favorite form?
**SA:** Poetry. Still poetry. I write *that* every day, all the time. Even being here, in New Zealand and Sydney, I've written fragments and pieces of ten or twelve poems—mostly about my sons' experiences here, the things they've said and seen. That's constant, that's *always* what I do—it's the way I look at the world. I write fiction to pay the bills, and I write poetry for the love of it.

**LA:** There are a lot of aboriginal writers here who talk about things they won't write. Some people won't write love scenes; some people won't write violence; some people won't write white people; they won't write ethnic characters. Are there things that you won't write?
**SA:** I prefer to write about violence, sex, and white people, actually. [Laughter.] I mean, I know growing up, there are all sorts of rules in our communities about ways you can talk and subject matter. So there is a really big cultural collision between growing up traditional and traditionally minded in our communities and then being an artist. An artist in a Native sense is somebody who is part of the community, who is enfolded in the community, whose job is no less or no more important than anybody else's, and all of it for the betterment of the tribe. But in the contemporary sense, art is about questioning, is about challenging, is about almost subverting the essence of tribe. And so we're always fighting that.

I have certain rules. To respect my traditional background, I don't write about ceremonies at all—but that's pretty much it. I don't write about ceremonies, but everything else is open. That whole idea of sex too—we have a real problem, Native writing is very neutered, which is sad because in our day-to-day lives, we are nasty, potty-mouth, sexually promiscuous panda bears. There's a whole element of literature we're missing out on. I think we're young in terms of writing—I mean, I'm the second generation that ever put pen to paper—so we're still catching up. As we assimilate and as we strengthen our tribalness, we'll be able to blend the notion of the artist as part of and separate from in a more effective way.

**LA:** You are also an outsider because as a writer you need to observe. So you have to distance yourself in a sense from your community in order to that.
**SA:** The younger generation of folks is much more up to this, this I-Podded, computerized generation. It's going to be much easier to be an artist coming from these backgrounds. You can still maintain your tribal ties and your culture while also having a much broader worldview. I think they're learning how to multitask.

**LA:** Unless riven by feeling a foot in both worlds. You know, our generation will write about that.
**SA:** I was taught that it was bad to write about that. But all these years later, I realize that it's pretty amazing. I have these two amazing cultures to choose from— this sort of world culture/American culture and then my own tribal background. They're both filled with magic, and I'm angry at the people who taught me I had to choose between them.

**LA:** You're also the world heavyweight poetry champion. You want to tell us about being the world heavyweight poetry champion?
**SA:** It's in Taos, New Mexico—they've since disbanded. But what they would do is bring in poets to perform against each other, and they'd set it up like a boxing match. There'd be rounds where each poet would read, there was a ring girl who was a transvestite, and you had to be poetic about it, there were three judges and a big crowd. And you had to read and perform while people were yelling and screaming like it was a boxing match, and you would compete against other poets. I'm the only four-time winner.

**LA:** So you were the Muhammad Ali of poetry?
**SA:** Yes, but it was just performance, which I'm very much into. There are a lot of writers who don't like it. But I'm also an athlete—I played basketball growing up—so I love to blend the idea of competition with art.

**LA:** Performing is a different thing compared to the social stuff?
**SA:** I'm in charge on stage; at a party I'm not. Nobody's ever as terrifying as you think they're going to be, but I always think they're going to be terrifying.

**LA:** Speaking of terrifying—you've been on *Oprah*.
**SA:** That's an interesting segue. [Laughter.] Is Oprah terrifying?

**LA:** She can be, I think.
**SA:** Well, she's the most powerful woman on the planet. If Oprah says it, it happens.

**LA:** So Oprah summoned you, and you came. How did that happen?
**SA:** A few years ago, I was part of an exhibit on genealogy at the Museum of Tolerance in Los Angeles. Which is funny because I've been in LA a number of times and seen their sign on the freeway: Museum of Tolerance, next exit. It always made me laugh because that's aiming low, right? That's aiming really low—"I tolerate you."

Then I found out it was a museum about the Nazi Holocaust, and since has broadened to include other notions of ethnic and cultural tolerance. They had an exhibit about American genealogy, about how we're all connected, and I was the Native American representative. Which is great because, I don't know about here, but only until very recently have *we* been included in those sorts of national discussions and national exhibits. On a pop-cultural level, I'm one of the very first who's ever been part of that sort of thing. I was in there with Kareem Abdul-Jabbar, Steve Young, Michelle Kwan, Billy Crystal, Maya Angelou. To be part of that exhibit was amazing.

Oprah had a show about it [the exhibit], invited me on, and I talked about my grandfather, who had won medals in World War II that we didn't know about. He died on Okinawa. And I had applied to get them [the medals] reissued, which is funny because at the same time I was part of the planning committee in Seattle for anti–Iraq-war marches.

**LA:** What happened? Did you trace the medals? Did you get them reissued?
**SA:** Well, I applied to get them reissued from the Army, and they said it would take years. My father was terminally ill, and I didn't know if I would be able to get them before he died. Oprah, during her show, surprised me by introducing "Special Forces Brigadier General Leslie [Fuller]—with your grandfather's medals." He came walking from backstage with my grandfather's twelve medals. All of a sudden it was a really weird episode of a reality show: "Survivor, Reservation Style." I got the medals and brought them home. My dad had them for three months before he died of kidney failure, due to a lifetime of alcoholism. It was Oprah, who delivered unto me these medals that represent my father's orphaned status at age six: his father dead, and his mother died of tuberculosis six months

after that. I was raised by a war orphan and a lifetime alcoholic, and so now I have these medals that represent war and pain and loss and fear and blood . . .

**LA:** The whole gamut of human misery there—but it must feel good that the circle is complete.

**SA:** Well, the door's not closed on it. Perhaps the old pain was numbed, but I have new pain, new wounds—I guess it's more personal now. The medals took it out of the historical sense and made it really about my father and me, and our failed relationship. That's what the medals represent now.

**LA:** Would you like to read for us from one of your books?

**SA:** Yes, I'd love to read something uplifting and warm after that—which I don't have. So now I'm going to read a feel-good story about a homeless Indian. I'll read from a story called "What You Pawn, I Will Redeem."

One day you have a home and the next you don't, but I'm not going to tell you my particular reasons for being homeless, because it's my secret story, and Indians have to work hard to keep secrets from hungry white folks.

I'm a Spokane Indian boy, an Interior Salish, and my people have lived within a one-hundred-mile radius of Spokane, Washington, for at least ten thousand years. I grew up in Spokane, moved to Seattle twenty-three years ago for college, flunked out within two semesters, worked various blue- and bluer-collar jobs for many years, married two or three times, fathered two or three kids, and then went crazy. Of course, "crazy" is not the official definition of my mental problem, but I don't think "asocial disorder" fits it, either, because that makes me sound like I'm a serial killer or something. I've never hurt another human being, or at least not physically. I've broken a few hearts in my time, but we've all done that, so I'm nothing special in that regard. I'm a boring heartbreaker, at that, because I've never abandoned one woman for another. I never dated or married more than one woman at a time. I didn't break hearts into pieces overnight. I broke them slowly and carefully. I didn't set any land-speed records running out the door. Piece by piece, I disappeared. And I've been disappearing ever since. But I'm not going to tell you any more about my brain or my soul.

I've been homeless for six years. If there's such a thing as being an effective homeless man, I suppose I'm effective. Being homeless is probably the only thing I've ever been good at. I know where to get the best free food. I've made friends with restaurant and convenience-store managers who let me use their bathrooms. And I don't mean the public bathrooms, either. I mean the employees' bathrooms, the clean ones hidden in the back of the kitchen or the pantry or the cooler. I know it sounds strange to be proud of, but it means a lot to me, being trustworthy enough to pee in somebody else's clean bathroom. Maybe you don't understand the value of a clean bathroom, but I do.

Probably none of this interests you. I probably don't interest you much. Homeless Indians are everywhere in Seattle. We're common and boring, and you walk right on by us, with maybe a look of anger or disgust or even sadness at the terrible fate of the noble savage. But we have dreams and families. I'm friends with a homeless Plains Indian man whose son is the editor of a big-time newspaper back East. That's his story, but we Indians are great storytellers and liars and mythmakers, so maybe that Plains Indian hobo is a plain old everyday Indian. I'm kind of suspicious of him, because he describes himself only as Plains Indian, a generic term, and not by a specific tribe. When I asked him why he wouldn't tell me exactly where he is, he said, "Do any of us know exactly where we are?" Yeah, great, a philosophizing Indian. "Hey," I said, "you got to have a home to be that homely." He laughed and flipped me the eagle and walked away. But you probably want to know more about the story I'm really trying to tell you.

I wander the streets with a regular crew—my teammates, my defenders, and my posse. It's Rose of Sharon, Junior, and me. We matter to one another if we don't matter to anybody else. Rose of Sharon is a big woman, about seven feet tall if you're measuring overall effect, and about five feet tall if you're talking about the physical. She's a Yakama Indian of the Wishram variety. Junior is a Colville, but there are only about 199 tribes that make up the Colville, so he could be anything. He's good-looking, though, like he just stepped out of some "Don't Litter the Earth" public-service advertisement. He's got those great big Indian cheekbones that are like planets, you know, with little moons orbiting around them. He gets me jealous, jealous, and jealous. If you put Junior and me next to each other, he's the Before Columbus Arrived Indian, and I'm the After Columbus Arrived Indian. I am living proof of the horrible damage that colonialism has done to us Indians. But I'm not going to let you know how scared I sometimes get of history and its ways. I'm a strong man, and I know that silence is the best way of dealing with white folks.

**LA:** Sherman Alexie, thank you very much for coming in and being on *Awaye* today.
**SA:** Thank you.

# Revising Sherman Alexie

Dave Weich/2007

Originally published in May 2007 as part of Powells.com online author interviews, http://www.powells.com/authors. Reprinted by permission of the interviewer.

Darkly funny, sharply observant, *Flight* lays bare the experience of a teenaged outsider circa 2007. Alternately heartbreaking and wondrous, Sherman Alexie's first novel in ten years tells the story of an orphan careening through foster homes until finally, not long after we meet him, he walks into a bank and comes unstuck in time. Gritty, intense, and especially timely, it's a lightning-fast read besides.

And according to Alexie, the story bound in these paperback pages is only a start. "*Flight* has been so extensively rewritten in my mind," he says, "that we think I'm going to rewrite it extensively and republish it in a year and a half."

Say what?

Having written seventeen books (prose *and* lots of poetry) and several screenplays, the Washington native is not afraid to flaunt convention. Sometimes at his readings, for example, he never quite gets around to reading. Or he'll simply use the book to get started. "My performances are a process of rewriting," Alexie explains.

Before his event downtown, Alexie stopped by to discuss the new book, slobbering on Stephen King, potlatch culture, pile of crap novels, and more.

**Dave:** Your book tour took you to Virginia on the day of the shootings.

**Sherman Alexie:** That day. It was an awful coincidence, being on tour for a book that features a disassociated kid grabbing pistols and walking into a public place. I felt it was my responsibility that night not to say a word about my book, so I didn't. I told a lot of other stories. I'm a performer, so I have a lot of material. I did the old bits. They didn't know it was the old bits. Nobody talked about the book.

*Flight* is heavily influenced by *Slaughterhouse-Five*. It has an epigraph from Kurt Vonnegut. Vonnegut died the week before that. A couple awful coincidences.

**Dave:** The first line of the novel recalls another classic of American fiction.

**Alexie:** *Moby Dick*. It's meant to be an interesting, funny opening. I tried—and

169

for some reviewers I failed—to point out that for teenagers the state of their complexion is at least as important as Moby Dick is to Ahab.

As somebody who had really bad skin and still struggles with acne, I know it's of vital importance. Perhaps there was a better opening, another allusion to some novel or poem that might have captured it better, but that's what I was trying to do: to show how much his scars affected him and how much they changed his outlook on the world.

**Dave:** In so much of your writing, the question of identity is front and center. In *Flight*, from that first line, "Call me Zits," we understand how he sees himself and how he believes other people see him.

**Alexie:** Physically marked. It was a way of talking about identity without going on and on about the damn Indian thing again.

**Dave:** Acne has nothing to do with his race. It's a problem of adolescence.

**Alexie:** Exactly. Which becomes a way in which everyone can identify with him. *My zits are me.*

**Dave:** Something that struck me reading *Reservation Blues*, in relation to *Flight*, was how ingrained boyhood violence is. And I don't mean boys walking into public places with pistols. I'm thinking of Thomas getting beat up by his friends.

**Alexie:** I grew up in a violent world. It's what I saw. Fistfights were incredibly common. I learned how to fight. It wasn't until I left the reservation school and went to the white high school on the border that I learned you don't throw a punch, that your automatic reaction was not to throw a punch.

It's still ingrained in me. I've met all sorts of people from other backgrounds, generally from poverty, whose first instinct is to throw the punch. Chris Offutt, an Appalachian writer. Black writers. Chicano writers. We've talked about this. As young men, we were taught to fight. It's still the case.

I've been on panels where a prep school, white, academic writer is being a smart-ass in one way or another and my first instinct is literally to stand up, walk across the stage, and pound him in the head. I have to actively resist that. I understand the motivation and the desire to commit violence because that's part of my hard-wiring.

**Dave:** In many of your books, there's an orphan or a character missing a parent. The child is missing too many pieces to form a complete or satisfying self-image.

**Alexie:** Well, that's a constant theme of any colonial literature. That's what I write.

**Dave:** How so in relation to colonial literature?

**Alexie:** Displacement. The killing of your birth father and the substitution of an adopted father. Think of your birth parent being your original culture and your adopted parent being the colonizing culture. In a sense, Native Americans, anybody who's been colonized, they're in the position of an orphan.

Look throughout the world. That missing parent is a constant theme in colonized people's literature. Literature out of Darfur, for instance, it's just starting—there hasn't been a major novel out of that yet—but, literally, parents are being murdered in front of their kids' eyes.

Now, here, after so many generations of being colonized, it's not about actual murder anymore. It's about the symbolic murder and the legacy of murder.

One of the ways in which colonization works is that it destroys family units, and it destroys generational contact. I had no grandparents because they all died for various colonial reasons. Without that connection to grandparents, I lost my connection to my history.

**Dave:** How have reservations and reservation life changed since you grew up on one?

**Alexie:** One of things we forget as natives and non-natives is that reservations were created as concentration camps. They were created so Indians would be shipped there and die. I really think that's still their purpose: to kill.

What has changed? Casinos have changed them. Not all of them, but a lot of them. So there's more money, more jobs, but there's still a distinct lack of education; there are still the same social problems. The joke is, instead of Chevys up on blocks in the yard, it's Lexuses on blocks in the yard. The amount of money flowing through any particular tribe has increased, but the social problems persist. They may not be as poor materially, but they're poor spiritually.

A big change: Almost 70 percent of natives live off reservations now. The flight from the reservation just keeps happening.

I lived in a pretty isolated reservation at a pretty isolated time. There was no Internet. There weren't five thousand channels on television. There were no satellites. Even reservation Indians don't feel as isolated as they used to.

Now even their social dysfunctions take on pop culture guises. You look at the reservations with really bad social problems, like some of the Plains Indians, the Sioux reservations—social problems among young men have manifested themselves in warring gangs called Bloods and Crips, which has nothing to do with Bloods and Crips but everything to do with watching *Boyz N the Hood*. There's no more cultural isolation. We're very much part of the cultural mainstream, even reservation life, because of technology. Being poor and outcast, we look more and more like all the other poor outcasts of the United States.

**Dave:** I saw you read "What You Pawn I Will Redeem" a few years ago at the *New Yorker* Festival.
**Alexie:** With Zadie Smith.

**Dave:** Right. I've read that story a couple times since. I love it. The guy spends every penny he gets, but only with or for other people. I love the ambiguity, that friction. Is he doing a good thing or a bad thing? Are we with him or against him?
**Alexie:** Part of that is growing up in a potlatch culture where the wealth of an Indian is determined by how much he gives away. That's still part of who I am.

It was an attempt to write a Spokane Indian without ever being so explicit in his Spokaneness. It was a very subtle way to write about being a Plateau Indian, giveaways and potlatches. It's a very Plateau experience.

It's hard to talk about that story because I wrote it in about two drafts, and I didn't think it was all that good. The *New Yorker* called and asked if I had any stories to submit. I had two that were done, that one and another. I thought they'd take the other. They took "What You Pawn."

It got published, and I still thought it was just okay. Then as soon as it was published, there was a firestorm, in a way I hadn't experienced since my first book, *Lone Ranger*. I got fan letters, hundreds of them. And other writers were sending me fan letters, which was shocking.

Even though I attend those festivals, I'm not really included in that world. I'm still, in a sense, the Indian guy. They're my peers in terms of awards and publishing and reviews and sales, but I'm still not really a part of their gang. It's not like Franzen and I hang out. Suddenly I was getting fan letters from people I never would have imagined. T. C. Boyle sent me a fan letter. I was, *What?!* And then the story ended up in *O. Henry* and *Best American Short Stories . . .*

**Dave:** It's a great story!
**Alexie:** I know. I know. You work so hard on some of them, though, and you think, *That's it.* And then others just appear. This is one of the ones that just appeared.

I don't know how I did it!

I don't know. What did I do? I read it, and I think, *This is really good.*

I'm adapting it into a screenplay now, and the people I've sent it to for financing can't handle the ambiguity.

**Dave:** Not Hollywood enough?

**Alexie:** Not at all. Even independent producer sources cannot handle the ambiguity.

One of the ways I wanted to preserve it cinematically . . . At the end of the story, he's dancing in his outfit and traffic stops. In a story, that feels low-key. It does. It's just an emotional ending.

In a movie, that would end up looking like *Hoosiers* or *Rudy* or something, some triumph, which is not the feeling I want. In writing the screenplay, I thought, *There can't be the swelling music. It has to be a silent dance.*

Then I remembered an interview I gave when the story came out. The guy asked a great question. He said, "What do you think happened to Jackson Jackson the next day?" I said, "He probably pawned the damn thing back." So in the screenplay, after that ending, when he's dancing—and I imagine emotion swelling in the theater, everybody's going crazy, that dance has the big music, and you think, *That's it*—

No. Cut to the next day. He's sitting in the alley with the outfit. He walks to another pawn shop, walks in, walks back out counting money. He walks out of frame, and we hold on the store window as a new pawn shop guy walks into the display window and hangs it up.

**Dave:** Which would be true to the story.

**Alexie:** Yes. But people have an issue with it because *he does not triumph.*

**Dave:** But after everything that happens, it wouldn't make sense if he turns his life around. It wouldn't be the same story.

**Alexie:** Exactly. And that's the whole notion of Hollywood movies: utter transformation.

My feeling is that it should feel like the story title, which is taken from a Lucille Clifton poem, "What You Pawn I Will Redeem," but it should also feel like, "What I Redeem I'm Going to Pawn."

**Dave:** If the response to "What You Pawn" took you by surprise, have you had the opposite experience? What's thrilled you that didn't resonate with readers or critics?

**Alexie:** Oh, the thing is, I'm never happy with anything I've done. I'm such a self-hater. I'm mortified by my own books.

It's been the case more often where something I thought was shit got a lot of attention. Like *Indian Killer.* I think it's a pile of crap novel.

**Dave:** Did you think that at the time?

**Alexie:** Yes.

**Dave:** What don't you like about it?

**Alexie:** Everything. Its tone. Its characters. It feels to me like a big cartoon. And the fact that it gets taught so seriously when I feel like it's really a cartoon, that bothers me. I love it when people teach it as a cartoon.

**Dave:** When you were working on it, what was interesting to you about it?

**Alexie:** The range. But I didn't go far enough. And I didn't complete it as a mystery novel. I was trying to write an actual mystery novel, and I ended up getting too fucking literary and didn't solve the mystery. That's really what bothers me.

I think all the other stuff is really just a way of talking about the fact that I wrote a genre novel that I didn't complete as a genre novel. If I had, it would be a far superior book. If I'd kept that in mind instead of turning it into some pretentious murder literary piece of shit.

**Dave:** This is the self-hating part?

**Alexie:** Yeah.

**Dave:** I'll put the question another way. If you had to create a Sherman Alexie box set, what would go in it?

**Alexie:** Ha!

**Dave:** I'm not sure who's forcing you, but you can't publish another book until you put this set together.

**Alexie:** "What You Pawn I Will Redeem." There are about eight stories. I've written about eight stories that measure up to just about anybody's stories. Probably ten or fifteen poems. That's probably it.

**Dave:** What if I asked the same question about other people's work. What would you include?

**Alexie:** "Because I could not stop for Death— / He kindly stopped for me— / The Carriage held but just Ourselves— / And Immortality." I'd start with that poem.

*Great Gatsby. Invisible Man. The Things They Carried*, Tim O'Brien. The poem "She Had Some Horses" by Joy Harjo. *Fire Water World*, Adrian Louis.

Adrian Louis has a poem in his new book, I can't remember the title, but it's about him having to make the decision to have his wife's—she has severe Alzheimer's and rheumatoid arthritis, and he had to amputate a finger, he had to sign the permission to get her finger amputated. I mean . . . That poem is the most painful thing I've ever read. So, that poem.

I could go on and on. I'm a fanboy, across all genres, from the most mainstream pop culture writers to the most obscure literary theorists, so I could go on and on for days about that box set. But one book? If I only had one book, Ralph Ellison's *Invisible Man*.

**Dave:** When you say you're a fanboy, have you actually had fanboy encounters?
**Alexie:** Neil Gaiman. We both fanboyed each other. He was a fanboy of me, which was great.

It was in Sydney, Australia, last spring, at the Sydney Book Fair. I rarely go to the parties because I'm shy. People don't believe that, but those situations make me horribly uncomfortable. This one was in my hotel, so I went up there. I'm hiding in a corner, and I see him. So I walk up, and as I'm walking up to him he turns. His eyes light up with recognition, and he says, "Sherman Alexie." I was so happy. I was going over there to slobber all over him, and he slobbered on me! So we slobbered on each other.

Stephen King, I slobbered on. The first time I met Lorrie Moore, yeah. Gosh. Toni Morrison.

Most of the experiences have been positive. The thing I do now, I actually send fan letters. When I read something I like, I'll send an email or a letter. I send notes of appreciation for poems, stories, books, music.

I like getting the letters from anybody. I love reading them. It's fun. It's such a lonely job. We have to deal with so much potential rejection and real rejection. I mean, no matter how good you are, 99 percent of the world doesn't give a shit. Getting a letter from someone who's in the same boat, I think it's polite in a job field short of politeness.

**Dave:** I assume that most of the people at your readings enjoy your writing and have read at least some of it, but do you get many people who are not so fond of your work?
**Alexie:** The ones who are uncomfortable come in a few categories, and they're pretty easy to figure out. The ones who come because I'm an Indian, so they expect spiritual shit. The ones who come because they've only seen *Smoke Signals*, which is a very sweet and tender movie. They expect me to be like Thomas, rather than being the profane, mouthy asshole I can be, performing.

It generally has to do with people's perception of what kind of Indian I'm supposed to be, why they're offended. I think vegans hate me now because I make fun of them. I'm on some vegan boycott list, me and Oscar Mayer.

In Eugene last night, a few people walked out while I was telling a story. What really gets people walking out is when I talk about sex.

**Dave:** What were you talking about?

**Alexie:** I told a story about the night before my reading in Virginia, in the hotel. I went down to get a couple bottles of water from the vending machine, and in the room next door I heard people having sex. I stayed there through the whole thing as they got louder and louder. And of course as I tell the story I exaggerate and improvise. Then I talked about my own sex life in relation to this couple in the hotel room.

Four or five people walked out. Generally, sex will send people running, which makes me want to talk about it even more. It makes me want to write a really horny book, which I've never done.

**Dave:** You've done stand-up comedy, though. I would imagine you have to be working an edge there if you're going to be interesting at all.

**Alexie:** The very nature of my performances pisses some people off. They come expecting a reading. They're used to some spectacled writer standing at a podium, intoning. I don't do that. I don't even read necessarily. Sometimes I don't get to the book.

And every night is different. I never know what I'm going to do when I stand up there. I have standard bits, standard material, different stories that I tell. Or, tonight, I might talk about my day, about feeling like a zoo animal while I was doing a photo shoot on the Portland waterfront, and what an idiot you feel like when people stop and give you the look of, *Oh, it must be somebody.* Then they look and, *No.* Next they think, *Oh, it must be a fashion shoot,* until they look at you and think again, *No.*

They go through the list of reasons why someone would be taking a picture of you, and they never get to *writer.* Your value in the country as an artist, even as successful as I have been, you get put in your place quickly during a public photo shoot. Maybe I'll talk about that. Certain people get bothered.

I did the keynote at an American Literature conference in Louisville a few months ago. By and large, people liked it, but I got emails and I got comment cards later. One guy wrote, "I hated him. All he was was funny."

**Dave:** Nailed!

**Alexie:** I often make T-shirts with negative comments about me. I play basketball in them. *Time* magazine, for *Indian Killer,* wrote that I was "septic with my own unappeasable fury." I had that T-shirt for a while.

I haven't done it yet, but I'm thinking about "All he was was funny."

**Dave:** You could create a whole line of Sherman Alexie gym wear.

**Alexie:** With negative comments, yes.

**Dave:** But to do something different and stimulating, something potentially offensive to convention—readings could use more of that, in my opinion.

**Alexie:** A huge part of my success has to do with my performances, with me going on the road and building an audience through word of mouth. Being unafraid of any venue. Because of my performance ability, I now get to take my stories into places that other literary writers don't go: Christian conventions; I do diversity training for corporate gatherings; reservations; poor communities.

If you compare me to a literary writer, where do they go?

**Dave:** The 92nd Street Y.

**Alexie:** Right. And I'm in a high school gym in Shiprock, New Mexico. I'm at multimillion dollar retreats in Oahu, talking to twelve of the richest one hundred guys in the world. That spectrum is what I've worked on, and it's because I can tell a story aloud.

What gets me angry is that this is where it all started, some caveman or woman sitting around a fire, and somebody saying, "I'm bored." That's where it began. That's what I do. I would die if all I could do is write books.

**Dave:** How does one outlet feed the other? You've written a lot of books.

**Alexie:** Now, with *Flight*, when I perform it, I rewrite it. I don't read from the text. Or if I have the book in front of me as I'm reading, I'll jump off as something occurs to me. Whatever I'm performing, I'll improvise. Great ideas will come. Other images, parts of other books, other characters. I'll bring in characters from books that I'm working on *now*.

My performances are a process of rewriting. Even a book that's already published, I have no problem rewriting in the context of telling a story about it.

*Flight* has been so extensively rewritten in my mind that we think I'm going to rewrite it extensively and republish it in a year and a half. I'm of the mind that I'll keep doing it. I'll have no problem rewriting this book every two or three years and watching it change. To think in terms of a career and one book, I think it's a fascinating exercise. Nobody's done it. I can't believe nobody's done it. It's what you talked about earlier [prior to the start of the interview], the notion of books being static.

**Dave:** And sacrosanct. Once the binding is stitched, that's the book.

**Alexie:** My culture doesn't treat storytelling that way. I've never treated the text as sacred. Why not take that feeling into the publication itself?

**Dave:** In an interview you gave a while back, you talked about *Reservation Blues*, how some of that story came out of your regret over not being able to sing. So you wrote about a musician and a singer. Your idea for *Flight* makes me think of the way restless musicians will constantly reinvent their songs. The songs change from tour to tour, year to year, the instrumentation changes, or the tempo.

**Alexie:** When you know music well enough—and I know it *just* well enough to hear the stuff inside the music—it's almost always the mistakes that are more interesting, the deviations, the errors, the recovery, the experiment inside the song.

I would love to think of being a musician-as-writer, a writer-as-musician. That's a great way to talk about it. Like I said, I really think it's why I've done well. I've been that, unofficially. Maybe by republishing *Flight* I'll be that officially.

**Dave:** What were the particular challenges of writing a book of this length? What were the opportunities? It's a lot longer than a short story, but it's only a third the length of *Indian Killer*.

**Alexie:** It was a challenge. I knew it was going to be short when I started. I felt that. Even though it had these time travel and historical elements, I knew it was going to be concise. Again, *Slaughterhouse-Five* being its primary influence.

I kept thinking about it as a poem, as if I was writing a really long, formal poem. So the key in my head was repetition: the same smells, the same sights, using repeated phrases the way you would use meter and rhyme in a poem. I thought that would make the book hold together more and make it more of an experience, to feel fuller.

I didn't want it to feel slight. I wanted it to feel intense.

**Dave:** Who makes the best fry bread?

**Alexie:** Ha! Wow. There's a woman on my rez, Flossie Abrahamson.

**Dave:** Flossie Abrahamson.

**Alexie:** Best of all time.

**Dave:** Any particular quality?

**Alexie:** A thin and crunchy exterior and the softest inside imaginable.

**Dave:** We haven't talked about the Northwest, but you live right up I-5.

**Alexie:** I love being from the Northwest. Certainly I take a lot of comfort and challenge in my career from being Native American, but there's something special too about being from the Pacific Northwest, which is by far the most literate region of the country and one of the most literate regions of the world. The Seattle to Portland corridor is powered by books.

I love being here in Portland. It feels like I'm directly connected to a really powerful literary culture. I'm glad I'm from here. I don't know that I'd be a writer otherwise. Recently we've gotten more respect as a literary region in terms of our writers, but I think by far we have the best readers.

**Dave:** It's fun when readers visit us in Portland. The American Booksellers Association held its Winter Institute here in January. Five hundred booksellers converged from around the country. It was great bringing them to Powell's. So many said, "I wish my hometown could support a bookstore this big."

We take it for granted sometimes. You don't find that everywhere.

**Alexie:** A few weeks ago, I was doing an interview, and the guy asked, "How many bookstores are near where you live?" I started counting bookstores within a fifteen-minute drive, used bookstores, new bookstores, chains, independents. Nineteen.

*Sherman Alexie visited Powells.com on May 15, 2007. We started talking; before I knew it, an hour had passed. As will sometimes happen when a transcription runs sixteen-plus pages, bits and pieces of conversation wound up on the cutting room floor. But this belongs in here somewhere:*

**Alexie:** There are great books about childhood. The latest one is *Black Swan Green* by David Mitchell, an incredible book, one of my favorite of the last few years. But that kid is not twelve. That kid—no way is that a twelve-year-old kid. That's a twelve-year-old filtered through the genius that is David Mitchell.

I worked really hard to make Zits sound like a bright fifteen-year-old. Even when he inhabits an adult body, with adult concerns, he's still very much a kid.

# Interview with Sherman Alexie

James Mellis/2007

Originally published online in conjunction with Alexie's appearance at the 2007 Decatur [Georgia] Book Festival. Reprinted by permission of the interviewer.

*Jim Mellis conducted the following interview with Sherman Alexie by phone on July 10, 2007. They discussed Alexie's two new works; the first,* Flight, *is a novel about a young half-Indian, half-Irish teenager named Zits, who, immediately before committing a mass murder at a bank, goes through a transformative experience by traveling through time, occupying the bodies of both Indian and White characters; the second,* The Absolutely True Diary of a Part-Time Indian, *is a book aimed at young adults and based on Alexie's own experience transferring from his reservation school to the wealthy, white, Reardan High School.*

**Interviewer:** Why don't we start with *Flight*: Zits seems to have trouble with his mixed heritage, so much so that early on he states, "I'm not really Irish *or* Indian, I'm a blank sky, a human solar eclipse." His dual identity seems to be one factor in his troubled consciousness insofar as his identities seem to cancel each other out rather than form a hybrid identity for him. Do you think that Native American children have to struggle with a similar dilemma—that is, having to negotiate being both Indian and American?

**Alexie:** Well, I don't think that Zits has a problem with either identity; I think he has a problem with having no identity. Like he says, being Indian and Irish would be the coolest thing in the world. I think he has a problem with nobody teaching him how to value either culture, so I think that Native American kids' problem is not being a hybrid—not being two things at the same time—I think the problem is when people tell them they have to be one thing or the other. (I prefer mixed breed dogs and mixed breed humans.)

**Interviewer:** When Zits is transformed into Hank, the FBI agent working for HAMMER [a FBI task force assigned to suppress IRON, a militant Indian Civil Rights organization], he learns that Horse and Elk, two Indian heroes for IRON, are actually double agents working for the FBI. Zits realizes that the two "aren't freedom fighters or anything like that. They don't care about protecting the poor and defenseless. No, man, these guys just like to hurt people"—a sensibility he also recognizes in the FBI agents. Given the brutality of both the Indians and the FBI agents during this experience, I'm wondering what you're saying about the nature of men and the myths built around them.

**Alexie:** (*Laughs*) That whatever our politics, we always find ways to justify violence. For me, there's really no difference between the left and the right when it comes to justifying violence. Worldwide, you know, the Palestinians and the Israelis aren't all that much different to me.

**Interviewer:** In other scenes in the novel, Zits occupies the bodies of both a Native American boy at the Battle of Little Big Horn and the elderly Indian tracker Gus, who at first leads a slaughter of an Indian village, and both these scenes are filled with brutality but also a sense of redemption: both the unnamed Indian boy and Gus eventually refuse to engage in the surrounding slaughter. These scenes seem to foreshadow Zits' eventual refusal to shoot up the bank at the end of the novel. Given the brutal history of American and Indian relations, how do you see these two scenes offering a new vision of the relationship between the two groups in the United States?

**Alexie:** Well, I don't know if it's as much a new vision as a different way to take lessons from it. . . . We did plenty of killing on our own and I think the sort of centuries' long effort to completely villianize and demonize white folks is very self-destructive to us.

**Interviewer:** And is that where the character of Justice comes in?

**Alexie:** Yeah, he has the inability to find the goodness in other people and other cultures. He can only see what's wrong.

**Interviewer:** As I was reading, I was struck by the physical features of Crazy Horse as he appears in the novel in that he kind of reminds me of Justice. Their representations seem very singular—were you trying to create the two as foils for each other?

**Alexie:** A little bit, but also the fact is that by all accounts Crazy Horse was a pale light-haired dude, so it's quite probable that one of the great heroes in Native American history was part white, so that I think it renders the whole notion of . . . you know, it makes all of us look like fundamentalists. I mean identity is far more complicated than history teaches us.

**Interviewer:** Given the delineation between the white world and the Indian world, I'm curious about the ending when Officer Dave rescues Zits from himself.

This marks a significant change in his life and I am wondering if there's a degree of irony in that, given the brutal characterizations of the FBI agents in the novel, to have a representative of the state or government be the impetus of the turn-around in Zits' life?

**Alexie:** I suppose irony is a term; I prefer to think of it as the evolution of a country. You know if someone breaks into my house, I'm not calling a member of the American Indian Movement, I'm calling a cop. My house catches on fire, I'm not calling Jesse Jackson, I'm calling engine number nine down the block. You know the mark of a successful society really is the quality of its civil service. You know, Zits says he feels like he's in the civil service hall of fame—there's a nurse, a cop, and a fireman—so that's less about an ironic look at American history and what has happened and more of a small celebration of civil servants.

**Interviewer:** It is a really poignant ending.
**Alexie:** Yeah, well, I believe in civil servants.

**Interviewer:** I know, I spent all morning at the DMV.
**Alexie:** I wish some civil servants were faster.

**Interviewer:** Ok, my final question regarding *Flight* has to do with the character of Justice, who is preoccupied with the Ghost Dance, the ritual that is meant to bring the dead back to life. And *Flight* reminds me somewhat of Eugene O'Neill's *The Emperor Jones* in that it's populated by ghosts, both dead and alive, but instead of the dead rising up to take vengeance, the novel ends positively with Zits seeming to assimilate into the white world, accepting his Christian name, and moving in with officer Dave's brother and sister-in-law. And my question is how do you see modern Native Americans engaging with the white world today, given that your books are filled with both mainstream pop-culture references and the possibility to retain, like the Ghost Dance, a traditional cultural legacy and still have an American identity?

**Alexie:** Well, the Ghost Dance itself is something pretty ironic; it was not native theology. Wovoka, who created the Ghost Dance, was a Methodist minister, so the Ghost Dance is actually very much Christian apocalyptic thinking . . . it's really funny that the U.S. cavalry massacred Indians for being Christians. So, once again, it was a subtle questioning and criticism of cultural purity. The Ghost Dance was essentially a completely impure cry for purity, so assimilation . . . people who are worried about assimilation are always worried about some romantic notion of purity. With assimilation, people always assume that it's a one way bridge—Native Americans, all of us, whatever we are, have had influence and been influenced by the common culture, we've all worked together to create it. Certainly, history books focus on one group or another as being the originators of our country, but we all know in reality George Washington's wife had as much to do with it. I refuse to take a lesser recognition on this, we've all been here together making it work. Or not work.

**Interviewer:** And what about humor, and how that serves your novels? Your works are quite serious but also very funny, despite the brutality that goes on within them. How do you think humor operates for contemporary Native Americans?
**Alexie:** You know, Shakespeare was hilarious. This is always a funny question for me because if you asked my mom and siblings about me they'd say I was the morose one in the basement playing Dungeons and Dragons. So I'm the least funny member of my family. . . . I have found personally that, if you're funny, people will listen to everything you say and that being funny is also [the mark of] people who haven't given up.

**Interviewer:** So do you think it's less of a coping mechanism than a reflection of . . .
**Alexie:** A reflection of strength.

**Interviewer:** That is a pretty good segue into the next book I'd like to talk about, *The Absolutely True Diary of a Part-Time Indian*, and my first question is that it represents a bit of a change for you, in that it's being advertised as being for young adults. I know that in some of your "adult works" there's been some debate as to what audience you're writing for, and by shifting gears this way, did you have a particular young audience in mind?
**Alexie:** Well, you know, do you know who reads my books? Do you know who reads all literary work? Any book, every book, all of them? The primary audience is college-educated white women, so that's who reads everything. If you want to talk about an indication of that—certainly this book is geared towards young adults, but I was at the American Library Association convention in DC a couple of weeks ago, and there were something like 15,000 librarians there and 99 percent of them were white women so . . . Thank God . . . they seem to be the people most willing to ignore barriers and boundaries and to reach across, so that's who my audience is in reality. In this book, specifically, I'm really hoping it reaches a lot of native kids certainly, but also poor kids of any variety who feel trapped by circumstance, by culture, by low expectations, I'm hoping it helps them get out.

**Interviewer:** That sense of being trapped is all over the book, obviously, and there are a lot of heartbreaking scenes, and I know some parts of the book are based on events in your life. To me, one of the most heartbreaking scenes is when after transferring to Reardan, Arnold is rejected at a basketball game when everyone in the audience turns their back to him. I'm curious, was this based on a real event in your life?

**Alexie:** Not quite that dramatic, but it was a football game actually that is not in the book, a flag football game in eighth grade. I transferred in eighth grade, and my former friends and [their] family members and everybody else on the other side were cheering against me, and the whole tribal team we were playing against quit having a game plan to win the game, and all they were focused on was knocking me down. They were running plays so that people could hit me and coach was willing to take me out, but I stayed in and took the hits the whole game. So when you look up in the stands and see people's parents cheering for their children to brutalize you, you sort of think "wow, I'm banished."

**Interviewer:** And in the book Arnold's sister seems to express a similar desire to get out and escape and she takes a somewhat different trajectory and dies tragically, and I'm wondering about the two different reactions on the reservation regarding the attempted escapes of Arnold and his sister and how you account for that?

**Alexie:** Well, she married an Indian and moved to another reservation, so she stayed within the community in that sense, plus she was just nicer. Arnold is a mouthy little bastard.

**Interviewer:** I like him, though.
**Alexie:** I like him too, he reminds me of somebody (*laughs*).

**Interviewer:** Ok, getting back to the scene of the basketball game, it's interesting that basketball appears a few other times in your work—as a pivotal scene in *Reservation Blues* when the Indians play the reservation police and at the end of *The Lone Ranger and Tonto Fistfight in Heaven*. How important is basketball to reservation life?

**Alexie:** It's every bit as important as it is in inner-city black communities. Number one, it's cheap. All you need is something resembling a hoop and something resembling a ball, and you can play it with any number of people. I really think it is a function of the simplicity of the game and also it sort of rewards, I'll get in trouble for saying this, but it really is an effeminate game. . . . Indian men are, you know, among the most effeminate on the planet. It rewards a certain body type and a certain level of grace and beauty that is not always seen as being masculine. I think that's part of it, sort of, the androgyny of the game.

**Interviewer:** It's interesting that you mention that it [basketball] is as important as it is in inner-city black urban life, because as I was reading *The Absolutely True Diary of a Part-Time Indian,* I noticed a lot of similarities between the cultures, not only the emphasis on basketball but also motifs that appear in a lot of African-American fiction like racial profiling, marginalization and ghettoization, lost cultural heritages, wise elders, etc. I'm wondering if you see these parallels, and if so, is there a lot of contact between the two cultures?

**Alexie:** No. By and large, no. That's one of the problems with contemporary civil rights and contemporary liberalism. . . . People march for their own rights so you don't see a whole lot of people working for [groups] outside of themselves. One of my jokes is that every year we should have a liberal giving tree where every liberal has to pull down a piece of paper from the tree and support that group for a year (and it can't be their own). So you might get a piece of paper that says "gay Black Panthers for Iowa corn farmers, Native American urban liberals for single mothers," so . . . no, it's a long way of saying there's not a lot of interaction or cooperation. One of the big things is that black folks are really powerful, economically, politically, culturally, and they don't really need our help.

**Interviewer:** How do you account then for the lack of power amongst Native Americans?

**Alexie:** We have no natural allies. We are on our own. The only people rushing to our defense are those white women.

**Interviewer:** Like in *Reservation Blues.*

**Alexie:** Exactly.

**Interviewer:** Ok, well the portrayals of whites in *The Absolutely True Diary of a Part-Time Indian* seem particularly interesting in that Arnold realizes when the book begins, he says that white equals hope, but as the novel progresses he sees the guilt ridden Mr. P, Penelope struggling with anorexia, the embarrassment of Billionaire Ted and realizes that whites are as troubled and ridiculous as everybody else. Do you think that seeing their problems is a fundamental part of his path of self-identity and self assurance?

**Alexie:** Definitely. The maturation process is of seeing that, for lack of a better term, everybody's screwed (*laughs*). That reminds me, I was watching the movie [*Léon:*] *The Professional,* have you ever seen it? With Jean Reno and Natalie Portman. And in one scene her face is all beaten at the beginning and she asks him, "Is life always this hard or is it just when you're a kid?" and he says, "It's always this hard." So we can [see] Arnold being Natalie Portman and white culture being

Jean Reno, "is life this hard or is it just because I'm an Indian?" and no, he learns that no, life is hard for everybody.

**Interviewer:** The character of Rowdy in the novel is very compelling. At the end of the novel he calls Arnold "an old-time nomad" who will wander the earth, and it seems that that prediction or characterization of Arnold allows him to retain his Native American identity by leaving the reservation and becoming that nomad, but also lose the modern Native American identity through that same departure. My question is, then, what do you think needs to be done either on or for the reservations to change the attitudes reflected in the novel?

**Alexie:** I have no idea. All I know is that just a few years ago when I realized that I traveled the world telling stories and that's how I make my living, I was on stage when I said that and I realized that and I thought, "wait a second, what's more Indian than that?" and it sort of collapsed all these notions I had about myself and all these struggles and all these ideas about my connection to my culture and my people and all of that. I realized that my culture was inherent in me. I came from a storytelling family. Maybe my stories have more dick jokes in them but they're still traditional. . . . To change the cultural idea about that? All I can do is live my life and write my books and tell my stories, and I know for a fact that it's influencing all sorts of other Native American people and pushing them to embrace their own eccentricity and to get nomadic, so I'm not worried about chronological definitions of identity whether it's old or new. I just know that I'm doing now what I would've been doing two hundred years ago, but now instead of somebody throwing me a salmon for a story, they pay me.

**Interviewer:** And you grew up listening to stories?
**Alexie:** Yep, my grandma's traditional stories and my dad's alcoholic ramblings.

**Interviewer:** And both are reflected in your stories?
**Alexie:** I like to make the profane sacred and the sacred profane.

**Interviewer:** It's a fine line. What's next for you?
**Alexie:** A new book of poems next year, called *Thrash*, and a family memoir I've been working on for a long time about the history of the men in my family and war, and there's another novel out there.

**Interviewer:** Do you ever struggle with honest portrayals about reservation life? With all its violence and alcoholism?
**Alexie:** No, the people who have an issue with that are the ones who are still drunk.

# Sherman Alexie

Tanita Davis and Sarah Stevenson/2007

This interview originally appeared 7 November 2007 on the *Finding Wonderland* blog as part of the 2007 Winter Blog Blast Tour, a multi-blog interview event organized by Colleen Mondor at *Chasing Ray*. The Winter Blog Blast Tour and Summer Blog Blast Tour feature online interviews with numerous children's and young adult authors and illustrators. Reprinted by permission of the interviewers.

If you go to Sherman Alexie's website and read his biography, one thing that's immediately striking is the similarity of his childhood to that of Arnold Spirit, the main character in his recently released novel for young adults, *The Absolutely True Diary of a Part-Time Indian*. In that respect, the story is absolutely true. And it's that ring of truth that gives it such power and makes Arnold the character so fully realized. In our review of the book on our sister site *Readers' Rants*, we wrote: This story "reflects the complexity of real life, with painful and haunting details that could only come from real experiences of reservation life—making Junior a sort of every-boy who both suffers greatly and finds strength and friendship in unlikely places" (http://readersrants.blogspot.com/2007/10/escape-from-spokane.html).

Of course, Mr. Alexie also has a way with words, injecting keen observations and pithy humor into his writing for adults as well as his YA work. As *Publishers Weekly* described *Absolutely True Diary*, "Jazzy syntax and Forney's witty cartoons examining Indian versus White attire and behavior transmute despair into dark humor; Alexie's no-holds-barred jokes have the effect of throwing the seriousness of his themes into high relief" (20 August 2007: 71).

It's not surprising to find out he's received awards and accolades such as a National Endowment for the Arts Poetry Fellowship, a PEN/Hemingway Award for Best First Book of Fiction (for his collection of short stories *The Lone Ranger and Tonto Fistfight in Heaven*), and numerous short-story prizes. And then there are the Sundance Film Festival awards for his film, *Smoke Signals*, which was based on his short story "This Is What It Means to Say Phoenix, Arizona." Oh, and that little matter of being a finalist for the National Book Award in the category for Young People's Literature. Did we mention that?

I have to admit, when we took on this interview we were really intimidated. Sherman Alexie is a celebrity in the literary world, especially with respect to writers of color. He's a National Book Award Nominee and a Cybils [Children's and YA Bloggers' Literary Awards] Nominee, for crying out loud. Even though we've interviewed some pretty intimidating people—authors included—between the two of us, I just about gulped when we sent off our list of impudent and nosy questions.

**Finding Wonderland:** Much of your work written for adult audiences is—adult. Graphically depicted alcoholism, obscenity, and profanity is just an everyday— every moment occurrence. Was there any point at which you felt that you could not write for young adults? Did you sense any indrawn breaths or resistance when you broached the topic with agents or publishers?
**Sherman Alexie:** I really didn't feel the need to censor myself when writing YA. And my agent and publisher also felt no such need. In fact, at one point in the process, my editor Jennifer Hunt asked that I put back in a few curse words that I'd deleted. Teenagers curse. And think and worry about sex and drugs and booze and violence. My previous books for adults have always done well with YA audiences, and have been taught in numerous high schools, and have always been challenged and banned in a few places, so I already knew what to expect with my YA. So far, I haven't heard of any bans or challenges, but I'm sure that's going to change.

**FW:** Zits, the main character from your novel *Flight*, is much more hard-edged than Arnold Spirit, from *The Absolutely True Diary of a Part-Time Indian*. Both stories end with a message of hope, but Zits and Arnold take very different journeys toward finding that hope. Could you talk a bit about these two teenage characters and the different perspective each one provides about life as a young Indian?
**Alexie:** Well, Zits is utterly disconnected and lost, unmoored in identity and in time. This is very much unlike Arnold, who certainly struggles through life, and has many identity questions, but is not unmoored, so to speak. Simply stated, I'd say that Arnold is struggling to reconcile two identities (rez Indian and off-rez Indian) while Zits first has to learn how to be human, rather than a feral orphan. I would bet that Zits would think of Arnold as a very lucky and spoiled whiner!

**FW:** Arnold has a unique and quirky perspective on his life as a kid with physical difficulties growing up on the reservation, but also as an Indian kid going to an all-white school. What did you hope to convey to your audience—whether white or Indian—about reservation life? About "mainstream white" life as it appears to an outsider?

**Alexie:** The reservation system was created to disappear and murder Indians. And I still think to some large degree that reservations still serve that nefarious function. I think Arnold, by leaving the rez, is escaping a slow-motion death trap. But I would also love my readers to recognize that a small white "mainstream" town can be a kind of death trap, too. If you asked Gordie and Penelope, two of Arnold's white friends, I think they'd feel just as trapped by their town and "tribe" as Arnold feels by his. Metaphorically speaking, we all grow up on reservations, don't we?

**FW:** Where did the character of Arnold come from? What made you want to tell this story through his eyes?

**Alexie:** Arnold is me. Well, he's twice as smart and funny as I was at the same age. But he's largely an autobiographical character and I wanted to tell this story for artistic and political reasons. Artistically, I just wanted to write a funny, moving tale. Politically, I want all those folks, Indian and not, who celebrate me to realize that they are also celebrating the fact that I left the rez. All of my books and movies exist because I left.

**FW:** Could you talk about the role of Ellen Forney's wonderful illustrations in this book? How closely did you work together in bringing Arnold's cartoon visions to life?

**Alexie:** I made Arnold a cartoonist about ten minutes into the first page of the first draft of this book, and emailed Ellen a few minutes after that, and asked her if she wanted to be the illustrator, and she sent back her first Arnold drawing just a few minutes after. Ellen and I have been working together since the very beginning. I'd guess that a third of the cartoons were dictated by me, another third were true collaborations, and a third were Ellen's ideas. I've learned that most YA illustrators are brought in after the fact, but that was not the case here.

**FW:** In your recent NPR interview with Renee Montagne, you said that anyone who thinks that the problem of alcoholism on the reservation is just a stereotype is a "romantic fool"—that it's truly an epidemic. Do you see books with teenage characters as a way to reach young reservation kids before it's too late? As a way to educate mainstream America and rouse them to action? Are you writing for "your community" or for young adults as a whole?

**Alexie:** There's really nothing that any book, or any work of art, can do to combat the epidemic of alcoholism in the Indian world. It's really a matter of this one book reaching particular kids, who will find sobriety, inspiration, and love in the words, and let them change their lives. With books, social change happens on a micro level.

**FW:** In the same interview, we find out that in the beginning of Arnold's story, he feels like he doesn't belong anywhere—either on the reservation or in the all-white high school. By the end, though, he's discovered that he "belongs to more than one tribe." To what extent is this based on your own life experiences? Did you learn the same lessons that Arnold did, or is this something that has changed over time—is the transition between "worlds" easier now, maybe?

**Alexie:** For many years, I've said that my two strongest tribal affiliations are not racially based. My strongest tribes are book nerds and basketball players, and those tribes are as racially, culturally, economically, and spiritually diverse. And, like Arnold, I also belong to a hundred other tribes, based on the things I love to read, watch, do. Ever since 9/11, I have worked hard to be very public about my multi-tribal identity. I think fundamentalism is the mistaken belief that one belongs to only one tribe; I am the opposite of that.

**FW:** When writing on ethnic issues, the temptation is to be either an apologist or a sensationalist. Do you feel that mainly centering your writing on a subculture, for the consumption of the dominant culture, is risking that your writing will be taken as caricature—writing Indians who fit into the dominant culture's precon-ceptions about reservation life?

**Alexie:** But doesn't everybody belong to a subculture? And doesn't every writer work out of a subculture? John Updike is not universal. He's writing out of a Northeastern American white subculture that is every bit as strange as my Spokane/Coeur d'Alene background. Lorrie Moore's white folks are vastly differ-ent than William Faulkner's white folks. Louise Erdrich's Indians are vastly dif-ferent than my Indians. In fact, as I write, I think William Faulkner's white folks and my Indians are more alike than one would suspect. And for that matter, I also see my reservation in the work of Flannery O'Connor.

**FW:** Many authors who write about racially charged subjects for young adults run into the attitude that there is a way to talk about race, and at times face a sort of editorial interference as they are urged to talk about it in one way or another. Do you feel that having a touchy subject matter interfered with your editor's ability to give you feedback? Are you willing to talk a little about what your experience has been in this area?

**Alexie:** My YA editor, Jennifer Hunt, is African American, and grew up in the very white American West, so she was the perfect editor for this book. She and I can have absolutely frank discussions about race and racism that I might not be able to have with a white editor.

# Index